What This Book Will Do for You

There are few businesses today that represent greater opportunity for entrepreneurial success than manufacturers' agencies. One-person agencies frequently report personal incomes well in excess of $100,000 after only a few years of operation. And larger agencies not only provide significant income and personal economic advantages, but also give owners an opportunity to create wealth by building a saleable property of impressive proportions.

This book will *not* tell you how to sell, but it will tell you how to create and multiply personal wealth in one of the fastest growing fields today. Manufacturers, large and small, are selling through agencies not only because of the economic advantages of having fixed overhead, but because of other very important advantages agencies have over a salaried sales force—such as, instant coverage of a territory, zero cost until a sale is made, multi-person professionalism that can't compete with direct coverage, plus much more.

There are many benefits for the manufacturer, and they translate directly into major advantages for anyone with selling skills, entrepreneurial drive, and a head for business.

A head for business doesn't mean that you need an M.B.A. from Harvard to make it. You simply must have the business information at your fingertips—and that's just what this book is all about. Whether you're just starting out, building your agency, or planning to sell it or pass it on to someone, you'll find everything you need in this handbook.

How You Can Draw on the Successes of Thousands of Agencies

The information on the following pages has been distilled into practical, problem-solving guidance from the experiences of the thousands of agencies that have been part of the Manufacturers' Agents National Association (MANA) since its inception, as well as from my own experience as an owner of a successful agency and as vice president of marketing for two international firms. For forty years, MANA has conducted extensive research and compiled vast data banks on virtually every element of agency success. The Association has also identified the pitfalls that can be encountered along the way. The information in this book—which is the only complete source of its kind—will help you plan, anticipate, and manage your business for maximum success, regardless of what stage of agency growth you are in now.

Practical, Easy-to-Use Advice and Case Histories

This is *not* a textbook. And it's not a get-rich-quick volume, either. Rather, it's a practical guide created to meet the day-to-day needs of the busy manufacturers' representative. It will save you from plodding through pages of text to get the answers to problems that have already been solved efficiently by others. With condensed text, checklists, and practical illustrations, you will find the help you need to succeed in every aspect of your business.

Because of the very personal nature of a manufacturers' agency, the book was also written with your personal and financial growth in mind. The two just can't—and shouldn't—be separated. Therefore, each topic is covered completely, but only in the detail you will need to solve your own problems. Additionally, specific case histories are included that not only illustrate important points, but also provide practical models you can adapt directly to suit your own needs.

WHAT THIS BOOK WILL DO FOR YOU

First and foremost, this book will let you concentrate on what you do best and what will make the most money for you—selling. But when you need answers to problems of management and growth, you will have them. Here are some of the many topics that are covered in detail:

- How to build a strong multi-person agency
- How to succeed with direct mail
- How to evaluate and sell your agency
- How to find and hire the best salespeople
- How to analyze and control your selling expenses

How to Start and Build a Successful Manufacturers' Agency

James J. Gibbons

President, Manufacturers' Agents National Association
Laguna Hills, California

A James Peter Book
James Peter Associates, Inc.

PRENTICE HALL
Englewood Cliffs, New Jersey 07632

Prentice-Hall International (UK) Limited, *London*
Prentice-Hall of Australia Pty. Limited, *Sydney*
Prentice-Hall Canada Inc., *Toronto*
Prentice-Hall Hispanoamericana, S. A., *Mexico*
Prentice-Hall of India Private Limited, *New Delhi*
Prentice-Hall of Japan, Inc., *Tokyo*
Simon & Schuster Asia Pte, Ltd., *Singapore*
Editora Prentice-Hall do Brasil, Ltda., *Rio de Janeiro*

© 1988 *by*

JAMES J. GIBBONS

10   9   8   7   6   5   4   3   2

This publication is designed to provide accurate and authoritative information in regard to the subject matter covered. It is sold with the understanding that the publisher is not engaged in rendering legal, accounting, or other professional service. If legal advice or other expert assistance is required, the services of a competent professional person should be sought.
. . . *From the Declaration of Principles jointly adopted by a Committee of the American Bar Association and a Committee of Publishers and Associations.*

Library of Congress Cataloging-in-Publication Data

Gibbons, James.
  How to start and build a successful manufacturers' agency.

  "A James Peter book."
  Includes index.
  1. Manufacturers' agents.   2. New business enterprises.   3. Success in business.   I. Title.
HF5422.G53   1988   658.8'6   87-35730
ISBN 0-13-434705-6

ISBN 0-13-434705-6

PRENTICE HALL
BUSINESS & PROFESSIONAL DIVISION
A division of Simon & Schuster
Englewood Cliffs, New Jersey 07632

Printed in the United States of America

- How to find and work with subagents
- How to locate and prescreen prospective principals
- How to conduct an interview with a prospective principal
- How to resolve commission disputes
- How to use a computer to build your business
- How to turn service calls into sales calls
- Successful advertising and sales promotion
- How to sell the corporate giants
- What is the best form for your business?
- How to organize your office
- How to make manufacturers' literature pay off
- How to analyze and control your cash flow
- How to establish practical commission rates
- How to deal with the problems of product liability
- How to negotiate contracts that protect you and your manufac-turer relationships
- What's the best name for your agency?
- How to handle the house account problems
- How to run efficient sales meetings
- How to handle split commissions
- Planning a practical benefit package for your agency
- The agency and tax laws
- How to evaluate your principals in terms of your own growth plan
- Why the opportunities in agency ownership will continue to expand
- How to be an effective member of a Rep Council
- How to find and work with overseas manufacturers
- Personality and success—a checklist of personal characteristics of successful manufacturers' representatives
- How to plan and manage a territory

- Should you stock products—have a warehouse?
- How to handle credit and collection problems
- plus much more

A Promise to the Reader

Everything I have learned by running a major multi-person agency for more than thirty years, everything I have learned as president of MANA since 1970, and everything that the MANA research projects have identified that leads to success are in this book. When I undertook the writing of this book, I told the publisher that it would have to be practical and real-world material, and not a how-to-get-rich-quick book. There's no doubt that you can get rich as a manufacturers' agent—but this book will not fill you with empty promises. Rather, it gives you every practical fact that has been field-tested and proven effective that leads to agency success. It also gives you a single volume filled with the knowledge that is necessary to run an agency on your own. You now have the collected wisdom of thousands of successful agencies in the pages that follow.

Jim Gibbons

Contents

CHAPTER 1

How to Harness the Five Keys to Agency Success

HOW TO MEASURE AGENCY SUCCESS

Agency success stories are told against a background of many individual successes. The agency that grows, whether it is a one-person or multi-person operation, is one that considers everyone and every company with which it must interact. This includes employees, customers, principals, suppliers, creditors, and even competitors. Let's look at each before we present a picture of agency success from the owner's point of view.

Employees Success in the agency business means either maximizing your own time as a solo or adding people to help you build the business. Today, though, the multi-person agency is the rule—not the exception. In 1987, the average manufacturers' agency had three salespeople on the road and one person in the office. And the average agency had been in business for nearly fourteen years.

The measure of success of an agency in employee terms is usually portrayed in terms of turnover. Manufacturers' agencies are seldom thought of as revolving doors. In fact, more than a few people who join agencies as employees frequently are given some form of ownership as their value becomes apparent.

Customers   This is a more complex group than you might imagine. At first, you might think that simply getting and holding customers is all that is needed. However, when you consider that more than a few companies split their buying based on elements of specific satisfaction provided by different agencies, you can focus on the issue. For example, one agency may carry the best line of valves, but the customer may split his valve buying with other agencies for price and delivery reasons.

Although an agency has no real control over the quality of most products, it can frequently exercise considerable control on principals to see that the buying is no longer split, and that the agency's principal gets all the business. It should be noted that the customer picture is usually a critical element in the sale of an agency. No one buys from an agency that isn't respected on several dimensions by its customers.

Principals   The agency that holds on to its principals is a successful agency, in most cases. However, it's important to understand why agencies keep their principals. If the agency is doing a good job by the usual standards, the answer is simple and uncomplicated. But many manufacturers keep their agencies for other reasons as well. For example, many manufacturers consider their agencies as prime sources of new product and competitive information. When you try to define the reasons for the success of your agency, be sure to do it in terms of the *total* value to the principals.

Suppliers   Few agencies depend as heavily on outside suppliers as do their principals. However, with the enthusiastic backing of your automobile dealer, insurance broker, typing service, and accountant, you have the strength of important allies. Without this strength you can flounder.

Competitors   Why should you measure the success of a sales agency by how your competitors feel about you? In more than a few cases your success may depend on just how you position yourself relative to your competitors. Competitors are a fact of life, but the agency that goes out of its way to be hostile will be repaid in kind. It's the friendly competitor that keeps other agencies guessing. Hostile people are very obvious, and easy to read and get the jump on. Limit your competitive activity to products, price, quality and delivery, and stay away from getting personal.

HOW TO MEASURE
YOUR OWN PERSONAL SUCCESS

When you can define success in terms of your own world of business, you have a much more realistic picture—one that will help you to be even more successful in the future. Let's look at some of the ways you can judge yourself personally as you build your manufacturers' agency.

Since there are as many people who claim that the reason they start agencies is to make more money than they could as employees working for someone else as there are those who feel that the personal, psychological, and emotional rewards come first, let's toss the coin and begin with the financial rewards for starting an agency.

Absolute Income   This is a critical factor for most agents who want to measure their progress. Unlike other small business operators who frequently talk in terms of their businesses' gross income, the average agent is quite realistic about the exact amount of money that goes in his or her pocket.

Owners of small advertising agencies, for example, tend to picture themselves in terms of their gross billings. Billing of $3 million with a four-person agency sounds impressive to those unfamiliar with the business. Though sales at this level seldom put more than $150,000 a year in the pocket of the owner. Manufacturers' agents are, of course, concerned with their gross figures from a cost accounting point of view. However, they are generally very realistic and get their pleasure in terms of the actual money that the business gives them.

Return on Net Worth   This is a factor that is very meaningful for businesses with a heavy capital investment. But for the average agency, the biggest investment will be in people and possibly a building. Therefore, few manufacturers' agents are in a position to get a picture of success in terms of return on net worth.

Return on Invested Time Time is money for the manufacturers' agent. Since selling and the management of a sales agency are time-intensive activities, most owners, consciously or unconsciously, calculate just what they earn for every hour spent. Although this has been included under a financial heading, the return on time spent has a very real psychological effect—when the business pays off. In fact, it's not uncommon to hear two friendly agents comparing notes in terms of what they perceive to be their hourly income. More than a few agents who have been in the business for a while have said: "I make as much per hour today as I did in a week just a few years ago when I was working for someone else." And this is seldom an idle boast.

Security This may seem out of place, but believe me it isn't. Most of the people who don't go out on their own, and those who took a long time to make the decision to break away, claim that their prime fear was the loss of security that accompanies a weekly paycheck and a place to go every day. But when you talk with agents who have been in business for a few years, whether they are marginally successful or are making it big, they will tell you that security as an employee is an illusion. Cutbacks, transfers, obsolete products, and a host of other things over which you have no control can put you on the street—regardless of how good a job you have done.

Once your agency is up and running, you can control most of these elements. Sure, you can lose a valued principal and a big customer can switch to your competitor's product for obscure reasons, but you can always dig in and get the business back up to speed. You know how you did it in the first place. It's usually just a matter of kicking the wheel harder, and possibly from a different direction.

The psychological factors Those who like to peg stones at the capitalist system will tell you that greed greases the wheels of industry. But contemporary business psychologists have revealed the truth. People who own their own businesses and like what they are doing get much more satisfaction from their work than those who dislike their work. There are some pretty well-paid and discontented people in industry, but there are very few agents who don't look forward to the start of each day.

The past few years and the years to come in this decade will reveal another reward that most entrepreneurs appreciate—personal recognition. Because most agents are gregarious people, they are usually quite sensitive to the way people think of them. We have come a long way from the drummer and peddler image of pre-World War II days. And we are currently beginning to get the personal recognition that is being accorded to all entrepreneurs—those who start computer companies, those who settle in small country towns to practice law, and those who stake everything on building a successful manufacturers' agency.

HOW TO STACK THE DECK IN YOUR FAVOR

"It took two tries to get here," a very successful agent told me. Here, for him, was his own building and a sales agency that employed six people. He was obviously quite proud of his achievement.

"The first time around," he said, "I thought I had it all together. I had been a successful salesman for a manufacturer and I had even spent a few years in the field working for another agency. I parted from my employer on the best of terms, I had a few good lines, and I had the contacts I had built up for almost ten years. But within a year I had to call it quits. I just didn't estimate my time and investment capital closely enough," he said. "Two years later," he continued, "I was back in business with a tight handle on my investment requirements and the time I had to spend on all aspects of the business."

More than a few of today's top agents didn't make it the first time, or they came close to going bust before they became successful. In fact, most new businesses, whether they are sales agencies or pizza stands, go through a similar cycle.

Here's how you can insure success in yourself as an independent manufacturers' agent.

Make a Definite Commitment to Yourself and to Your Agency

I have talked with thousands of manufacturers' agents over the years. Many were just starting out, and others were at various stages in the growth of their business. The one fact that stands out when reviewing these meetings is that those who have made it have made a definite commitment. Those who were vague about the whole thing didn't, or it took them much longer to get to the top.

Committed agents are almost totally absorbed in their business. Uncompleted projects and unresolved commitments are burrs under their saddle. However, the commitments they make relate to their personal needs as well as to the needs of a growing business.

It's not enough to shout out loud, "I'm going to be a successful manufacturers' agent." You have to know in advance what it's going to take to be successful, and you have to make the commitments that will get you there.

For example, if you know that it takes an average of six calls before you can expect an order, you must make the commitment to make those six calls. It's tempting to spread them out a little or to make just five when you have such other things to do as bookkeeping and correspondence with your principals. But if six calls are needed, you better make them and do your office work at night. It's as simple and direct as that. Some day, of course, you won't have to burn the midnight oil. But for now, lay in a good supply and be prepared to make a lot of personal compromises to get your business on sound footing right from the start.

> *Ask yourself this:* Are you prepared to make a strong commitment to yourself and to the future of your agency? Are you willing to put in the kind of hours early on that insure success? Investing early in the development of an agency is critical to success.

Take Risks, But Be Certain That They Are Calculated Risks

Contrary to conventional wisdom, manufacturers' agents aren't big risk-takers—they seldom gamble on the most speculative opportunities. And this is one of the characteristics that business psychologists have identified as being important for business success.

If it's the thrill of big risks you want, race motorcycles. But if it's a challenge and the opportunity to build a profitable business you want, choose moderate risk opportunities. Agents are achievement-oriented people, and as such they gladly shoulder responsibility for projects that they feel they can handle themselves. They are aggressive, but realistic. And they make commitments to projects that reflect an assessment of their ability to insure a successful outcome.

Pick low-risk tasks, and the chances are good that you will achieve everything you set out to do. But a lot of low-risk tasks don't lead to the kind of business success that most agents want or can achieve. Choose high risks, and the probabilities of your success will be diminished. However, when you are realistic about the moderate risks you will assume to build a successful business, you will be psychologically better tuned to success than you would at either end of the risk scale.

Ask yourself this: Do you prefer a moderate risk solution to a business problem after you have studied the alternatives thoroughly? Or do you prefer to go very slowly, or take the plunge? Choosing the moderate risk alternative may not be as exciting as taking a plunge, but it's the best way to go with a small business.

Look for and Seize Opportunities

Most successful people will tell you that they were blind to far too many opportunities during the early stages of building their businesses because they were too concerned with less important details. You can't let the details slip by unhandled, but you must also remain alert to opportunities in their obvious and subtle forms.

Successful agents are usually very good at turning opportunities into active achievement. "I was only in business for four months," an agent said, "when a manufacturer came to me with a very fine line. It was a great opportunity, but I wasn't sure I could handle it with the commitments I had made. But it was a once-in-a-lifetime deal. Rather than turn it away, I added a man, even though I couldn't afford it at the time. It was the best move I could have made—even though it gave me more than a few sleepless nights during the first year."

Agents are realistic people. They have the ability to anticipate and plan carefully just where they want to take their business. But they prefer making logical predictions that are based on sound research rather than running by the seat of their pants.

Those who lack the characteristics attributed to the entrepreneurs of today tend to be overwhelmed by the obstacles that are part of every business. However, agents who are successful all claim that some of the greatest challenges of their lives came as the result of facing obstacles that they had never considered when they first went into business. Most of them came up with innovative ways of handling the obstacles, rather than following the well-worn paths that others had taken when faced with similar problems.

This characteristic is critical today, especially in the wake of the criticism that has been leveled at the case-method training given at some of the country's leading business schools. It has been shown that some of these highly paid individuals fail to solve more than a few problems mainly because they tend to rely on solutions tried by others, rather than by seizing opportunities imaginatively.

> *Ask yourself this:* Do you prefer innovative solutions to maximize opportunities, or is your approach more traditional? Most successful agents are ever vigilant; they are always looking for opportunities in every situation and they prefer to make the most of them in imaginative, rather than stereotyped ways.

Maintain Objectivity in Everything You Do

Agents are, perhaps, the most realistic businesspeople when it comes to themselves and the goals they want to achieve. They have to be to get into a profession that is based solely on personal performance. Sell nothing; get nothing!

According to business psychologists, success in the field depends quite heavily on remaining impersonal about the one thing that is frequently closest to an agent's heart—his or her agency. Rarely do agents let personal likes and dislikes get in the way of the things they want to accomplish. And when they need help, successful agents turn to experts, rather than to friends or relatives. In other words, they take a very professional attitude toward their business.

> *Ask yourself this:* When you need help, advice, or any kind of assistance, are you more likely to turn to those with the answers or to those who are likely to tell you what you want to hear? The ability to take the advice of an expert, even when it may sound distasteful, is critical for success. You may turn to friends and relatives for consolation once in a while, but you must make certain that advice comes from those who are most capable of giving it to you. You must also be objective at all times.

Keep Your Ear to the Ground

One of the biggest problems of being a manufacturers' agent is the isolation you will experience. Factories seldom call unless it's to complain. And you usually hear from customers more when there are problems than when they want to place orders.

Every agent needs to get input from a variety of sources. And they need to know from those who are important to them just how their performance stacks up. "I had a fifty percent increase in the territory," an agent told me a few years ago. "But at the end of the year," he continued, "they dropped me. I should have paid more attention to the signs. When the sales manager mentioned that my commissions exceeded his salary, I should have known I was in for trouble."

It's true that situations like this one occasionally crop up. It's also true that manufacturers' agents thrive on and need information— whether it's directly relevant to what they are doing or comes from left field. More often than not, the good agent can make sense of the bits and pieces better than most. I know more than a few manufacturers' agents who have been able to advise their principals on new products and competitive situations mainly because they were obsessed with all kinds of information.

Ask yourself this: Is it important for you to know how well you are doing for a principal, even though you have a clear picture of your effort in terms of commissions? Are you constantly combining pieces of seemingly unrelated information to make a picture that has meaning in unexpected ways? If you are, you are in good company with the successful agents of the country.

Be Optimistic in Unfamiliar Situations

Successful agents are very optimistic when they find themselves in unfamiliar situations. They may not have a clear picture of the odds, but the opportunity to be the master of a situation is always very appealing. According to social psychologists, entrepreneurs seldom see why they can't win in unfamiliar situations just by relying on themselves. They take bold steps where there aren't any clear guidelines. And they usually make more of the opportunities in unusual situations than do those who are more cautious.

Perhaps more important than the optimism agents show in unfamiliar situations is the fact that they learn very quickly from what they have done. There are usually things in every unique situation that can be applied to other situations in the future. Successful agents are able to catalog these experiences and the things they did to insure a positive outcome mentally, and to draw on the experience readily when the need arises. They also are able to move from vaguely defined situations to positive solutions to the use of what they have learned in other situations.

> *Ask yourself this:* Do you welcome the opportunity to take on an unusual problem? Are you optimistic that you can handle the novel situations and learn something in the bargain? For most successful manufacturers' agents the answer to these questions is a resounding *yes*.

Have a Positive Attitude Toward Money

Agents have a real respect for money, but they are not greedy. Seldom do they see money as something to hoard. And few of them feel the need to display their success to everyone they know and don't know. Most agents view their wealth as a sign that they are winning the game rather than as a personal adornment.

Making and losing money gives agents the signals they need to play the game harder or to change the rules to suit themselves. A profit tells the successful agent that what he or she has done is right and that he or she should do more of it. A loss tells the agent that he or she has to do something differently. Unfortunately, too many beginning entrepreneurs, including manufacturers' agents, tend to intensify what they have been doing when the game turns to losses, rather than to look for the causes and how best to correct them. As agents gain experience, this approach seems to change to problem seeking and solving.

> *Ask yourself this:* Why is it important for you to make more money as an agent than you could ever make as an employee working for someone else? If you see the practical value of money as well as the signals it sends when you are doing things right and wrong, you are in good company with successful agents.

Be a "Proactive" Manager

This is, perhaps, one of the most difficult skills for an agent to learn. Most agents get into the business after they have proven themselves as salespeople for manufacturers or for other agencies. However, it takes more, much more, to run an agency than just good selling skills. It takes management ability—even if you have no one to manage but yourself.

Unfortunately, most new agents are what the management buzz-word specialists call *reactive managers*. They are always putting out fires. That is, they react to problems when they occur, rather than anticipating them and heading them off before they get out of hand. Those who have this skill are called *proactive managers*. They have everything under control.

> *Ask yourself this:* Do you like to plan ahead rather than just letting things happen? Remember that planning in this sense refers to general directions. You can't possibly nail down every contingency. Besides, if you could, business would be a very dull thing. Planning ahead isn't done to eliminate all problems or to reduce the ambiguity that makes business fun. Planning ahead is mainly done to give you and your business a positive trajectory.

Examples of What Being in Business Means to Agents

In the next chapter, you will meet several agents who started from scratch and built very successful businesses. But I'd like you to read what a few agents have said about the business of being in business. These are the warts and the roses. Remember each if you can and try to apply what they have said to what you will hear from the three agents in the next chapter.

> "There is an awful lot of satisfaction being your own boss. You can do things your own way. When you succeed, you get all the credit. When you fail, you also get all the credit. But at least you know that the control is in your hands—not in someone elses."

> "There's more than making a lot of money in running your own sales agency. You can guarantee your future whether you take the money and invest it personally or use it to build an agency that you will sell someday. And then there's the satisfaction of giving jobs to others, helping them to make it. I can't imagine any other business that offers all of these satisfactions."

> "You can win the respect of other people. I have been called to serve on more than a few community committees just because I run a successful business in the area. At first I thought that I could use these committees to get more business. But once I really became

involved I decided that the rewards of community service were important without getting more business.''

"It's a mistake to think of yourself as your own boss in the popular sense. You have a lot of bosses when you start and run your own agency. Your principals are your bosses. Your customers can exert some pretty tough pressure, too. And meeting more and more governmental regulations makes me wonder who really is in charge—me or the IRS, the Federal Trade Commission, and every other department in our vast bureaucracy.''

"You are limited by your resources. Of course, this may not be a problem, but there are too many opportunities that require investment that a small agency owner is unable to get or afraid to risk.''

"At first I believed all those stories about the family forgetting who you are when you start your own agency. But I solved that problem by getting them all involved—my wife and the two kids. Most agents come home and gripe to the family about their problems. My wife and kids live the business with me. The children do office chores after school, and my wife handles some of the correspondence. I did this not to save money—although it helps— but to make sure that the business I was building was part of them as well as it was part of me. It's too soon to tell now, but I bet I'm raising the two owners of my agency right now. They love it.''

CHAPTER 2

Profiles of Professional Sales Agencies

This chapter presents case histories on which you can pattern your own business. I did not use people's real names because it allowed me to build on the work of these people and to add material from other people's experiences, which should prove very helpful to you. But keep in mind that real people did the things described.

A ONE-PERSON AGENCY THAT COVERS THREE STATES

Technically, Tom runs a one-man show covering three eastern states, and he is incorporated. He does, however, have part-time secretarial help.

Tom is a graduate engineer and worked for about fifteen years designing hydraulic components for a major manufacturer. He was good at it, but he was getting bored. When his employer asked him to make a few field trips with the agents who represented the company, a whole new world opened up to him. As he put it: "I never realized how interesting face-to-face selling was." In short, he was hooked.

During a one-year period, Tom was able to spend about one-third of his time working in the field. Each time he returned to his engineering office, he was less and less comfortable doing the work that had sustained him for fifteen years. But he knew that he was poorly equipped to be successful in a field that was as competitive as selling. Therefore, he took a few courses at a local college on sales and marketing and became very attentive when he was in the field with one of his employer's agents.

As you might expect, this kind of enthusiasm didn't go unnoticed by his employer and by the agencies with whom he worked in the field. His employer got a little anxious about losing Tom, as he was a good engineer. But he recognized that Tom was still very much on the company's side.

It wasn't until one of the agents decided to expand that Tom had to make a decision to move. With his boss's blessing, he left the firm that had given him a computer, a cubicle, and a salary for fifteen years for the uncertainty of selling with a manufacturers' agency. He had a lot to learn, but was a fast learner.

After a few years working for the agency, and still selling the products manufactured by his former employer, he had the opportunity to open a new territory for his former employer—as the owner of his own manufacturers' agency. It was a big step because it required a move for his family. But Tom decided the risk was worth it. He also decided that for the time being he would operate as a one-person agency.

Now, let's pick up on Tom four years after he moved and opened his own agency. He represents four other manufacturers. Two of his principals were referred to him by his first employer and two he acquired about six months after he opened the doors. He covers his three states himself by car and with an occasional regional airline flight. He has plans to grow, and is growing. However, he is very much contented with his one-person agency. Since you are probably wondering whether a one-person or multi-person agency would be best for you, let's get right to Tom's ideas.

"The products I sell," Tom said, "are specified as OEM components. The first sale is the toughest. After that it's mainly a matter of servicing the customer. That can be difficult, but it frequently doesn't take the same concentrated effort as it takes to crack a new account. In my first few years in business, I worked night and day getting a customer base. Now it's less a matter of chasing new customers but serving the customers I have developed. It's true that there is more business in my territory and I get more and more of it every year. My principals and I agree on the increases they would like to see. And we both know who the customers are that they would like to get. We work on this together and they are quite happy. I think that if I were a one-person agency in a territory and was only bringing in a fraction of the business, I wouldn't be doing the best thing for my principals and for my agency.''

Tom and his principals recognize the potential in the territory and they know that it can be covered adequately with a one-person agency. But let's look at some reasons why Tom might want to expand to a multi-person agency.

- *Expanded product lines.* If any of Tom's principals expand their lines to the point where his one-person coverage becomes inadequate, Tom should seriously consider expanding his agency.

- *Adding new lines to the agency.* At the moment, Tom has a very successful business in terms of his own needs, the needs of those manufacturers he represents, and the needs of his customers. However, if he should decide to want more, for whatever reason, he will have to add people. Adding people usually requires adding internal support services and often necessitates larger quarters. Although this is the way that most multi-person agencies grow, there are more than a few that still operate from a small office. However, the people generally cover remote territories and seldom have a need for fixed office space. These people often work from their home offices and visit agency headquarters only for meetings.

- *To insure continuity.* One of the strongest advantages of the manufacturers' agency for a manufacturer is the continuity in the territory. Employed salespeople come and go with alarming frequency. However, the manufacturers' agency represents stability in a territory. And even though the working life of the one-person agency may be 20, 30, or more years, manufacturers like to have some assurance that their interests will continue to be served when the one-person agency decides to retire and take up professional golf. For this reason, many one-person agencies often become multi-person agencies in later years. And more than a few merge with other similar agencies to provide this continuity for their principals.

- *To build a saleable business.* After World War II, a group of entrepreneurs recognized that there was a lot of growth potential in the American economy. Many of these people had the skill to create and develop businesses, and they did so with the sole purpose of building something that could be sold. No agents that I know of have done this. But it does point up the fact that there will always be buyers for good businesses. Unless you are able to make and save a lot of money during your working career as a one-person agency, you ought to think about expanding simply because you will have something significant to sell. Such a sale could sustain you rather comfortably in old age, or provide a decent legacy for your heirs.

The decision to expand should really be made on the basis of every event that impinges on your business. You may be more comfortable as a one-person agency, but market circumstances and principal pressure may make the decision for you. The best word of advice I can give is to keep an open mind. It's not easy to be too flexible, though, after you have built a successful one-person agency over a ten- or fifteen-year period. The comfort factor, strangely enough, can make life more than a little uncomfortable.

The story of an agent who faced this situation highlights the profile of a multi-person agency.

A MULTI-PERSON AGENCY THAT COVERS ONE STATE

Let's call this agent Bill. He took pretty much the same route as Tom, in our previous example. However, Bill only covered one state. It's a big one, though—California.

"At first I could do it with ease," Bill related. "I had three principals whose main customers were in Silicon Valley. I had San Jose and the surrounding territory covered like a blanket all by myself. But you know how this business has expanded, especially in the West. When I found myself commuting from San Francisco to San Diego and back up to Los Angeles in one day, I knew that I either had to give up some of the territory or expand. I didn't want to give up the territory."

Bill didn't have the kind of capital needed to set up another office in Southern California, so he decided to make a working arrangement with another agent in that territory. "He acted as a subagent for me, but we discussed long-range plans early on," Bill explained. "I knew that I wanted to have a bigger business, and working with subagents gives you coverage, but it doesn't exactly build a business for you," he said.

After a few months, Bill and his subagent knew that it would be possible to merge and open an office. Since Bill brought more to the table than his new partner, he had the controlling share. However, this was agreeable to both parties.

Armed with existing business in the territory and a good track record, Bill was able to borrow the money he needed to fund an office in the Los Angeles area. "We decided that we both wanted to build something that represented equity," Bill explained. Although he had made a lot of money solo, he now felt that the promise of owning something was valuable to him. "Apart from the pure financial picture," he said, "I have a son and a daughter who would like to be part of the business. My daughter is already working in the office. As she gains experience with the products and the customers, she will start making calls with us. She has already expressed an interest in running a territory by herself. Who knows, perhaps we'll expand with the right person?"

This little vignette has identified some of the more important characteristics of the people who decide to build larger manufacturers' agencies. Although there are probably as many one-person agencies as there are multi-person agencies, there are some decided advantages to expanding. However, expansion just for the sake of expansion doesn't make sense. For those who would like to consider the possibility of building a larger agency, I have devoted an entire chapter (14) to the subject.

ANOTHER ONE-PERSON AGENCY— WITH A DIFFERENCE

Art has been in business for almost twenty years. He covers one midwestern state by himself and makes a good living. His principals are satisfied, and his gross sales are about $3 million.

Three million! That may seem like a lot, but Art sells two lines of hand tools to distributors. His customers don't use the products, they buy them, stock them, and sell them to those who will drive the nails and turn the screws.

Art bought this agency from another man about twenty years ago. He worked for the man from whom he bought the business for about two years, and this is what makes the story really interesting. In a sense, it's not Art's story, but the story of the man from whom he bought the agency, Paul.

Paul had run his agency as a one-person agency very successfully and with no thought of adding people, until he wanted to take it a little slower. Taking it slower meant that sales were sure to drop off and that his principals would have doubts about the future of the agency. Therefore, Paul, having no kids to bring into the business, took on Art as a salesman with the agreement that Art would buy the agency after a few years. Both men were smart enough not to announce their intentions immediately. "No need to make the principals and customers nervous," they both agreed.

Art explained: "We wanted to make sure that our customers were accustomed to working with me before we let the world in on our plans. Once customers and principals were comfortable, it was just a matter of Paul phasing out. Actually, we never really did announce this. I just spent more and more time with the customers and Paul spent less and less. Everyone was pleased. Even when Paul was almost fully retired, we still gave the outward impression of being a two-man agency."

It's interesting to note that even though these men perceived the problems that can occur in a single-person agency, they both decided to continue operating in this fashion. When I then asked how they handled it, Art explained: "We have always insisted that our agency be measured by results, not by the number of people we have on the payroll. And that has always been the strength of our operations. The few times we looked for new lines, we never acted defensively at all about our size. We did, however, act very dramatically in terms of the results we had produced for our other principals. Good corporate managers look at the bottom line. They were buying results, not a lot of people."

It's important to note that this attitude can and does work in many circumstances. But you have to make absolutely certain that you are dealing from strength. If a particular principal has a wide territory for you that requires a heavy specification type of contact, the chances are that you will have a tough time getting the line as a one-person agency. However, if the business is established, as it was in this example, and it's more a matter of seeing that the business is protected, there should be no problems.

IS ONE FORM BEST FOR EVERY AGENCY?

The answer is no. However, one of the things I have noticed over the years is that two agencies doing almost exactly the same thing in different territories may do things exactly opposite from each other. This, of course, translates into an understanding of the human equation. Where one person may feel perfectly comfortable covering a territory alone for four principals, another would want help.

Throughout this book, you'll be given practical information that has been derived from my own experience and the experience of thousands of manufacturers' agents who are active members of the Manufacturers' Agents National Association (MANA). It's important that you review this material not in the absolute, but as it relates specifically to you as an individual—to the territory you cover or will cover, to the markets within the territory you will serve, to the customers you serve, and to the needs of the manufacturers you serve or are planning to serve. Only when you look at every dimension will you be able to decide which form will work best for you. And even then, the decision should not be irreversible. You may be firmly convinced that your needs are best served by running a one-person agency. But when a new and big principal knocks on your door with a line that needs more than one person in the field, you'll probably do more than just think about it.

PROFILES OF MANUFACTURERS' AGENCIES

The Manufacturers' Agents National Association periodically surveys its members and develops composite profiles. The most recent survey indicates that today's agency is more than just an independent sales organization. It's a team of well-educated professionals who are carrying their principals' products to domestic territories as well as to other countries.

It's no wonder that manufacturers are turning to agencies. The sales agency of today is more often than not a corporation run by a person with solid professional, practical, and sales skills. The average agency produces sales for its principals in excess of four million dollars annually, covers five states, and fields a team of three highly qualified salespeople. Moreover, this agency may be carrying the sales banner to foreign shores. The owner is mature, well educated, and well paid. And often the agency is part of Fortune 500 selling teams as well as a part of smaller companies that traditionally sell with agencies.

How Agencies Are Organized

Most agency owners have chosen the corporate form for their business. The conventional corporation and the S Corporation account for 69% of the agencies that responded to our survey. The corporate structure seems to represent a form that is better suited to the complex businesses that agencies have become. Pension plans, continuity protection, and other benefits are often more easily structured for a growing agency that is incorporated.

Corporations	S Corporations	Sole Proprietorships	Partnerships
58%	11%	27%	4%

A Picture of the Average Agency

The average agency is a composite, made up of corporations, partnerships, and sole proprietorships. Although profiles for each type of business organization form have been provided in this chapter, the composite (Figure 2-1) provides a view that summarizes, in a sense, the state of the sales agency today.

Of particular interest in terms of the international shift we have been experiencing is the number of agencies selling foreign products domestically and marketing American-made products abroad. Unfortunately, we have no baseline on which to judge the picture. However, our general observation is that this growth has been relatively recent, and it appears that it will be a trend that will continue for years to come.

FIGURE 2-1
A Composite Profile of the Average Agency (1986)*

Average number of offices	1.5
Average number of states covered	5.2
Average number of manufacturers represented	10.1
Average number of salespeople	3.5
Average number of office staff	1.7
Average number of years in operation	15.06
Average gross revenue in 1986	$ 280,099.61
Average gross sales	$4,402,986.34
Average agency net (after taxes)	$ 55,922.49
Established agency	83%
Acquired agency	16%
Agency is the result of a merger	4%
Agency represents foreign manufacturers	45%
Agency selling products overseas	10%
Agency planning to become involved in international trade	17%
Agency provides warehousing	30%
Agency also acts as a distributor	43%

* This profile was created by averaging responses from agencies operating under all forms of organization: sole proprietorships, partnerships, corporations, and S Corporations.

THE SOLE PROPRIETORSHIP

Twenty-seven percent of the agents who responded to our survey said that they operated as sole proprietorships. However, it's important to remember that not all sole proprietorships are one-person agencies. Many have sales and support people working for them. Remember, the less than one figure for office staff is an average, but the average sole proprietor has two salespeople. The net incomes for the owner and his or her number-two person are not insignificant, indicating that the sole proprietorship is not necessarily the stereotype of the mom-and-pop shop. Data gathered in interviews and other studies show that these organizations are using sophisticated telecommunications and comput-

FIGURE 2-2
Sole Proprietorship (Average Profile)

Average number of offices	1.18
Average number of states covered in territory	4.25
Average number of manufacturers represented	7.95
Average number of salespeople	1.95
Average number of office staff	.86*
Years in operation	9.88
Average age of principal owner	46.89
Gross revenue, 1986	$ 117,700.70
Gross sales	$2,137,419.91
Agency net	$ 53,611.60
Principal owner net	$ 51,985.92
Partner net	$ 32,838.71
Established agency	84%
Acquired agency	9%
Agency is the result of a merger	1%
Representing foreign manufacturers	35%
Selling products overseas	7%
Planning to become involved in international trade	18%

* Since most of the sole proprietorships are operating out of their homes, they do most of the office work themselves.

ing equipment, and that they are turning in strong sales for their principals. Average gross sales of $2.2 million for sole proprietorships is nothing to sneeze at. They are very much a force to be reckoned with. (See Figure 2-2.)

PARTNERSHIPS

The small percentage of partnerships, 4%, compared with corporate forms of ownership, should not be thought to mean that they are a minor force in the marketplace. With about four people selling and a coverage of nearly five states, the average partnership produced impressive net figures. It's interesting to note that the average partnership has

FIGURE 2-3
Partnerships (Average Profile)

Average number of offices	1.73
Average number of states covered in territory	4.85
Average number of manufacturers represented	11.27
Average number of salespeople	3.55
Average number of office staff	1.73
Years in operation	15.42
Average age of principal owner	50.55
Gross revenue	$ 243,172.41
Gross sales	$3,309,534.48
Agency net	$ 131,078.95
Principal owner net	$ 58,401.81
Partner net	$ 44,686.84
Established agency	85%
Acquired agency	15%
Result of a merger	21%
Representing foreign manufacturers	55%
Selling products overseas	3%
Planning to become involved in international trade	21%

been in existence in its present form for 15 years. Those who responded apparently felt no need to modify their business structure to the corporate form as their fortunes and size grew. (See Figure 2.3.)

THE CORPORATION

Those who have chosen the conventional corporate form for their business report average sales of over $5 million annually. They cover a little more than five states with four salespeople, and represent 10 principals. On the other hand, the average S Corporation reported annual sales of $3,741,468.24. The S Corporation agencies are fielding about 3 salespeople, and they cover the same number of states and represent about the same number of manufacturers.

Although corporations dominate the financial statistics, it's unwise

FIGURE 2-4
Corporations (Average Profile)

Average number of offices	1.60
Average number of states covered in territory	5.30
Average number of manufacturers represented	10.28
Average number of salespeople	4.03
Average number of office staff	1.50
Years in operation	16.78
Average age of principal owner	49.65
Gross revenue	$ 362,693.18
Gross sales	$5,349,249.83
Agency net	$ 56,787.88
Principal owner net	$ 70,278.69
Partner net	$ 51,342.38
Established agency	77%
Acquired agency	19%
Result of merger	4%
Representing foreign manufacturers	45%
Selling products overseas	11%
Planning to become involved in international trade	17%

to assume that the act of incorporating leads to growth. Generally speaking, when agencies acquire more principals, customers, employees, and debts, the corporate form offers greater advantage. (See Figure 2-4.)

S CORPORATIONS

For all practical purposes, we could have lumped S Corporations in with conventional corporations, except for one significant fact: The average conventional corporation had about $2 million more in sales than did the average S Corporation. Remember, though, that Sub-S corporate profits are ordinarily taxed and allocated on a pro-rata basis to shareholders. This is done to eliminate double taxation, and may be reflected in our data. (See Figure 2-5.)

FIGURE 2-5
S Corporation (Average Profile)

Average number of offices	1.31
Average number of states covered in territory	5.43
Average number of manufacturers represented	10.32
Average number of salespeople	2.60
Average number of office staff	1.38
Years in operation	13.13
Average age of principal owner	50.84
Gross revenue	$ 184,377.92
Gross sales	$3,741,468.24
Agency net	$ 35,309.96
Principal net	$ 50,826.78
Partner net	$ 41,646.03
Established agency	83%
Acquired agency	16%
Result of a merger	2%
Representing foreign manufacturers	52%
Selling products overseas	9%
Planning to become involved in international trade	11%

THE MONEY PICTURE

Sales, gross revenue, agency net, and the net to the owners, in general, are up over our last survey, taken in 1987. (See Figure 2.6 for details.)

THE PERSONAL PICTURE

As the laws say, an incorporated agency may exist as an artificial being. However, every agency, regardless of its business structure, is a living, breathing, selling machine. The people are professional, well educated, mature, and take good care of themselves financially. An after-tax income of $63,121.18 (see Figure 2-8) is no small figure, especially when you consider that most agencies are able to throw off considerable benefits as well. The only fly in the personal-picture ointment seems to be the 33% of the respondents who have no continuity plans for their agencies. However, despite any lack of plans, many of them will probably sell to employees or pass the business to family members. At least that's the picture that seems to emerge from stories we're told.

FIGURE 2-6
Regional Representation of Agency Income Statistics**

Regions***	Percent of Respondents*	Gross Sales	Gross Revenue
New England	13%	$7,497,212	$261,649
Mid-Atlantic	13%	$4,002,920	$318,968
Southeast	16%	$4,099,174	$229,460
South Central	10%	$4,769,221	$344,361
Rocky Mountain	4%	$4,206,303	$358,755
Southwest/Hawaii	12%	$3,660,911	$267,569
Pacific Northwest/AK	5%	$2,484,257	$195,786
North Central	4%	$4,013,957	$270,961
Great Lakes	24%	$5,097,310	$287,264

Regions***	Agency Net	Owner Net	2nd Person Net
New England	$ 84,799	$80,515	$58,100
Mid-Atlantic	$ 71,123	$64,264	$58,235
Southeast	$115,253	$96,687	$53,241
South Central	$ 73,507	$75,705	$50,390
Rocky Mountain	$ 39,572	$48,791	$43,407
Southwest/Hawaii	$ 35,351	$59,421	$47,251
Pacific Northwest/AK	$ 28,032	$50,174	$41,099
North Central	$ 9,813	$63,351	$38,484
Great Lakes	$ 50,123	$62,235	$52,159

* Figures indicate percent of respondents, not the actual percent of agencies in regions.
** These figures are based on the data provided by all those who answered this question. However, not all respondents did answer the question. The inclusion of nonrespondents would have skewed the results.
*** See Figure 2-7.

FIGURE 2-7
Regional Representation

New England:

Maine
Vermont
New Hampshire
Massachusetts
New York
Connecticut
Rhode Island
Ontario, Canada

Mid-Atlantic:

Pennsylvania
New Jersey
Delaware
Maryland
D.C.
West Virginia
Virginia

Southeast:

Tennessee
The Carolinas
Georgia
Florida
Alabama
Mississippi

South Central:

Texas
Oklahoma
Kansas
Louisiana
Arkansas
Missouri

Pacific Northwest:

Alaska
British Columbia, Canada
Washington
Oregon

Southwest:

California
Nevada
Arizona
Hawaii

Rocky Mountain:

New Mexico
Colorado
Utah
Wyoming
Idaho
Montana

North Central:

The Dakotas
Minnesota
Iowa
Nebraska

Great Lakes:

Ohio
Michigan
Indiana
Kentucky
Illinois
Wisconsin

THE AGENCY OF TODAY

The use of agencies has been growing steadily since the end of World War II. The economic downturn of the early eighties, however, has had a geometric effect on the trend of the curve. And it appears that

FIGURE 2-8
A Personal Profile*

The principal owner's employment background:

Former sales manager—45%

Former salaried salesperson—24%

Former purchasing agent—6%

Other employment—34% of the respondents indicated experience in these fields: engineering, manufacturing management, commission sales, and the ownership of another business.

Educational background of the principal owner:

Some college—21%

Associate degree or technical school completion—7%

Bachelor's degree—59%

Advanced degree—16%

Average age of the principal owner:

51 years

Average net income of the principal owner:

$63,121.18

Average net income of partner, or number two person:

$47,917.95

Owner's plan for continuity of agency:

No plans; agency will cease to exist upon retirement—33%

Plan to sell agency to employees—43%

Plan to pass agency on to heirs—27%

* These statistics are based on a composite of all agencies sampled.

the return of a stable economy has not lessened the trend. This is probably because of the professionalism that exists in the contemporary manufacturers' agency. As you can see from the profile outlined in this chapter, the agency of today is a financially solid organization run by experienced professionals. It provides a practical way to reach virtually every domestic and foreign market professionally and economically.

3

How to Choose the Best Business Form

Let's talk about successful sales agencies, looking at the business from a structural point of view. After all, a business should be like a well-tailored suit of clothes for the owner. It has to fit, complement, and enhance. If your business doesn't do these things, something could be wrong.

HOW TO DECIDE WHICH FORM OF BUSINESS IS BEST FOR YOU

Technically, you can go into business just by announcing that you are in business. But how many principals would give you their lines? How many customers would listen to your story? And how many bankers would lend you money to get your venture off the ground?

There is more to setting up a business than just creating an entity that stands for the product or service you have to offer. For one thing, you have to consider the matter of legal protection. Far too many agents have not thought this detail through and, to their dismay, have found themselves the victims of product liability lawsuits. "I thought liability was the responsibility of the manufacturer," an agent related in a counseling session recently. I had to explain to him that agencies are being named by plaintiff's attorneys, along with anybody with "deep pockets," as also being responsible. However, because manufacturers' agencies do not take title to the goods and do not alter them, label them, and package them, their liability is generally limited to the legal fees to prove that they are *not* liable. Therefore, one of the first things you should do when you sign a contract is to ask the manufacturer to include you in a rider to its product liability coverage.

Protection is important. But for most people contemplating a business of their own, the question of taxes—the payment of the least amount of taxes—is uppermost in their choice of structure. If you see your agency as an organization that will grow based on invested capital or even if you plan to run solo, it's critical to make the right decision early in the game.

Following are the main types of business structures and the advantages and disadvantages of each.

Sole Proprietorship

About three quarters of all the businesses in the United States are sole proprietorships. Don't think that this form is only for a mom-and-pop grocery store and not for a sophisticated manufacturers' agency. The vast majority of consulting firms operate as sole proprietorships. From a practical point of view, this is the easiest type of business to form legally. Actually, when you go this route, you and your business are for the most part one and the same. For example, the laws of most states say that if you use your personal name for the business, you do not have to file under an assumed name. But remember that your business income is your personal income. This can make things difficult for you in terms of taxes when you really start pulling in a lot of commission income. Also, you and your company cannot be separated in terms of liability. And, as mentioned, product liability awards have been staggering recently.

Although these points may scare you some, think of the tradeoff. You and you alone make the money that your business generates. You don't have to share it with anyone. But make sure that you make good financial plans because, according to law, your company dies when you die.

Partnership

You've got a choice when you go the partnership route. If you choose the general partnership form of organization, you and your general partners will control the day-to-day operations of the agency. But general partners have unlimited liability for the agency's debts. Limited partners, however, exercise no control over the daily opera-

Generally speaking, when agencies are formed as partnerships, each of the partners goes into the field to bring in business. And the experience of each of the partners generally complements the experience of the others. However, you should be aware that among the many members of MANA, only four percent are organized as partnerships. This small number confirms the experience of agents who have gone this route—partnerships are usually not the best way to go.

In small agencies, such as those just starting out, conflicts between partners can often lead to the dissolution of the businesses. Legally, the loss of a partner automatically terminates the business. However, the loss of a stockholder in a corporation doesn't mean that you have to start all over again.

There are also tax consequences you should consider in the partnership form of organization, such as:

- The formation of a partnership and the incorporation of a business can ordinarily be accomplished without any recognition of gain. However, a partnership can usually be liquidated without recognition of gain, and a corporation generally cannot.

- In general, partnerships can be merged without recognition of gain, but corporate mergers can't be accomplished without the recognition of gain unless there is compliance with certain rules.

- The income of a partnership is attributed and taxed to the partners. But the income of a corporation is taxed to the corporation and again to the stockholders when the money is distributed as dividends. However, S Corporations can elect to have income taxed directly to stockholders, thus avoiding the double tax. You should note, though, that a corporation may avoid the double taxation if the stockholders' reasonable salaries absorb practically all of the corporate net profits. But a regular corporation can, to some extent, defer the distribution and resulting taxation of earning to stockholders.

The Corporation

In legal terms, a corporation is an independent entity. It exists apart from you or any other officers or stockholders. Most of the larger U.S. businesses are incorporated, and for some very good reasons.

The corporation offers its owners permanence; it continues to operate despite a stockholder's death. And your personal liability for the firm's debts is limited to the amount you invest in stock. Also, depending on your tax bracket, there are more than a few tax advantages to be achieved with this form. When you decide to grow and need an infusion of capital, the corporation is attractive for inducing outside equity investment.

There are some disadvantages to the corporate form, though. In general, it is subject to higher taxes and fees. The cost to incorporate can run from a few hundred dollars to many thousands of dollars, depending on the complexity. And the red tape that federal and state taxing authorities demand can be quite difficult to handle. Unlike the unlimited power you have with a sole proprietorship, your control within a corporate structure is limited to those stated in your charter. You also could have difficulty doing business in another state because of its laws governing corporations. And the people, other than you, who invest in the corporation may not share your devotion to the agency.

Many consultants today operate as sole proprietors. Consultants, however, seldom face liability suits, and they seldom have business structures that need to be defined as carefully as those of sales agencies. While most agents have started out as sole proprietors, more and more are electing to abide by the rules of the S Corporation. This is a unique form of corporate organization that offers considerable protection for the individuals involved. In return for this protection, however, you will give up some of the tax benefits. Before you choose this or any other form, you should get advice on your situation from an attorney.

You should be aware that a corporation runs the risk of severe tax penalties if it accumulates earnings unreasonably or turns out to be a personal holding company. Though, operating a business as a family partnership may permit splitting of business income among family members. However, similar benefits are available within the corporate S structure.

The laws governing these business forms are much more complex than presented here, but this overview will give you an idea of where to start. *Important:* You should not make the decision on the form of your business without competent legal and accounting advice. When you do, be sure that you have your business plan in hand. No lawyer or accountant can be of much help unless he or she knows what you are immediately planning to do and what you plan to do when your sales agency grows.

The trend today is definitely toward the corporate form right from the start. Some attorneys agree that the fear of costly lawsuits is behind this movement. It seems to be the least expensive form of protection in a world where protection is not only important, but more and more difficult to get.

SHOULD YOU BUY OR START AN AGENCY?

Buying an Agency

Buying an agency is an attractive way to get into business, but you really have to look closely at the entire situation before you make a decision. Just listen to what a disappointed agent related to me:

> I had worked for another agency for about nine years—I knew the business and I knew how to sell. I was ready to move, but the agency I worked for was not for sale. Even if it were, I wouldn't have been able to afford it. But then I heard of a smaller agency that was available in another state. It sounded like a dream come true. I visited with the owner, talked with his principals, and even made a few field trips with him to see how his customers responded to him. Everything was A-OK. Armed with an accountant's analysis of the financial health of the agency and with good feelings, I made an offer that was accepted. I then became the owner of a going and successful agency.
>
> But I had neglected to look at the trends carefully. The current numbers I looked at were strong. However, as I found out all too soon, the major principal was headed for an acquisition which, when it took place, replaced the agencies with factory people. In addition, a smaller customer was relocating his plant in another territory. That resulted in a split commission arrangement for a couple of years. And another principal had cut back on his research and development expenditures. His competitors came into the territory with their new equipment and "ate our lunch."

This situation may seem unwieldy, but I'd like to report that the agent who bought this business not only survived these calamities, but he has grown and prospered. The point is, you should look at every detail *very* carefully before you consider buying an agency from someone, whether it's on the way up or on the way down.

The agency on the way up represents to many people an opportunity to latch on to a business that has already gained momentum—a business that you can take over and run just as it has been run in the past. This may be possible. But be absolutely certain that you are bringing to the agency exactly what those who started it have brought to it. For example, if the founder is an engineer and the products the agency sells are technical, you should have a background that matches this profile. Since the agency business is a very personal business no matter how large it gets, it's very important that you will fit in all the way when you decide to buy a going agency.

More than a few of the successful agents today bought their agencies from those who had started them a number of years ago. But you'll find that most of the present owners worked for a number of years for the agency they eventually bought. Many started as salespeople, moved up to sales management, and then acquired the whole show when the owner decided it was time to play some golf. In some cases, especially in larger agencies, several people pooled their resources to buy the agency when the owner retired.

Starting an Agency

Starting an agency from scratch is not as formidable as you might imagine. But the cost of starting an agency is, of course, higher today than it was ten years ago; and it will even be higher next year. This, however, is a misleading statistic. Everything costs more today. And if you look at the bottom line of the average agency today compared with the same agency ten or twenty years ago, you'll see that the owner is better off now—and he will continue to be better off as the years go by.

This interesting statistic isn't predicated on anything as unreliable as inflation or the cost of money, which can vary widely from year to year. But it's based on the fact that each year more and more manufacturers are turning to agency selling. In the early days of rapid sales agency expansion, just after World War II, there were thousands of new and small companies just getting started. And most owners of these firms soon discovered that they could have a national sales force (manufacturers' agencies) that didn't cost them a nickel in overhead.

Today the main reason for using agencies is not just this fact alone, but because they consistently do a better job of selling a manufacturer's products. This event has not gone unnoticed by some of the biggest manufacturers in the country, including some on the Fortune 500 list. This means that, at least for the foreseeable future, there will be more than enough room for new agencies.

However, this doesn't mean that every part of the country can soak up a lot of new agencies. In some areas, agencies are strongly competing with each other for principals as well as for customers. In others, however, the competition just isn't as intense, or it's almost nonexistent. Since conditions change so quickly, it would be misleading to give you any specific guidance on territories. However, it's safe to say that expanding areas are the better choice.

Expanding areas can be difficult to spot and difficult to interpret. Silicon Valley is still a center of solid-state manufacture but, as of this writing, it's slowing down. It would be an iffy choice to build an agency in this area. However, recent reports indicate that the industrially slow areas of the Northeast are coming to life with light industry and research and development activity. Reading any good business publication such as *Business Week* or *Forbes* should give you some idea of the trends and what to expect from them in the future.

Trade magazine publishers and editors in your field also are often good sources of information on growth areas, because they have to keep up to date on happenings in their field in order to keep readers informed. And they have to be especially sensitive to the trends that affect the advertisers in their magazine. More spending for advertising in one area and less in another, for example, could be the signal you are looking for.

As it turns out, though, most people who start agencies do it right in their own backyard. And they usually succeed because they have an intimate knowledge of their industry, its markets, and the specific territory in which they worked before deciding to start an agency. And most of these people have many of their contacts already set up. It's just a matter of getting the business into action—just about everything else falls into place.

Conversely, people who buy agencies that they hadn't worked for previously usually buy them in areas outside the geographical region they had worked in before. These people often worked for an agency or manufacturer in a sales capacity, and wanted to get into their own business. However, many times they discover that the opportunities are limited in their own area and seek businesses elsewhere.

HOW TO FIND AGENCIES THAT ARE FOR SALE

One of the most active marketplaces for those who want to buy and sell agencies is in *Agency Sales* magazine, published by the Manufacturers' Agents National Association. This inexpensive classified advertising is read by close to 90,000 readers every month. For information on classified advertising in this magazine, write to MANA at P.O. Box 3467, Laguna Hills, California 92654.

According to many agents who have bought agencies from others, a lot of their leads came from contacts in the field. One very successful agent revealed his story to me. "I was a sales manager at the time and thinking about getting into my own agency," he explained. "An agent I knew who operated in our headquarters territory mentioned to me one day that the agency he competed head-to-head with was up for sale. That was the trigger. I bought the agency, and I compete with the guy who tipped me off; but we're friendly competitors."

The larger metropolitan newspapers usually carry extensive "Businesses for Sale" advertising sections. Although very few agents I know have bought agencies in this way, it is an avenue to explore, but not to count on heavily. I would say it's probably a waste of time to run an ad in the "Business Wanted" section of these newspapers looking for an agency. There just aren't too many agents who try to sell their businesses this way. And there are more than a few aggressive and tenacious business brokers who scout these columns for leads. More than likely if they don't have a sales agency on the block, they'll try to sell you a farm.

One of the best ways to get leads on agencies for sale is to put out the word that you are looking. Sometimes this may not be practical, especially if you're trying to hang onto a job until the right agency comes along. However, you can begin by making discreet inquiries from the people in your company who buy from the agencies in your territory. They may know of an agency that is up for sale.

If you belong to local or regional sales organizations, such as those sponsored by groups that offer training and courses in selling or public speaking, your contacts within the group could prove fruitful. Even local business service clubs such as the Rotary can provide you with some contacts.

4

How to Find
—and Land—
the Lines That Will
Make Your Agency
Grow

In the strict sense of the word, you are not an agency until you have products to sell or manufacturers to represent. But more than a few agencies "existed" long before they had either. They existed in the minds of the people who started the agencies and they existed, at least legally, before any principals came on board.

This, of course, is the perennial dilemma. Which comes first—the agency or the principals. The answer to this must be the result of looking at each individual situation. Let's look at a few cases just for perspective.

Joe Thomas was a sales manager for a large manufacturer of plastic parts that were sold to the OEM. Joe did a good job, but recognized that the only path to the top of his company was through engineering experience, not sales experience—no matter how good it was. So Joe, an ambitious guy, decided to start an agency on his own. Since he had always sold through agencies, he figured right when he asked his firm's president if he could have a territory as an agent. Joe then started with a principal, a product, a territory—and an awful lot of experience. His first line paid the rent and a little more, but he still needed other lines.

Bill Williams worked for a sales agency. He started out new in the field and moved up to sales management. His request wasn't unreasonable when Bill asked for a piece of the action. However, the owner, strictly for personal reasons, wasn't ready to share his business on any terms. So Bill decided to take the bull by the horns and left and opened his own agency—without principals. However, the contacts that he had made at his previous job soon resulted in two lines that paid the rent and a little more. He got the lines from the recommendations of his former employer who didn't hold a grudge when Bill left.

Our third story is about Mike Jacobs. Mike, another successful manufacturer sales manager, wanted to run his own show for many of the same reasons as most who go into the agency business. But he had never worked for a small company. Mike got his lines by starting as a subagent for another agency that operated outside of his area but needed extra coverage. Eventually, Mike became more than a subagent, he became part owner of the agency that had given him the lines. As of this writing, it appears that Mike will have the opportunity to buy the whole show soon.

Three agents. Three ways to get started. And these only scratch the surface. The point is this: There are many ways to get started and to get the lines you need. The technique you choose will depend almost entirely on your personal circumstances. However, once you are able to put yourself in the picture clearly, there are a number of ways to get lines that will work for you. And that's what this chapter is all about.

HOW SUCCESSFUL AGENCIES GET TOP LINES

First of all, let's define success. For one agency it means covering 4 states with 10 men and having a 10,000-square-foot warehouse. For another, it means covering one major city with one person and doing it from a home office. In other words, you have to look at success from your own perspective. But no matter how you define your own success, getting lines will always have priority in your agency. When you get started, you will need a stable of principals in a hurry. Then you will need to expand your lines as you expand your agency. And you will also need lines to replace lines. Some of these lines you will lose through no fault of your own, and others will drop for your own reasons. In any case, the search for lines will be an ongoing process throughout your agency career. It will be intense early on, but become a background activity once you get your feet on the ground.

It may be putting the cart before the horse by telling you how successful agencies get the top lines if you are just starting out or are in the formative years of building your agency. However, the points worth remembering are more valuable in terms of attitudes than they are in terms of technique. Later on, specific tips on how to attract and get the best lines for your agency will be given.

The reason for putting the cart before the horse is because top lines for one agency may not be top lines for another. A top line may not necessarily be the line that nets you the biggest commissions. It may be the line with the prestige to open the door for customers. Or it may be the line that opens the door with other principals. Let's look at both of these concepts in some detail.

An agency owner I know has had for years a principal who is one of the country's major manufacturers. However, his income from this line is smaller than the income from any of the four other lines he carries. As he explained: "This manufacturer advertises heavily, has a class-A reputation, and is known by everyone. The line I represent for it is relatively small compared with its other products, but it is profitable and it does enhance my agency's reputation. If it hadn't been for having this line and for the recommendation from the sales manager, I probably wouldn't have been able to get the lines that are most profitable for me."

Another agency owner explained how he uses a prestige line to sell his other lines. "We've had this line for years. It's the top line in the country, but for the market we serve, it's a marginal line for us. However, when I sell this company's line, I have almost immediate access to just about any customer in our territory for the other products I sell."

This agent, too, made a profit on his prestige line, but it was the effect the line had on his customers and prospects that had the most impact for him. As you can see, top lines are not necessarily the lines that make the most profit. Remember, though, you can't afford to have too many "top" lines and not enough of those that bring in the money.

Successful agencies usually get new lines because they are known by the sales managers of the top lines. However, you cannot afford to sit back and wait for a call. You continually have to promote your business by letting people know who you are and what your agency is all about. It's a matter of doing not only an effective, but a steady public relations job.

How would you let manufacturers know about your agency without actually contacting them? Most agencies who have manufacturers calling them about their lines do such things as participate in industry associations, take part in seminars, and a few even write articles for the national, regional, and local publications that are read by the people they want to influence. And, of course, when an agency does a good job for its present principals, others hear about the agency and seek them out when the territory needs coverage.

Furthermore, those who buy from manufacturers' agencies usually know who the good agencies are, and they frequently are willing to share this information with other manufacturers who are seeking agency coverage. "There are two agencies that call on me," a purchasing manager told me recently. "Each of them does a lot more than just make calls. Both of these agencies bring me solid information that is not only useful in terms of the products they sell, but also in terms of other aspects of my work. For example, just the other day one of them called to say that the product he sells is going to be modified in a few months. This modification will make the product better for us. The agent thought it would be better for us to wait before placing our next order until the modification was available. This guy did me a favor. Sure I'm going to buy the products, but when he told me to hold off for a month, he was putting himself on the line for a slight delay in the sale—and a delay in the commission. But he wanted me to have the best. I like that. I've already recommended him to two other manufacturers who have asked me about agencies in the territory. I know that he has gotten one of the lines and will probably get the other."

As you can see, getting the lines you want takes two things: imagination and persistence. When you first get started, you may have to scramble a little; but once you have your feet on the ground, using these two human qualities, you should have very little difficulty locating and landing the lines that will make your agency grow.

Why You Don't Have to Be a Big Agency to Deal With the Fortune 500

The myth that big companies deal only with big agencies just isn't so. Some of the largest companies in the country that sell through agencies are using some very small agencies—including one-person operations. It's not bigness that smart companies want, it's coverage. Of course, if a company is looking for an agency to cover Texas, Oklahoma, and Louisiana, and each state represents strong potential, the chances are the company will either look for many smaller agencies to cover parts of the territory, or it will look for one larger agency with branches to reach the market it has defined.

The point is you, as an agency owner, have to look at the situation rationally to understand what the company wants and whether or not your agency is going to be able to provide the coverage. It doesn't make sense to push for a line of oil-field drilling accessories for the state of Texas if you're a one-person agency; you'd have to be all over the state daily. But it does make sense to pitch for a line of process instruments if you have coverage in the refineries because you have some well-defined geographical areas that can be covered in regular sweeps.

More than a few of the largest manufacturers in the United States sell through manufacturers' agencies. Some, especially those with a number of different lines that are sold into a number of different markets, have a hybrid marketing system. That is, they sell some of their products to some of their markets through agencies, and they sell to others either through distributors or direct. Even when companies sell through distributors, they frequently use sales agencies to set up and manage their distributor network.

Smart manufacturers today don't make the kind of distinctions about large agencies that were commonly made a few years ago. A sales manager related that the decisions on agencies made by his company a few years ago were weighted heavily on a "glitzy" impression and less on just what they could do for the company. "We had a few big agencies back then," he said, "that never did a nickel's worth of business. Today we have a real mix of large and small agencies. But the decision in each case was made specifically on what we thought the agency could do for us in the territory."

HOW TO DECIDE WHICH LINES WILL BE BEST
FOR YOUR AGENCY

Reaction time is often slow in the agency field. If you are planning to expand or are looking for lines for a new agency, don't expect that any one technique will get you the lines you want overnight. You might get lucky and find a manufacturer with the line(s) you want, but this will probably be the exception—not the rule. Locating and screening the lines that will make your agency grow is as tough as selling the products you now represent.

There is no question that the best way to expand your business is to go after lines you can sell to your existing customers. And, of course, they should be compatible with the lines you now carry. When you can cross-sell from one product to another on the same call, you are making the most efficient use of your time. And, of course, this is one of the reasons that so many manufacturers are turning to agencies for their marketing needs.

Many agents, however, don't make use of the full power that exists in this situation to attract and get the best lines for their agencies. They usually just review their lines, analyze their customers' needs, and then look for the lines they know that will be best for them. This is only a good first step. It's safe to say that for every product you know of that is manufactured by a company you have heard of, there are many similar, and possibly better, products being made by companies you don't know. It may turn out that some little resistor manufacturer in Montana is poised to give the industry leaders a kick in the pants—with agencies! The point is this: Some of the most dramatic growth in American business has come from the smaller, faster moving companies. Look at the lines you feel you need for growth everywhere; don't just settle for the familiar.

More than a few agencies have had the misfortune of taking on a line that offered a higher commission than all the others, only to build a territory and then have their principal fold unexpectedly. Commissions are important, of course, but as long as they are within the range of industry standards, there are many other points for you to consider, such as the following:

1. *Product compatibility*. There's more to this than just taking on related products that can be sold to your existing customer base. Product compatibility must be considered in its broadest sense. For example, is the product you are considering selling manufactured to the

same qualitative standards as the other products you sell? You might have quality lines now, and do a lot of damage to your image and sales potential by taking on lower quality lines. Even though you have nothing to do with the product's manufacture and quality control, your customers will surely include you in the blast directed at the manufacturer when your new products fail to meet anticipated standards.

2. *Manufacturing capacity.* One agent I know took on a line that complemented his other lines perfectly. The quality was first rate. His major customers placed a large stocking order of OEM components of the new line, but the order failed to materialize on the date it was due. The customer's production line ground to a stop . . . and so did the relationship with the agency. You know your customers and you know their needs. Therefore, when you consider a new line, make certain that the principal is going to be able to deliver. Any failure in this department is going to rub off on you.

3. *New product development.* You may, at the moment, be satisfied with the products manufactured by your prospective principal. But this isn't all you should consider. If your customers are in industries that feed on new products and new ideas, make sure that your prospective principal is involved in new product development. Some industries don't pay as much attention to R & D as others. If, for example, you're in electronics and computers, it's better to have a principal who can outthink as well as out-manufacture the competitors.

4. *Corporate mentality.* Most sales and marketing managers come up through the ranks of the sales department. By the time they take command of an agency sales team, they often have some pretty fixed ideas. You should try to discover these fixed ideas as soon as possible. For example, is the sales chief going to get nervous when your commissions exceed his take-home pay? Also, make sure that the sales manager and his management see eye-to-eye. Most corporate salespeople are volume-oriented. And good management is usually profit-oriented. The difference between gross sales and net profits may come down on your neck if you misread the signals.

5. *Sales leads.* In most fields, manufacturers advertise to generate sales leads for their agencies. Since it's all but impossible to make smoke-stack calls and cold calls on unqualified leads these days, it's important to have a good understanding with your principals on the question of lead qualification. Leads should be pre-qualified by your principals.

6. *Sales commissions*. More than just establishing the best rates, it's important to have a firm understanding of when and how the commissions are to be paid. The trend these days is payment upon shipment and invoicing.

7. *The contract*. Actual contractual details are discussed in considerable detail in Chapter 5. However, you should note that even the most appealing product may not be right for you if you can't negotiate a favorable contract with a principal.

8. *Internal contracts*. Be sure to know just how deeply you will be able to penetrate a principal's organization for the help you need. You'll need to know whether you'll have access to the people in the engineering, manufacturing, marketing, shipping, and accounting departments—and even to the president. You should be able to talk, without restriction, to those who will have a direct effect on the work you do for the principal.

9. *Corporate stability*. It's no secret that in some industries, companies come and go at an alarming rate. It has always been so in smaller companies, especially those that are undercapitalized in growth industries. Now, however, the same phenomena has been seen in industries that most people considered to be rock stable. Just look at the microcomputer industry if you need an example.

10. *Attitude toward agencies*. This isn't easy to assess in some cases. However, it can be done by talking with agencies that are already a part of the team. Look especially for whether or not the company keeps its promises. See if they really treat their agents as professionals, and especially if they have a tolerance for ambiguity. The last point can be critical. Many manufacturers tend to run their businesses by the book, often out of necessity. But any salesperson, whether on staff or selling as an agent, is dealing with conditions that are often ambiguous. Signals are seldom strong in the early stages of a sale, and they're often difficult to interpret. Manufacturers who have difficulty with ambiguity usually want concrete answers at every step of the way. It just may not be possible to do this; reports may have to be best-guess until the sale moves further along. If you are talking with a manufacturer who is this rigid, you could be in for trouble.

These are the main variables that can put a relationship on or off course. The best lines for your agency are usually made by those manufacturers who come up positively on most of the points in this checklist.

HOW TO FIND THE LINES AND PRINCIPALS THAT ARE BEST FOR YOUR AGENCY

Successful agents claim that the best place to begin your search is with the products you already know. The chances are that the products that would fit your organization and style are already being represented in your territory. But this isn't as bad as it may seem. You at least have the opportunity to get to know the kinds of products that are available and who makes them and sells them. This exercise gives you some perspective and several other directions to take.

It's often best to begin with an off-the-wall sheet. List every manufacturer you know that manufactures products you feel you could sell profitably even if you know that they are already being represented by someone else in your area. Then, check off those that are definitely out of the question—those that are already being handled by another agency. However, be sure that you know the complete picture on each company from a technical, application, and sales point of view.

Obviously, if any of the products that show up on your preliminary list are not being represented in your territory and you feel that there might be a match, consider them as prime candidates. (I'll talk about making the actual approach later on.)

Now that you have identified the obvious lines, the real detective work begins. You want to try to locate the other manufacturers that are not quite as obvious. Some may be marginal, some may be start-ups, and others may be on the skids. But the chances are that when you use the techniques described here, you'll turn up more than a few solid candidates.

1. Begin with published directories. Virtually every field has an association that publishes the names and addresses of its members. You won't get every one that is in the field, but you will get those who belong to the major association in the field.

2. Read the magazines and trade journals that cover your field. Look for the companies that advertise the products you'd like to sell. You'll find them in the ad pages as well as in the new product pages.

You will probably come across more new companies in the new product pages than anywhere else. Newer and smaller companies tend to watch their advertising dollars very closely and go the new-product-release route because the price is right.

3. Talk with other agents in other fields. Often they will know of new products, will have swapped a lot of information with other agencies, and will be more than willing to pass along good leads.

4. Talk with your current principals. Most manufacturers are interested in seeing their agencies grow, even though they don't like the idea of sharing your time with other manufacturers. You can usually get their cooperation if you explain that your search for new products will probably result in your hiring additional people. This, as you might imagine, translates into strong benefits for all your principals.

5. Talk with your customers. They are usually aware of products that are related to those which they now buy from you and which may not be represented in your territory. In fact, if manufacturers without representation are trying to get business in your territory, your customers will probably know about it. This can be a very beneficial situation. Simply having one of the manufacturer's prospects suggest that regular representation might help the case can often give you an immediate line—if you want it!

6. Exploit companies that sell to manufacturers in whom you are interested. One agent I heard of sold electronic components to a contract assembly firm. The assembler had customers all over the country, many of whom had products that the agent felt he could sell. The right word got this agent interviews and some very good lines.

7. Put someone in business yourself. This has been done by more than a few agencies in the past, and I feel that the technique will be even more effective as our economy grows. You may see a strong need for a product in your territory, but when a search turns up no available lines, you can try to get one of your present principals into the business. For example, an agent in an oil-producing territory knew he could sell pipe fittings by the ton, but virtually every line he wanted to be associated with was already represented by other agencies. This enterprising agent looked at the manufacturers he represented, made a survey of their manufacturing capabilities, and then talked the owner of one firm into making the fittings. At first this agent accounted for all of the output. Before long, the manufacturer's other agencies began moving the

fittings in their territories. The pipe fitting is now a major line with this manufacturer.

8. Keep an eye on the personnel columns of the publications that serve your fields. This is somewhat of a long shot. But when you see a new appointment in a company that manufactures products that interest you, a letter from you just might give him or her a chance to be an overnight success. The new executive might have to build a sales team.

9. Watch for new contracts being awarded in your territory. For example, when United Consolidated announces that a new power plant is to be built in your territory, and you know that it will need to buy a slew of pen recorders (a product that belongs in your line), get in touch with the best manufacturer of these recorders and explain why you should have the line. There are a number of newsletters published in a wide range of fields that can give you a jump on this kind of information.

10. Create a package. You may have one product that, by itself, is not especially profitable. But when you sell it during the course of making calls for other products, it pays the freight. However, that one product may be enough for you to attract several other directly related products into a package deal. And the people who can best help you to put together the best package deals are those at the plant who make the one product you now have. They want more sales, and if you can make a strong case for additional closely related lines, more than a few will actually help you to negotiate with other manufacturers.

11. Advertise for the lines you want. You can try the magazines that serve your fields, but you will probably have greater general exposure by advertising in *Agency Sales* magazine, published by the Manufacturers' Agents National Association. Write to the association at 23016 Mill Creek Road, P.O. Box 3467, Laguna Hills, California 92654 and ask for a recent issue of the magazine and a current advertising rate card.

12. Go to as many trade shows as you can. You'll see the products you want and you'll be able to talk with the people who make them. If you can't make it to a show, ask the show management to send you a show guide. The show directory can be a powerful tool in your search for new products to represent.

If you go to a show and see a product you like, it's usually best not to jump on it right away—unless you are absolutely sure of the line and don't mind feeling a competitive agency breathing down your neck. If you can, do a brief selling job on the person from the factory and try to set up a meeting at the plant after the show closes.

Is There Good-People Chemistry?

So far, products, markets, and customers—all things that are relatively easy to nail down—have been discussed. However, people are important in the equation as well. Here are a few pointers to help you put the personal equation into perspective:

1. Does the person or people to whom you will report within the corporation see the problems and prospects of the territory? Are they willing to help every way they can?

2. Does the sales manager take all the credit for himself, or does he see himself as an effective member of a winning team? Look for the secure people who are willing to give credit when and where credit is due.

3. Does the sales manager understand the nature of agency selling? Make sure that all the differences between agency selling and running salaried salespeople are understood—especially the fact that no call reports will be issued.

4. Do the people involved have an understanding of ambiguity? Too often when people reach the top, they assume that everything that must be done will be done right. However, when any activity varies from the norm, whether it fails or succeeds, these people can get very nasty.

A good agency is always working with new approaches. The agency that gets into a routine is in trouble, and the sales manager of a principal who seeks a routine, rather than some experimentation, will be difficult to work with. Most agents are not especially afraid to fail, therefore they frequently try different approaches. This mode of operation can send some of the corporate sales-types into a funk. Be sure you know who you are dealing with before you sign the papers.

5. Check to see if the person with whom you will work has the ability to act independently. Corporations do many of the things they do because of the way individuals interact. A stifling chain of command and a fearful sales manager can be a deadly combination. The line may seem to be worth a million—until you see that your contact won't move without checking himself every step of the way.

6. Make sure you are working with a "people" person. Recently, a major manufacturer recruited for its top marketing job a fellow who came from its competitor's marketing department. A good match? It would seem so, except that this man was a market planner who had never made a trip to the field or sold anything to anybody. You can just imagine the disaster. Since sales is a people-to-people business, you must make sure that your contact understands you, and not just the computer.

7. The corporate person should have high integrity. It's a problem being between an agency team and management. You know where your paycheck comes from and where your loyalty belongs. But beyond these basics, you should feel that you are dealing with a person for whom issues are important. Not that he's going to turn on the company when it's done something wrong. But he should be secure enough to deal with problems and people in a forthright way.

PRACTICAL WAYS TO APPROACH MANUFACTURERS FOR THEIR LINES

Before the approaches that have worked for many very successful agencies are given, I'd like to say that there is *never* any justification for trying to take a line away from another agency. The agent with the line may be doing a poor job, but he still has the line and that fact should be respected. We may compete head-to-head when we sell competitive products, but the tradition in the agency field is and always will be one of honor. Sure, there are those who don't care for such a personal code. Fortunately, though, there aren't very many of them.

Now, let's assume that you are going to contact manufacturers that have products you'd like to sell and who do not have representation in your territory. The techniques described all work and there are none that work better than others for all agents. The methods that will work best for you are those with which you'll be most comfortable. For example, if you can handle yourself well on the telephone, the chances are that you will make a better first impression when you initiate contact this way than if you were to write a letter. Review the following ideas within a personal frame of reference that you know has worked in similar situations in the past.

1. How to use your line card effectively. Virtually every agency has a line card, whether it's just a list of your principals printed on your

letterhead or an elaborate multicolored folder. However, by itself as a mailer, the line card will do very little for you; it will supply the basic information. With it you must include a letter that tells the sales story. And don't be afraid to be active in your letter—that is, use the word "you"—and talk in terms of benefits that will accrue to the manufacturer when he appoints you his agency.

2. When to write a letter without sending a line card. If you feel that you can write a compelling letter, you might want to send it without sending your line card. If you take this approach, it's best to begin with the benefits that are most important to the principal. For example, if you know of sales that could be made immediately, you might write a letter something like this:

Dear _____:

The other day, while calling on one of our long-time customers, I discovered that they are planning a change in the manufacture of their thermostats. My contact asked if we could supply the mercury switches he wants to use, but none of our principals makes such a switch.

Since the initial order will be sizeable and the reorders should go on for many years, I am interested in keeping the business within our agency. I have researched the firms that make mercury switches that will work with the customer's thermostat, and it appears that yours meets all the specs.

I know that you are not represented in my territory, and I would appreciate the opportunity to discuss our working together.

This letter would conclude by asking for a meeting at a specific time. However, contrast this letter, written in terms of the manufacturer's interests, which is agency-centered:

Dear _____:

We represent Continental Corporation and sell to one of the largest manufacturers of thermostats in the country. We can sell your mercury switches to this company because we have been working with the customer for many years and have qualified sales engineers on our staff.

The second letter is all about the agency, and the prospective principal really won't be especially interested. The principal wants to know right up front what's in it for him. The first letter does the job; the second doesn't.

3. Get one of your customers to write a letter for you. This is a powerful way to get attention. Suppose that you have turned up a need for a product that you don't carry but your customers could use. If you are close enough to the customer, he or she might be willing to make an inquiry about the product and suggest that a local agent—you—could do the job. If you take this approach, be sure to do it out in the open. Don't try to pretend that it was all the customer's idea and that you are surprised and flattered. If there is merit in the opportunity for the manufacturer and you know that you can do a good job with the line, there is no need for subterfuge.

4. Phone calls can be very effective, too. Agents are generally more accustomed to talking with prospects, rather than writing to them. However, if you choose this route, use the phone to establish the reason for the call, to describe the benefits of the situation for both of you, and to suggest further action. Progressive manufacturers who are interested by a phone call or letter will frequently pay your fare to visit them at plant headquarters. Your own sense of time and sales response will tell you how far you can carry the meeting approach.

5. Use another agent to make contact for you. If you know an agent who has a different territory for the manufacturer you'd like to represent, it's often appropriate to have the agent provide the contact. When you are recommended by an agent who has been successful with the line, the agent's success will put you in a good light right from the start.

6. Make contact at trade shows. This approach must be handled carefully. Remember that manufacturers spend quite a bit of money to take part in trade shows and they are most interested in making profits with prospects—not with agencies. This isn't always the case, but it's generally wise to qualify any attempt to make contact at a trade show. You can usually make points by saying that you know how important the show is for making customer contact and that you will call at the plant after the show. Be sure to leave your card as a reminder when you make that call.

HOW TO MAKE MANUFACTURERS SEEK OUT YOUR AGENCY

This, of course, not only does wonders for cash flow but it also does a lot for the ego. But how can you get the manufacturers you want to seek you out and can you afford to play a reverse game while another agency may be taking a direct approach?

There are no hard and fast rules, except that if you have the time and are not under the gun, you can build a much stronger relationship with a manufacturer if you can "arrange" for him to contact you. It's no different in agency/manufacturer relationships than it is in any other business or social situation.

To put this into perspective, here is a scenario that is common with most fast-growing agencies:

1. The agency has been around for a few years, is successful, and is generally respected by its principals and customers.

2. The agency has reached the limit of its facilities and manpower capacity.

3. Several principals would like to see more attention paid to their lines, but the resources aren't available to support this in the agency.

4. The alternatives include adding a full-commission person, biting the bullet with borrowed money, or trying to do more with the present people and facilities. And there is another possibility, one that would help solve the present problem and help by adding another dimension to the agency. That possibility is expansion by getting a new line so you could justify adding people.

5. There's no great rush, but you know that something must be done and that new lines must be acquired in the future. Since you are up to your ears servicing existing businesses, it just isn't in the cards to spend too much time actively pursuing new lines. Why not arrange it so that the manufacturers will seek you out? It's easier than you think.

An Eight-Step Plan to Get Manufacturers to Contact You

1. Before you do anything, you must first be able to put yourself in the "mental shoes" of the people you want to meet and influence. You must be able to think in terms of their needs—not yours—and how you can help the company fill its needs.

2. Get all the facts and figures about the firm that interests you and on the market that exists for its products in your territory. You might begin by reviewing competitive products that are sold in the territory and by making some estimates of the volume that exists. The chances are that the manufacturer has some figures of its own. This will show the manufacturer that you are not only serious about its line, but are quite capable of being effective with it.

3. When you have all the information you need and when you feel capable of discussing competition and applications intelligently, you are ready to start your campaign. There are a number of ways to get started; however, you should only choose those with which you feel most comfortable. The steps that follow will draw on this information.

This plan is essentially a public relations program designed to get the attention of the people you want to influence. In any public relations campaign, it's the cumulative effect that is most important. You will have no way of knowing whether any single element will work any better than others. But you will know that the number of positive exposures all add up to the development of a strong image.

4. Read the magazines in which these companies advertise. You'll know the shows they attend and be familiar with activities in their trade association. These will be the areas where you can get the most exposure.

5. Write an article in the magazine in which your principal advertises most heavily, or find a public relations counselor to do it for you. This magazine will be the one that is most often read at the plant, and that will get you the most points. Most of the articles in trade and professional journals in the industrial and commercial fields are not staff-written; they depend heavily on contributions from outside experts. Only rarely do they use professional writers, other than on special assignment or to work with content experts who are not experienced in writing.

Be sure to choose a topic on which to write that will be important to the client you want to influence. After you get the go-ahead from the editor, you can make points by contacting the principal and asking for information to use in the article. Everyone likes to be quoted, and this kind of request will get everyone from the president to the public relations people at the plant doing handstands to help you. Be sure to give that person plenty of credit in the article. This technique not only establishes positive contact for you, but it also shows the manufacturer just how easy it will be to work with you. These points will not be forgotten when the time comes to cover the territory with an agency— or even if you don't want to wait for the manufacturer to make the first move.

6. Many agents publish newsletters. However, most of them are aimed at drumming up prospects and customers' sales. Nothing is wrong with this; but why not create a newsletter—it doesn't have to go out more than a few times a year—that is sent to all the manufacturers you'd like to represent? Don't just blow your own horn, though. You can talk about how you solved problems for various principals and customers. And, if feasible, make the newsletter an open forum in which you get your customers and principals to write a few paragraphs. These become implied endorsements without seeming obvious. Even if you only mail as few as a dozen of the newsletters, they can be cost effective. Just don't think of them in the same way you think of a newsletter that may be sent to hundreds of prospects and customers.

7. Take part in seminars where you know that you will come into contact with the principals you want to influence. This opportunity comes most frequently during trade shows and industry or association conferences. You can always find out who is on the various panels before you volunteer. When your target principal is on a panel, make sure that you're on the panel, too. It's often easier than it sounds. Those who run seminars are always looking for good participants. When you have something important to say, they will most always make room for you.

8. Find out if someone you know knows the person you want to influence. If you fail to find a direct contact, you may be able to make a second-level contact through another person. This will become your grapevine. You can use the technique to get information that will guide you in planning and pacing your approach. And you can use it to plant seeds in the minds of the decision makers that you want to nourish.

The approaches outlined are ways that will bring you to the attention of the people you want to influence. However, if after you do all of this you still don't get the call you are waiting for and if you see that the time is right for the manufacturer to appoint an agency in your territory, you should then take the bull by the horns. Send a letter or phone and try to set up a meeting. Frequently, the manufacturer may be well aware of you from the steps you have already taken and think quite highly of you, but he may be under the influence of someone else over whom you have no control.

When you make contact, all of your past efforts will obviously weigh heavily in your favor. But timing can be everything. If you perceive that the company is looking for an agent in your territory and it hasn't made the move—you make the move.

Nothing succeeds like success. To be successful, you must first identify the principals that best suit your operation and set out to attract their attention. Remember, the best principals may not necessarily be the biggest. But they should be principals in whose products you have the most faith and those who have faith in what you can do to sell the products they make. It's this joint venture chemistry that will make the difference!

CHAPTER 5

How to Protect Yourself With and From Contracts

After reading agency contracts for years, and after listening to the problems that agents have had with their agreements, MANA thought it was time to create something that all agents could use. Note that I said "something." I didn't say contract.

Working with attorneys, the association has developed and refined a set of guideline agreements. They are guidelines in the sense that we feel that every contract should be created to meet the specific needs of the individuals involved. However, as you might imagine, there are many features of an agency agreement that are pretty much standard for agents in all fields and in all states. But, in spite of our attempt to create documents that could serve all agents, we clearly state on each of them the following:

DO NOT USE WITHOUT CONSULTING YOUR ATTORNEY. LAWS AND CUSTOMS VARY. This publication is designed to provide sample information in regard to the subject matter covered. It is furnished with the understanding that the publisher, MANA, is not engaged in rendering legal, accounting, or other professional service. The services of a competent professional legal and accounting person should be sought.

The two agreements (Figures 5-1 and 5-2) that follow will give you the essential ingredients of a practical working agreement for the single-person sales agency and for a multi-person agency. They should be used as a guideline to help you prepare your own agreement. MANA publishes a complete guide to this contract that includes extensive contractual guidelines. The association does make these available to members as well as to nonmembers. Nonmembers pay a small fee. For the current price of *Specimen Contractual Guidelines for the Manufacturer/Sales Agency Relationship* write to MANA, P.O. Box 3467, Laguna Hills, California 92654.

YOUR INDEPENDENT CONTRACTOR STATUS AND THE IRS

According to a research bulletin published by MANA: "The independent contractor relationship is that principle of law which establishes a professional manufacturers' representative as an independent entity, as one who offers his services to the manufacturing community for the performance of a specified task, namely sales, and who thus enjoys the freedom to pursue that activity in any lawful manner he so chooses."

Without this common-law concept of the independent contractor, our entire chain of commerce would buckle with inefficiency. Yet, as important as this concept is (it determines legal rights, responsibilities, and tax liabilities), it is often misunderstood by those who most depend on it—manufacturers as well as agents.

AN OVERVIEW OF AGENCY LAW

Understanding the legal nature of the independent contractor requires a look at the law of agency and its long-term development. Agency law grew out of the need for people to extend their activities

FIGURE 5-1

**DO NOT USE WITHOUT
CONSULTING YOUR ATTORNEY.
LAWS AND CUSTOMS VARY.**

**TO BE USED BY MANUFACTURER
AND SINGLE-PERSON AGENCY
SPECIMEN ONLY**

*This publication is designed to provide sample information
in regard to the subject matter covered. It is furnished
with the understanding that the publisher, MANA, is not
engaged in rendering legal, accounting, or other professional service. The services of a competent professional
legal and accounting person should be sought.*

SALES REPRESENTATIVE AGREEMENT

THIS AGREEMENT is made on the date shown below by and between _____

_____ ("PRINCIPAL") and _____ ("REPRESENTATIVE").

1. Exclusive Representative. Principal grants to Representative the exclusive right (to the exclu-
sion of Principal and all claiming under or through Principal), to act as Principal's SALES AGENCY, to solicit
orders for the Principal's goods and services ("Product"), within the following geographical area: _____

_____ ("Territory").

2. Sales Policies. The prices, charges and terms of sale of the products ("Sales Policies") shall be
established by the Principal. The Sales Policies shall be those currently in effect and established from time to
time by the Principal in its price books, bulletins, and other authorized releases. Written notice of each Sales
Policy change shall be given by Principal to Representative at least thirty (30) days in advance of such change.

3. Orders and Collections. Orders for products solicited by Representative shall be forwarded to
and subject to acceptance by Principal. The Principal agrees to refer all inquiries to the Representative and to
promptly furnish the Representative with copies of all correspondence and documentation between the
Company and Customer. All invoices in connection with orders solicited by Representative shall be rendered by
Principal, direct to the customer, and full responsibility for all products, services, collections and bad debts rests
with Principal.

4. Relationship Created. Representative is not an employee of Principal for any purpose
whatsoever, but is an independent contractor. Principal is interested only in the results obtained by Representative, who shall have sole control of the manner and means of performing under this Agreement.
Principal shall not have the right to require Representative to do anything which would jeopardize the
relationship of independent contractor between Principal and Representative. All expenses and disbursements
incurred by Representative in connection with this Agreement shall be borne wholly and completely by
Representative. Representative does not have, nor shall Representative hold Representative out as having
any right, power or authority to create any contract or obligation, either express or implied, on behalf of, in
the name of, or binding upon Principal, unless Principal shall consent thereto in writing. Designation by
Representative as "Sales Agent" or "Sales Agency" shall not expand the limited authority to conduct "Sales"
activities granted under this Agreement. Representative shall have the right to appoint and shall be solely
responsible for Representative's own salespersons, employees, agents and representatives, who shall be at
Representative's own risk, expense and supervision and shall not have any claim against Principal for
compensation or reimbursement. Unless expressly permitted in writing, Representative shall not represent
products which directly compete with the Products of Principal during the existence of this contract
relationship.

5. Representative's Commissions. The commissions payable by Principal to Representative on
orders solicited within or delivered to the Territory shall be _____ ("Commission Rate"). Commissions
shall be deemed earned by Representative upon acceptance or delivery of the order or any part thereof by

FIGURE 5-1 *(Continued)*

Principal, whichever occurs first. Commissions earned by Representative shall be computed on the net amount of the invoice rendered for each order or part of an order, exclusive of freight and transportation costs (including insurance), normal and recurring bona fide trade discounts and any applicable sales or similar taxes. All commissions earned by Representative shall be due and payable to Representative on or before the twentieth (20th) date of the month immediately following the month during which the invoice applicable to an order is sent by Principal.

6. Term. This Agreement shall continue in full force and effect until the date ("Termination Date") set forth in a notice given by one party to the other indicating such party's election to terminate this Agreement, which Termination Date shall be at least one-hundred twenty (120) days after the date notice of such election is given. Alternatively, this Agreement may be terminated at any time by mutual written agreement between both parties hereto. If this Agreement shall terminate for any reason whatsoever, Representative shall be entitled to receive Representative's full commissions determined in accordance with provisions of Paragraph Five with respect to orders solicited prior to the effective date of such termination, regardless of when such orders are accepted by Principal (provided Representative can demonstrate such orders were solicited prior to the effective date of such termination) and regardless of when such shipments are made or invoices rendered.

7. Hold Harmless. Principal shall save Representative harmless from and against and indemnify Representative for all liability, loss, costs, expenses or damages however caused by reason of any Products (whether or not defective) or any act or omission of Principal, including but not limited to any injury (whether to body, property or personal or business character or reputation) sustained by any person or to any person or to property, and for infringement of any patent rights or other rights of third parties, and for any violation of municipal, state or federal laws or regulations governing the Products or their sale, which may result from the sale or distribution of the Products by the Representative hereunder. This Agreement shall be subject to and shall be enforced and construed pursuant to the laws of the State ("Representative's State") where the Respresentative's principal office is located, as set forth below. Principal hereby appoints as its Agent for service for process in connection with any action brought by Representative against Principal hereunder the Secretary of State of Representative's state of residence at the time such action is brought. In the event of litigation, the prevailing party may recover interest, court costs and reasonable attorney's fees. If any part of this Agreement is held by a court of competent jurisdiction to be invalid, void, or unenforceable, the remainder of the provisions shall remain in full force and effect and shall in no way be affected, impaired, or invalidated.

8. Entire Agreement. This Agreement constitutes the sole and entire Agreement between Principal and Representative, and supersedes all prior and contemporaneous statements, promises, understandings or agreements.

9. Notices. Any notice, demand or request required or permitted to be given hereunder shall be in writing and shall be deemed effective twenty-four (24) hours after having been deposited in the United States mail, postage pre-paid, registered or certified, and addressed to the addressee at his or its main office, as set forth below. Any party may change his or her address for purposes of this Agreement by written notice given in accordance herewith.

(PRINCIPAL):_____

By:_____

Date:_____   **Title:**_____

Principal's address:_____

(REPRESENTATIVE):_____

By:_____

Date:_____   **Title:**_____

Representative's address:_____

FIGURE 5-2

SALES AGENCY AGREEMENT

THIS AGREEMENT is made as of the _____ day of _____, 19____, by and

BETWEEN _____, ("PRINCIPAL")

AND_____ ("AGENCY").

1. Exclusive Representation. Principal grants to Agency the exclusive right to act as Principal's sales representative, to solicit orders for the Principal's goods, and services ("Products") within the following geographical area: _____

_____

_____ ("Territory");

(exclusions, if any, are:_____

_____).

2. Sales Policies. The prices, charges and terms of sale of the products ("Sales Policies") shall be established by the Principal. The Sales Policies shall be those currently in effect and established from time to time by the Principal in its price books, bulletins, and other authorized releases. Written notice of each Sales Policy change shall be given by the Principal to the Agency at least thirty (30) days in advance of such change.

3. Orders and Collections. Orders for products solicited by the Agency shall be forwarded to and subject to acceptance by the Principal. All invoices in connection with orders to the Territory shall be rendered by the Principal direct to the customers, and full responsibility for all collections and bad debts rests with the Principal. The Principal agrees to refer to the Agency for attention all inquiries concerning the Principal's products received by the Principal from any source or by any means whatsoever from the Territory or for shipment of products into the territory. The Principal agrees to promptly furnish the Agency with copies of all correspondence and documentation between the Company and any customer covering any products ordered from within or for shipment into the Territory or sold to a customer within the Territory and to furnish the Agency with a statement on the twentieth (20th) day of each month covering the amount of orders and the amount of invoices for the previous month and the amount of commission due the Agency.

4. Duties. The Purpose of this Agreement is to promote Principal's products and services in the Territory and the long term goodwill of the Agency. The Agency agrees to diligently and faithfully work the Territory in an endeavor to secure business for the Principal and use its best efforts to promote Principal's products. Principal will use its best efforts to perform and provide its products in a good, workmanlike and marketable manner, provide marketing support for the sales effort of the Agency and protect and promote Agency-customer relationships within the territory.

FIGURE 5-2 *(Continued)*

5. Relationship Created. The Agency is not an employee of the Principal for any purpose whatsoever, but is an independent contractor. Principal is interested only in the results obtained by the Agency, who shall have sole control of the manner and means of performing under this Agreement. Principal shall not have the right to require Agency to do anything which would jeopardize the relationship of independent contractor between Principal and Agency, unless otherwise agreed in writing. Agency shall be responsible for Agency's taxes. All expenses and disbursements incurred by Agency in connection with performance by Agency or Agency's sales activities shall be borne wholly and completely by Agency. Agency does not have, nor shall Agency hold itself out as having any right, power or authority to create any contract or obligation, express or implied, on behalf of, in the name of, or binding on the Principal unless Principal shall consent thereto in writing, excepting to solicit orders as the same are more particularly defined in this Agreement. Agency shall have the right to appoint and shall be solely responsible for Agency's own sub-agents, sales-persons, employees, agents and representatives who shall be at Agency's own risk, expense and supervision and shall not have any claim against the Principal for compensation or reimbursement unless otherwise agreed to in writing between the parties. On termination of the Agency's right to solicit orders for new business for the Principal, the Agency shall promptly return to the Principal all promotional material, order forms and supplies provided by the Principal to the Agency prior to termination.

6. Commission. The Agency's commission rate is: _____.

6.1 Commissions are earned by the Agency on all "accepted orders" solicited within and/or delivered to the Territory, whether the orders are sent in by the Agency, received by the Principal by the mails, taken at the Principal's place of business, or otherwise. The Principal has the option of accepting or rejecting any order solicited within the Territory or any order for delivery to the Territory, except that an order will be considered an accepted order for the purpose of commissions, unless the Principal does not ship or invoice and notifies the Agency in writing of the order or orders rejected by the Principal within thirty (30) days of the submission of the order to the Principal whether submitted by the Agency, a customer or through some other source. If the order is submitted by mail, the order will be considered accepted, unless the Principal does not ship or invoice and notifies the Agency in writing of the Principal's rejection of the order within thirty (30) days of the mailing of such order by the Agency or the customer or otherwise to the Principal. Principal shall be entitled to charge back against Agency's commission a sum equal to the commission paid on orders on which the Principal has shipped the product, the customer has returned the product and the Principal has given the customer full refund or credit for the purchase price on such returned product. Commissions payable to the Agency shall be computed on the net amount of each invoice rendered for each order or part of an order on shipment, exclusive of freight and transportation costs, incuding insurance, normal and recurring bona fide trade discounts and any applicable sales or similar taxes. The Agency shall not be charged with or liable for advertising allowances nor any decrease or reduction of commission based upon volume or other discounts unless mutually agreed in writing by all parties prior to acceptance of the order. All commissions payable to the Agency hereunder shall be due and payable to the Agency on or before the twentieth (20th) day of the month immediately following invoicing. In the event of termination of this Agreement by either party, the Agency shall be paid commissions on all orders from or deliveries to the Territory which are substantially attributable in whole or in part to activities or services performed prior to the effective date of termination, regardless of the shipment and invoice date, except in the event of a "for cause termination" under Paragraph 7.1, in which event Commission obligation is limited to shipments made by Principal prior to the effective date of termination.

6.2 Principal in Principal's sole discretion has the right to split Commissions on Orders: obtained solely outside the "Territory" and in the exclusive Territory of another Sales Agency to whom Principal pays Commission on the Order; deliveries outside the "Territory" to the exclusive Territory of another Sales Agency to whom Principal pays Commission on the delivery to the extent that Principal pays Commission to the other Sales Agency; but in no event shall the Commission payable to Agency herein be reduced by reason of the split to less than fifty percent (50%) of the amount Agency earns pursuant to Paragraph 6.1 of this Agreement.

FIGURE 5-2 *(Continued)*

7. Term. This Agreement shall continue in force and effect for one (1) year and thereafter from year to year (not to exceed twenty-one (21) years unless renewed thereafter in writing by the parties) unless the first to occur of the following events, at which time the Agency's right to solicit new business shall terminate:

7.1 For Cause Termination

7.1.1 Commission of a felony by either party in the course of performance of the Agreement shall entitle the other to effect immediate termination upon the giving of written notice.

7.1.2 The election of one party (the "aggrieved party") to terminate this Agreement upon (1) the actual breach or actual default by the other party in the reasonable performance of the defaulting party's obligations and duties under this Agreement and (2) the failure of the defaulting party to cure the same within 15 days (the "cure period") after receipt by the defaulting party of a good faith written notice from the aggrieved party specifying such breach or default and (3) provided that the defaulting party has not cured the default and the aggrieved party may then give written notice to defaulting party of his or its election to terminate ten (10) days after expiration of the cure period.

7.2 Without Cause Termination

7.2.1 After the first year, on expiration of any one year term, provided written notice of election to terminate is given in writing to the other party sixty (60) days before expiration of the existing term.

7.2.2 After the first full year, either party retains the right to terminate at any time after one-hundred twenty (120) days written notice to the other party of election to terminate.

7.2.3 For each year of continuous service, after the first two years, the notice periods under Paragraphs 7.2.1 and 7.2.2, above, shall be extended an additional thirty (30) days. (e.g., in the third year—ninety (90) and one-hundred fifty (150) days; fourth year—one-hundred twenty (120) and one-hundred eighty (180) days, etc.)

8. General Provisions.

8.1 This Agreement may be modified or amended in whole or in part from time to time only by the mutual written agreement signed by all parties and delivered by each to the other prior to the effective date of such modification or amendment. Principal shall save Agency harmless from and against and indemnify Agency for all liability, loss, costs, expense or damages whatsoever caused by reason of any of Principal's products (whether or not defective or covered by warranty) and any act or commission of Principal or Principal's customers or vendees, including but not limited to any injury (whether to body, property of personal or business character or reputation) sustained by any person or organization or to any person or to property whether from breach of warranty, products liability, infringement or any patent rights or other rights of third parties and whether from any violation of municipal, state or federal laws or regulations governing the products or services or their sale which may result from the sale or distribution of the products by the Agency, and including any act by the Agency related to the design, alteration, modification or change of the product supplied by the Principal, except as to modification or change caused by or assumed in writing by Agency. Principal agrees to include Agency as an insured in all policies of Principal which provide protection or indemnity against any liability to customers, consumers or third parties as to any liability or responsibility above referred to. All provisions of this Agency Agreement, including the provisions of this Paragraph 8, shall be subject to and shall be enforced and construed pursuant to the laws of the State ("Agency's State") where the Agency's principal office is located, as set forth below. Principal hereby appoints as its agent for service of process in connection with any action brought by Agency against Principal hereunder the Secretary of State of Agency's state of residence at the time such action is brought. In the event of litigation, prevailing party shall be entitled to recover interest as may be provided by law, court costs and reasonable attorneys' fees.

FIGURE 5-2 *(Continued)*

8.2 If and in the event any portion of this Agreement is void or voidable under any applicable local or state law, such void or voidable provision shall not affect the balance of the Agreement which shall remain fully enforceable as if said void or voidable provision had been deleted by mutual consent of the parties.

8.3 The parties hereto agree that this Agency Agreement constitutes and expresses the whole agreement of the parties with reference to the exclusive agency and compensation for and respect to such agency created hereby and all promises, undertakings, representations, agreements and understandings and arrangements with reference to such agency representation and compensation are herein merged.

9. Notices. Any notice, demand or request required or permitted to be given hereunder shall be in writing and shall be deemed effective twenty-four (24) hours after having been deposited in the United States mail, postage prepaid, registered or certified and addressed to the addressee at its main office, as set forth below. Any party may change its address for purposes of this Agreement by written notice given in accordance herewith.

DATE:_____

(PRINCIPAL):_____

   By:_____

   Title:_____

Address of Principal's Main Office:

_____

_____

(AGENCY):_____

   By:_____

   Title:_____

Address of Agency's Main Office:

_____

_____

beyond the physical limits of their own person, a task that was originally handled by servants. But in seventeenth-century England, brokers began to play a prominent role in commerce, and it was the growth of this group that caused the focus of the law to change over the years from master-servant to principal-agent.

The term agent in its broadest sense, therefore, can include an employee who does nothing but manual labor. But common usage in language and evolution of the law's interpretation have redefined agent to mean one who conducts business transactions on behalf of another. Generally, anyone who is granted authority to change the legal rights and responsibilities of the principal is an agent. But even this definition is too broad to apply to manufacturers' agents and others who work independently, so the description of "agent" had to be further refined.

EMPLOYEE OR INDEPENDENT CONTRACTOR?

Today, an agent can be either an employee or an independent contractor. If he or she is an employee, the principal (employer) retains control over the entire scope of the task: determining the job to be done, supplying the tools with which to accomplish it, and overseeing all the activities of the agent (employee). If, on the other hand, he or she is an independent contractor, the principal has no right to control the agent's physical actions, and it is this fact which, in the eyes of the law, primarily determines the existence of an independent contractor relationship. If the principal is limited to controlling only the objective of the agent's work and defining the scope of his or her authority and retains little or no overview of the agent's physical conduct in reaching this objective, then it's safe to say that the agent is an independent contractor.

Manufacturers' representatives fall into this class. They are independent contractors whose authority in transacting the principal's business is generally limited to procurement of orders for goods within a predefined territory. Manufacturers' agents are not as a rule empowered to bind a principal to a legal obligation. They can't, for example, oblige a manufacturer to fill a specified order. Only the principal can ultimately accept or reject an order and dictate the final terms of the sale. But as independent contractors, agents may proceed in any lawful manner which they see as necessary to get that order for the manufacturer. That's why they are paid a commission.

Whether an agent flies or drives is of no concern to the principal. One hour or three for lunch makes no difference. That the agent sells on his own or hires a team of salespeople to sell for him is out of the manufacturer's hands. The sales objective of the principal-agency relationship is the primary concern. The way it's achieved is not.

How the Courts Determine the Legal Status of an Independent Contractor

Court decisions have had to be made in order to determine liability in cases where the actions of a principal or agent have in some way harmed a third party. For example, can a manufacturer be held responsible for injuries caused when an agent, in the course of business, injures someone in an automobile accident? Or can an agent be held responsible for losses caused to a customer by a manufacturer's failure to fill an order correctly or meet a properly supplied specification? The courts have answered these complex questions in part by examining the relationship between the principal and the agent.

Whether an agent is an independent contractor or an employee can be significant, and so the courts have outlined the following determinants of independent contractor status:

1. The extent of control which, by the agreement, the principal may exercise over the details of the work;

2. Whether or not the person employed is engaged in a distinct occupation or business;

3. The kind of occupation and whether it is one traditionally done without supervision or direction by the principal;

4. The skills required for the work;

5. Whether the principal or the worker supplies the tools needed to perform the job;

6. The length of time the person is employed;

7. Method of payment—whether by time or by the job;

8. Whether the work performed is part of the regular business of the principal;

9. The intent of the parties entering the relationship, i.e., if it's intended to be independent contractor/principal;

10. Whether the principal is an established entity.

Of the factors listed, the first—the right to control—is of paramount importance. In fact, in one 1976 Appeals Court decision, the presiding judge wrote in his decision determining liability for a construction site accident: "All of these factors are of varying importance in determining the type of relationship involved, and with the exception of the element of control, not all elements need to be present. It is the right to control another's physical conduct that is the essential and oftentimes decisive factor in establishing vicarious liability whether the person controlled is a servant (employee) or nonservant (independent contractor) agent."

How Independent Contractor Status Affects the Taxes You Pay

If the independent contractor concept is important to manufacturers' agencies and their principals from a strictly legal standpoint, then it's even more critical to that relationship where the IRS is concerned.

Since the late 1960s, the IRS has closely monitored—and more strictly enforced—the collection of payroll taxes, FICA, FUTA, and federal income withholding tax. Every employer and employee shares the Treasury's tax-collection burden through employment taxes.

Independent contractors require no payroll taxes to be paid by those using their services. Indeed, one of the major advantages of contracting with another for the performance of necessary business services is relief from payroll tax burden.

Instead of federal income withholding tax, those in business for themselves as independent contractors generally must make quarterly payments of estimated income and self-employment taxes directly to the Treasury. Principals who contract with independents must, in turn, file with the IRS Form 1099 for all those to whom they pay over $600 each year in nonemployee compensation. This allows the Service to monitor tax payment of self-employed independent contractors.

In the late 1960s and the early 1970s, it became apparent to many that the Internal Revenue Service was waging a major campaign to reclassify traditional independent contractors as employees, an action which critics said would fatten the Treasury's coffers at the expense of the business community, especially small business. In its past enforcement efforts, IRS training manuals, revised May 1971, expanded on the common-law factors used in determining independent status. The resulting horror stories from all industries, manufacturers' agents included, were legion. In one case, an audit of a manufacturers' representative turned up once-thought-innocent call report forms provided by one of his principals. Determination: Employee. Result: A back-payroll tax bill for the manufacturer, plus penalties and interest.

The IRS Training Manuals, in a chapter entitled "Employer-Employee Relationships," lists 20 common-law factors to determine whether for employment tax purposes an individual is an independent contractor or an employee. Compare this information which the IRS seeks with the criteria listed earlier.

1. Is the individual providing services required to comply with instructions concerning when, where, and how the work is to be done?

2. Is the individual provided with training to enable him or her to perform the job in a particular manner? (A common-sense approach to this point doesn't prohibit a manufacturer from providing product familiarization or other exchanges of information necessary for the agent to sell effectively.)

3. Are the services performed by the individual a part of the business operation?

4. Must the service be rendered personally?

5. Does the business hire, supervise, or pay assistants to help the individual performing under the contract?

6. Is the relationship between the parties a continuing one?

7. Who sets the hours of work?

8. Is the individual required to devote full time to the party for whom the services are performed?

9. Does the individual perform work on another's business premises?

10. Who directs the sequence in which the work must be done?

11. Are regular oral or written reports required?

12. What is the method of payment—hourly, weekly, commission, or by the job?

13. Are business or traveling expenses reimbursed?

14. Who furnishes the tools and materials necessary for the provision of services?

15. Does the individual performing the services have significant investment in the facilities used to perform them?

16. Can the individual providing the services realize a profit or loss?

17. Can the individual providing the service work for a number of firms at the same time?

18. Does the individual make his or her services available to the general public?

19. Is the individual providing services subject to dismissal for reasons other than nonperformance of contract specifications?

20. Can the individual providing services terminate his or her relationship at any time without incurring a liability for failure to complete a job?

How Written Call Reports Can Jeopardize Your Independent Contractor Status

It's apparent that the IRS guidelines for independent contractor determination—while paralleling the broader, theoretical tone of the legal doctrines—are significantly more detailed and seek to focus on the mechanics of an independent contractor-principal relationship. Of particular importance to agents and manufacturers are the questions regarding oral and written report requirements, whether the independent contractor can work for a number of firms at the same time, reimbursement of expenses, and continuity of the relationship. Also significant is question 20, termination without reprisal. Most agency agreements are written so that either party may terminate a relationship with 30-, 60-, or 90-day notice. This in and of itself is indicative of a business-to-business relationship, not one of employer-employee.

The one constant in both descriptions of independent contractor status—the one on which all other deciding factors are based—is the element of control. This is the first thing that will be examined if an independent contractor relationship is questioned for any reason, whether it's a question of law or a tax dispute. Following that will be the other criteria: Whether reporting requirements are present—they, too, indicate an element of control; whether expenses are reimbursed—implicit here is control over the manner in which the job is done; and whether the "tools" to perform the task are provided. No one factor proves or disproves the existence or nonexistence of an independent contractor/principal arrangement. Rather, all in combination with the circumstances surrounding any one independent contractor relationship will determine just where a manufacturers' agent stands with his principals, and where a principal stands with his agents.

HOW TO PROTECT YOURSELF FROM A COMPETING FORMER EMPLOYEE

Historically, the manufacturers' agent has been a one-man band, selling in his territory with little additional help except for that of a clerical nature. But the one-man band is being replaced by an increasing number of multi-person agencies, and this change has caused a number of legal problems.

After the agency and its salespeople have pioneered a project and territory, how can the agency keep a salesperson from taking on a competing line and selling it to the customers he or she and the agency have developed together? A non-competition covenant prepared by a lawyer, that is fair and legal, may be just about the only way to keep an aggressive employee from taking over. But there still may be legal problems that can result in trade suits filed by ambitious performers who become disgruntled. Even with a covenant, the court may decide that the agreement attempts to cover too much time or territory, or that no covenant exists because of the way it was entered into.

To protect yourself from an ambitious employee, assuming federal and local laws are strictly complied with, these are the basic guidelines for you to consider:

1. The agreement must be entered into before hiring the employee.

2. Mutual consideration is an essential element of the agreement. There is no legal contract if the employer fails to provide or promise something in return for the employee's promise not to compete.

3. For a covenant to be in effect, an employer must live up to all the terms he has promised in hiring the employee, i.e., wages, benefits, expenses, size of territory, etc. If he does not meet these terms, the court will probably deny the employer relief should the employee break the covenant.

4. No covenant exists indefinitely. If the employee leaves, rehiring him does not automatically renew the agreement. A new covenant must be agreed to in writing.

5. Don't make the contract too widespread or farfetched. If your employee doesn't know any trade secrets or doesn't have access to any secret customer or prospective customer lists that are not already public, you can't restrict him from divulging them. You may only protect truly confidential information or your substantial investment in an employee's training to make his service unique to your territory.

How to Add a Covenant to an Employee Who Is Already on the Payroll

Suppose an employee is already on the payroll without a covenant and the employer wants one? It's not too late to add one if you go about it in the right way. The courts are divided on whether the continuation of employment itself is enough consideration to make an after-hiring covenant stick. But many have decided that further consideration may be added to the employment agreement in order to include the covenant not to compete. In other words, if you add extra benefits or a thirty-day notice of termination or anything over and above what currently exists in the employment contract, you may also add the covenant. No agency wants to buck unfair competition from an employee or a principal, and it should not be necessary if the proper legal steps are taken.

The information related is intended to serve only as a guideline to help you avoid this type of competition. The only safe way to insure protection is to consult an attorney when drawing up a covenant not to compete.

HOW TO RESOLVE LEGAL PROBLEMS

No matter how hard agencies and manufacturers work at building trust, problems will arise sooner or later. Late delivery that makes the agency look foolish in the eyes of the customer is frequently viewed as a sign that the relationship is on the skids. An agency that seems to be paying less attention to the principal than it did in the past will send some manufacturers into a funk about the state of the relationship.

Problems that do occur should be dealt with immediately and

honestly in order to keep the joint-venture partnership of the manufacturer and agency alive. In most of the cases I have heard of over the years, small problems that could have been solved if they had been addressed immediately turned into big, unsolved problems when they reached expanded proportions.

Most people won't be upset or think you are nit-picking when you opt to solve a problem right away. However, if you feel the person could take the approach personally, it's best to explain up front that what you are doing is because you want the relationship to continue to grow.

You can set the stage for a strong relationship by stating that you want to hear about problems early on and that you don't want people to think that they will go away by themselves. Also, be sure that the other party knows that you are going to bring up things which concern you before they have time to grow into monsters.

FOUR WAYS TO CEMENT THE AGENCY/MANUFACTURER RELATIONSHIP

The following checklist was created by reviewing problems that I have discussed with agents and manufacturers and by suggestions offered during the MANA agent and manufacturer seminars:

1. Establish a working relationship only if you intend it to be a long-term one. When short-term relationships are practical for agencies and manufacturers, both parties should agree on the term.

2. Stay in touch, but don't violate the independent contractor status of an agency by requesting daily call reports.

3. First try to solve problems yourself. Agents and manufacturers who turn to lawyers or other intermediaries without trying to solve the problem themselves often create additional problems.

4. Start with the assumption of trust. Usually when you show another party that you trust him, he will work very hard to maintain that trust. But when a person feels that you don't trust him, he is less inclined to work toward maintaining a healthy relationship.

6

How to Build Strong Ties With Your Principals

Being an agent is being in the middle—between your principals and the customers you serve. You serve your customers well when you sell quality products at competitive prices, and when they are delivered on time. However, relations with your principals can be more complex. There's a lot of personal chemistry involved along with specific ground rules that each principal feels are important.

The following checklist will help you determine whether you and a principal have the same objectives:

I. Product information
   A. Give a short description and principal application of each product.
   B. List the advantages and disadvantages of each product in relation to competition and industry requirements. Be objective and include:

1. Quality/performance
2. Production
3. Current delivery time from receipt of order
4. Service policy
5. Are you prepared to communicate with your agency on all matters influencing the marketing of your products?
6. Are you prepared to inform all members of this agency of your product knowledge?
7. Are you prepared to work in the field with members of this agency?

II. Pricing information

  A. Describe the method used to establish price.
  B. Outline the policies on price (discounts, returns, allowances, etc.).
  C. Show your price for each product in relation to your major competitors' prices.
  D. If your prices are higher than those of your competition, can you justify them in terms of quality, service, and delivery?
  E. Are you prepared to provide quotes on time and follow them up in writing?

III. Market information

  A. Estimate the total industry sales and unit volume attainable on each product for this territory on a short- (1 year) and long-range (3 to 5 years) basis by classifications, i.e., commercial, institutional, school, and so on.
  B. Approximate the percentage share of the sales volume you now have and expect to have.
  C. Compute the share of this volume your main competitors have (short range by product).
  D. Give your annual volume for the last three years.
  E. Show the long-range trend for each product.

IV. Customer identification

  A. Estimate the number of customers for each product in this territory (short and long range).
  B. Describe the purchasing procedures for each product
     1. Initial orders:
        a) Primary buying influences
        b) Secondary buying influences

      2. Orders after being specified

         a) Primary buying influences

         b) Secondary buying influences

V. Competitive information

    A. Name the companies in competition by product

       1. Number and size

       2. Location

       3. Characteristics

       4. Policies

       5. How long have they been in business?

       6. Evaluate their trade relations.

       7. Are they making a profit? Estimate.

       8. Are they growing? How fast?

    B. Describe the competitive sales situation

       1. How good are their salespeople?

       2. What kind of reputation do their salespeople have?

       3. Is the morale of their contact people good?

       4. Do they have a high rate of turnover?

VI. Sales information

    A. Describe the internal sales organization.

    B. Describe the external sales organization.

    C. Tell about the system used for agent/principal communication.

    D. Give the methods used to evaluate sales representation

       1. Effectiveness

       2. Reputation

       3. Morale

       4. Training

       5. Reports

    E. Show the record of sales volume by product to date for this territory.

    F. Present the sales objectives for this territory for the next year.

VII. Production situation

    A. Show whether production is limited or flexible.

    B. Describe the difficulties in obtaining materials (projected).

    C. List pending production limitations and forecasts.

VIII.   Advertising and sales promotion information
   A.   Give the advertising budget for this region, if any.
   B.   Present samples of advertising developed.
   C.   Describe sales promotion activities (trade shows, films, etc.).
   D.   Describe publicity activity.
   E.   Give samples of competitive advertising and sales promotion.
   F.   Evaluate activities to date.
   G.   Estimate competitive expenditures and allocations
   H.   List policies on cooperative advertising, if applicable.

IX.   Sales leads
   A.   How are they generated?
   B.   How are they qualified?
   C.   How quickly are they furnished to the agencies?

X.   Agency/principal relationship
   A.   How is the exclusivity of this territory described and what are its boundaries?
   B.   Have you any house accounts and if so, what is the commission structure?
   C.   What are your policies on field back-up and visitation?
   D.   What is your commission structure?
      1.   Percentage amount
      2.   When paid
   E.   Do you currently work with a representative advisory council?

XI.   Written agreement with agent
   A.   What are the points you would like it to cover?

If you and your prospective manufacturer can agree on most of the answers to these points before the relationship begins, you'll be off on the right foot. You will both have an understanding of each other's position, and when difficulties arise, they will be much easier to solve.

UNDERSTANDING YOUR PRINCIPALS' NEEDS

It's easy to generalize and say that the only thing most principals want is for you to sell their products in sufficient quantities so that they (and you) make a good profit. But this is just a part of it. Manufacturers often have a rather large agenda, and their agencies play a major role in its implementation. For example, there is hardly a manufacturer that doesn't have growth plans. And the sales organization, of course, figures largely into these.

Manufacturers that are growth-minded want agencies of like mind. So if you want to build strong ties with a manufacturer that is committed to building a bigger business, you will have to share in their goals. In fact, there is probably no better way to build a relationship with a principal than to be able to relate your growth to his. If, for example, a principal looks to you for market intelligence, you can use this as a way to cement a relationship. But remember, you should expect to be paid for your effort when the research work that the manufacturer would like to have from you takes you away from the field or requires more than just some casual observation.

There are many other areas in which manufacturers expect their agencies to interact with them, and which will help to build strong agency–manufacturer relationships. However, keep in mind that a relationship is that of working partners. As an agent, you are an independent contractor, a businessperson working with another business. You are not a salesperson on the manufacturer's staff.

WHAT A MANUFACTURER LOOKS FOR IN AN AGENCY

Knowing what to cover with a principal is very important. However, it's just as important to know what a manufacturer is looking for in an agency. These are the points that most manufacturers concentrate on when they interview prospective agencies:

I. Agency size
    A. How many field sales personnel does your agency have?
    B. Do you work with subagents?
    C. Is the owner actively involved as a salesperson?
    D. What is the number of office personnel?
    E. Do you have any long-range expansion plans?
    F. Would you be willing to expand to accommodate a new account?
    G. If so, how would you go about handling the expansion?
    H. What is the business structure of the agency?

      I.   How many offices do you have?

      J.   Do you have plans to open new offices?

  II. Growth patterns

      A.   How long has the agency been in business?

      B.   What is your sales growth pattern since the agency was started?

      C.   What is your present sales volume?

      D.   How much does each agency salesperson contribute to total agency sales volume?

      E.   What are your sales objectives for next year?

 III. Territory

      A.   Describe the territory covered by your agency.

      B.   Are you willing to expand the territory?

      C.   If so, how would you implement the expansion?

 IV. Product line

      A.   How many lines do you represent?

      B.   Are your present lines compatible with our line?

      C.   Do you feel that there would be any conflict or competition?

      D.   Would you be willing to change from your present product market?

      E.   If so, how would you handle the new product line?

      F.   What would you consider the minimum sales you need to justify handling our line?

  V. Facilities and equipment

      A.   Do you have warehouse facilities?

      B.   If so, what size? Capacity?

      C.   What is your method of stock control?

      D.   Do you have any data processing equipment?

      E.   If so, describe.

      F.   What type of communication facilities do you have (TWX, Telex, WATS, etc.)?

 VI. Company policies

      A.   Describe your agency's program for sales staff compensation.

      B.   Do you have any special incentive or motivation programs?

      C.   How do you monitor sales performance?

1. Sales volume
2. Effectiveness
3. Morale
4. Reputation
5. Reports

D. Would you and/or your sales staff attend factory seminars?
E. If so, what expenses would you expect the manufacturer to pay?
F. What is your policy regarding field visitation by factory personnel?

VII. Customers

A. Describe the types of customers you are presently contacting.
B. Are they compatible with our product line?
C. Who are your key accounts?

VIII. Principals

A. How many principals are you now representing?
B. Do you have a line card?
C. Would you be willing to send us a copy?

IX. Marketing and sales promotion

A. Would you be willing to assist us in compiling market research information for making market forecasts?
B. Are you presently doing this for your other principals?
C. What media do you use to promote your principal's products?
D. If you use direct mail, how many customers are on your mailing list?
E. What type of brochure do you use to describe your agency?

X. Special services

A. Can your agency offer services such as writing quotes, making proposals, and helping with customer education?
B. Do you have a sales reporting system?
C. Do you consider yours a sales and service organization?
D. What do you consider to be your agency's major strengths?

XI. Have you made contingency plans for the continuation of the agency?

XII. References

A. Banks
B. Principals
C. Customers

HOW TO AVOID THE MASTER–SLAVE SYNDROME

One of the best ways to get the agency/manufacturer relationship off on the right foot is to have a firm and written contract. To continue to build on that relationship you must, right from the start, make sure that you are treated by your principals as an equal. When this is accomplished, interactions will result in mutual respect and a positive working relationship. You may feel that bending a little is necessary to keep a good principal, but it's important to establish the boundaries early. It's far easier to put a halt to unreasonable requests when you can remind the other party that you both had agreed on the rules than it is to handle a problem without any prior understanding.

HOW TO BUILD
THE AGENCY/MANUFACTURER RELATIONSHIP

MANA runs about a dozen seminars every year; half of them are for manufacturers' agents and the other half are for manufacturers who sell through agencies. One of the questions that both sides ask every time is "How can we effectively keep in touch?"

This seems like a silly question, doesn't it? After all, manufacturers' agents succeed because of their communicating ability. And most sales managers are more than verbal people. Yet, both groups seem at somewhat of a loss when it comes to staying in touch.

Let me begin by first telling you how you *should not* communicate. Then I'll get into some practical ways that you can use to build the bridges to your principals that spell a long-term relationship.

Call reports are standard operating procedures for companies that work with a salaried sales force. The salespeople are asked to fill out reports on each of the calls they make. The sales manager often uses these reports to measure the progress of the calls and to help the salespeople move closer to the sales. It is an effective way to help salespeople. But it can only be used by manufacturers who sell with salaried salespeople. If this approach is taken with independent sales agencies, the wrath of the IRS will fall on both parties.

Remember that you, as a sales agency, are an independent business, operating apart from your principals and receiving only commissions for your work. You are not paid a salary and your expenses are not paid by your principals. However, if you were to fill out regular call reports, the IRS would very quickly determine that the manufacturer was exercising direct control over your operation, and the whole relationship would change. Then you—and your principal—would be liable for the same taxes that would be paid if the principal were using you as a salaried salesperson. *Don't use call reports to build your relationship with your principals*.

How to Keep Your Principals Posted

There are, however, ways other than call reports that you can use to see that your principals get the information they need and that can build strong bridges without getting into trouble with the IRS. Let's, for a moment, stick with the job of keeping your principals posted on sales progress.

One agency I know has given each of its salespeople microrecorders to dictate reports after significant meetings. Their reports are first sent to the agency headquarters for evaluation, and then the agency owner sends the tapes on to the principal for review. Note that these tapes are sent voluntarily—the manufacturer hasn't asked for them. Also note that these tapes are sent only after meetings during which significant progress has been made, or during which major questions arose that the factory must resolve. This, of course, doesn't violate the agency's independent contractor status, and it gives both the agency and the manufacturer a good source of information on the progress of major sales.

Some agencies supply their field salespeople with post cards, which are preprinted with their principal's address, and ask them to jot down quick impressions of important discussions right after the call takes place. Usually, if these cards bring up an important point, either a follow-up letter or phone call is arranged to fill in the manufacturer on the details. This has the effect of passing along important information and helps to build strong agency/manufacturer relations.

Many manufacturers today have installed 800 numbers strictly for their agencies' salespeople to use whenever they have questions to ask or information to report. The phone is answered by a person who is best able to help the agencies.

It is possible to submit written reports, but they have to be done without the control of the manufacturer. Sometimes it's almost impossible to convey all the information that a manufacturer needs without some form of written report. The savvy agencies who do submit reports do them only when an important event has to be reported, and they do not do it on any sort of predictable schedule that could get them in trouble with the IRS.

Examples of How Some Agencies Have Built Solid Relationships With Their Principals

So far, you've seen some specific situations in which all agencies and manufacturers find themselves, and how an agency can make the most of the situation in order to build a strong relationship. There's more to a solid working partnership than this, though. In most cases, it's not too difficult to take the first steps in building a good relationship, but the real test comes in the long haul. Unfortunately, both agencies and manufacturers often start out with the best of intentions and then let things slide. Usually they assume that everything is going well and that it's no longer necessary to continue to do the things that were responsible for the strength of the relationship in the first place. This just isn't so. A good relationship takes work—all the time.

Perhaps the best way to tell you about how agencies can build and strengthen their manufacturer relationships is to describe how some agencies have done it. In some cases, these will be composite case histories, built on the experience of several agencies.

How to Use a Newsletter for Best Results

When newsletters are used, it's often from the manufacturer to his agencies. As a New England agent who felt that he should be able to work the other way, too, said: "We were always very impressed with the newsletters that our principals sent to us. Those that were most helpful were loaded with good product and application information. They told us about how other agencies have made sales so that we might use the same approach. So, when we began thinking about producing a newsletter for our principals, our first consideration was to give them solid information that *they* needed, not pictures of our agency bowling team.

"We have nine principals," this agent continued, "and, as you might imagine, each of them makes products that we sell to the same market—contractors. Since we didn't want to include specific information about individual sales in the newsletter for all the principals, we decided that the editorial content would reflect the needs of all these manufacturers. First of all, we include news of new projects that are going up in our territory. We talk about contacts with contractors and architects, as they relate to the interests of all. Frequently our customers are sources of good information that they don't mind sharing with us and with our principals. This type of information is often featured in the letter. We get their permission to use the material, of course.

"We also discuss product applications. Fortunately, applications for any one of our principals is of interest to all the others. It helps them in their market planning.

"And, of course, we do a little brag and boast in our newsletter. For example, we include information on agency people who are doing things that are of specific interest to our manufacturers. Recently, we featured an item about one of our field salespeople who had just passed the exams for professional engineer certification. Having a PE on the road is important for some of these people to know about.

"We also include reprint material from other publications (with permission) that we think will be of interest to our principals."

Sounds like an ambitious undertaking, doesn't it. It is, but this agency only does the letter four times a year. Since they don't have to contend with the problem of late-breaking news, a quarterly works well for them. The letter is typed on a good typewriter and reproduced on the company copying machine.

The circulation of this letter is as interesting as the approach to editorial content. "We see that everyone at each of our principals who has anything at all to do with us gets a copy," the agent said. "That is, the president, everyone in the marketing department, the expediters, the financial people, and even the people in shipping. Who knows, they may have to decide whether its your customer's order or someone else's that gets out that day. When you're paid based on day of shipment, it makes sense to include everyone who can benefit you."

The agent who has been producing this letter claims that it has been very successful in cementing relationships with his principals. "We still have our disagreements," he claims, "and there still may be some shouting, but nobody carries grudges. We like to think that a lot of this is due to the care with which we build our principal relationships. And I know that our little newsletter is a very big factor."

Use Field Sales Trips to Cement Principal Relationships

For some products, it just isn't necessary for a person from the factory to visit customers. But for most products engineered for industrial and OEM customers, visits from factory people can be very important. One agency I've heard of uses this time not only to solve customer problems but to cement relationships with his principals.

As this midwestern agent put it: "We need to have the marketing and engineering people from several of our principals make field visits with us fairly regularly. Most of them are more than pleased to make these visits because they know that they are being made for a specific reason. Too many people drag their factory people into the field just to have backup, even when the need isn't critical. When we set up a meeting with a customer and a factory person, it is for an important reason. But this isn't all. When a factory person takes the time to visit our territory, we like to make the most of it, and we schedule either a breakfast or a dinner meeting with the factory person and all of the agency staff. These meetings are informal, but we do have a basic agenda to cover. Everybody, including the factory person, gets a copy of the agenda several days before the meeting so that we can be more productive. The meetings seldom last more than three hours, and this includes the meal at a local restaurant. But we are able to get more helpful information in that time—and so is the factory person—than we could in just about any other way."

The principals this agent represents agree with his estimate of the value of the field visits and mini-meetings. In fact, some of them have been encouraging their other agencies to follow suit.

How to Make Good Use of Rep Councils

Rep councils can work wonders if the agencies and the manufacturer who sponsors the council understand the role the council should play in agency relations. Manufacturers shouldn't use the council to further ideas that might be difficult to promote to individual agencies, and agencies shouldn't view the rep council as a union surrogate. Rep councils should be used to provide regular and active communications between the agencies and the manufacturers. Both agents and manufacturers can use them as a source of information and guidance in the management of the affairs that affect both organizations.

The following are topics that are most often included in rep council agendas. If you are an agent member of a council, you can probably contribute most to the success of the council if you keep yourself up to date on these subjects.

Communications   This topic, like ones often discussed at rep council meetings, will overlap with others. For example, advertising is included under the topic of sales policies, but it could come under communications. That is, what agencies are expected to do with advertising leads after the manufacturer has qualified them. Communications is a broad category and additional discussion questions under this subject might include: Are agents and the manufacturer communicating effectively and frequently enough? Are they communicating too frequently and not resolving very much? Are both parties really listening to each other?

Delivery and Service   This is an item that is likely to raise hackles at some rep council meetings. When you close a sale, you want to see the product delivered quickly, and so does the customer. It's a problem that should be approached maturely by both parties, despite the big differences that can exist when a manufacturer pays less attention to delivery than to other operations.

Commissions   Commissions are discussed occasionally, but because each agency has a signed contract before coming on board, there is seldom much to discuss. If the discussion ends up being a pressure session by either party, the effectiveness of the rep council will be wasted. Commission problems are usually individual, and they should be discussed individually, not at council meetings.

Competition   Here's a topic that can benefit agents and manufacturers considerably if it's handled in a mutual way. That is, if the council members don't get defensive, a good discussion of the strengths and weaknesses of the competition, relative to the strengths and weaknesses of the principal and the agency team, can do more to create effective strategy than many other topics. When everyone accepts the fact that competition exists and that it may in some ways have better products than the principal's products, the groundwork has been laid for a fruitful discussion.

New Products   The marketing concept states that product ideas should come from those who will use them—not from engineers who are sitting in isolated cubicles in the plant. Agents are, perhaps, in the best position to bring in ideas for new products. When an agency doesn't have a product a customer wants but knows how one of its principals could make it, there is room for synergy. This can be one of the most productive topics for rep councils to discuss.

Sales Aids   Again, this could be under other headings, but it warrants one of its own. Sales aids range from catalogs and samples to active participation in trade shows and conferences. Agents should be given the opportunity to help shape the type of sales aids that are prepared—catalogs, direct mail, and so on. Remember that the actual development should be left to advertising agencies or other creative services specialists. But there is no better place to get input on what will and will not work than from the people who will use the sales aids—the agents.

Motivation   Every principal feels that somewhere there is a secret motivation technique that will double the sales of its agencies and insure that they will devote all their time to the agency's products. Obviously, no such system exists. However, motivation is a good topic for rep council discussions. Motivation, as most sales managers define it, is the sound application of good management techniques with the agency sales force.

Growth   Growth is an important topic for rep council members to consider. Agents want to make sure that their principals are committed to growth, and the manufacturers want the same commitment from their agencies. When growth is brought up at rep council meetings, however, discussion should be limited to the collective scene. Don't bring up individual issues.

As you can see, rep councils can be used to build strong ties with principals. However, the council should only be used to build strong ties with the agency team in general—not to further your own individual goals. Although, as an active and productive member of a rep council, you just can't help but build up the stature of your agency!

How Best to Handle the Problem of House Accounts

Nothing seems to cause anger quicker in an agent than the mention of a house account. And most manufacturers are usually bewildered and upset when agencies refuse to take on their lines as long as there are house accounts in the territory. However, since the purpose of this chapter is to discuss building strong ties with principals, I'd like to introduce you to a concept that has worked for many agencies on this front. Perhaps the best way to explain this approach is to let an agent tell it in his own words. This agent was offered a line in a territory in which there was one major house account. Here's his story:

> "We were offered the line, but there was one proviso—the major customer in the territory was to remain a house account. As close as we could estimate, this customer accounted for about 25 percent of the volume in the territory. We could have made it with the other accounts, but I just didn't like the idea of a house account.

> "It seemed that no amount of discussion would shake the manufacturer from his position until I offered this suggestion. I told him that I would service the existing business at the account for half of the normal commission. I also said that I wanted the full commission on all the new business I was able to bring in from the account. Since the manufacturer had been making calls on this customer from the plant only three or four times a year, I knew that the almost weekly calls we were making on the customer for other products in our line had to pay off. We did this for a year and increased the business by 23 percent. Needless to say, this isn't a house account any longer."

This not only resolved a house account problem, it dramatically showed the manufacturer just what a good agency can do.

How to Resolve Commission Disputes

There is little chance of their being a commission dispute if you have a solid contract with your principals. There may be some misunderstandings, but when the foundations are laid in a contract that both agree on before any selling begins, the disputes can usually be resolved quickly. I'm not talking about the individual intransigency you occasionally encounter but just plain pig-headedness. These are problems that mature businesspeople can deal with in terms of agreements that have been made.

Most problems should try to be solved by the individuals involved before bringing in a lawyer. When all your efforts have failed to get results, you will probably have to seek legal assistance. It's rare that the relationship will continue after an attorney has been brought in—no matter who wins.

As Alvin Greenwald, an able attorney, has put it: "It is highly recommended that potential litigants review time, costs, and stress aspects before filing suit. An example of the risk that can be borne by the party bringing action, if such party can be charged with breach of contract, disparagement, interference with economic right, and abuse of process of other actionable circumstances, includes liability that may far outweigh the potential judgment. Another example is if a party attaches or garnishes to secure ultimate payment and then loses the action, the penalty for wrongful attachment or garnishment is severe and includes recovery by the prevailing party of attorney's and witness' fees, as well as compensatory and consequential damages. Merely because the remedy is available does not mean that one should pursue it. Remember that one who does not properly and wisely pursue substantial legal rights is an automatic winner. The world loves winners!''

Commission disputes are, more often than not, the result of misunderstandings and not out-and-out cheating. However, if you know and can prove for a fact that you have been cheated, the courts will probably be your best bet.

Strong Sales Build Strong Ties

Manufacturers appoint agencies to sell for them. While they do like to hear from their agencies as often as possible and they are usually impressed with such things as agency growth and expansion, their bottom line is sales. Therefore, to be successful, do everything outlined in this chapter, but do it in addition to bringing in sales. If you do, it will be a win-win situation for everyone.

7

How to Create Successful Advertising, Sales Promotion, and Public Relations Programs

Most manufacturers' agencies don't pay too much attention to advertising when it comes to their own business. As one agent explained recently: "My territory is two small states. If I were to advertise in the magazines that cover our industry, I'd have to advertise in magazines that cover all fifty states. Two-fiftieths efficiency just isn't worth it."

This agent makes a valid point, but only as far as he has gone. It seldom pays for an agency to advertise in nationally circulated magazines. However, this doesn't mean that sales agencies can't make use of the power of advertising in other ways. Agents can, indeed, advertise in *some* magazines, make use of direct mail, use the telephone, take advantage of many of the publicity avenues, and make excellent use of the sales literature produced by their principals. In this chapter, you'll see, in some detail, just how you can use each of these, no matter the size or location of your agency.

HOW ANY SALES AGENCY CAN PROFIT FROM MAGAZINE ADVERTISING

There are probably a few regional magazines in which you can advertise, depending on your field. For example, the Instrument Society of America has many regional journals, and most of the advertisers in these journals are manufacturers' agencies. These local publications are usually well read and the societies are well thought of. This means that your advertising will be in good company.

The rates charged by these publications are seldom crushing. More often than not, those who publish these journals are operating on a not-for-profit basis and have to keep the rates at a point where they do nothing more than cover the expense of publishing the journal.

Agents who have advertised in local and regional magazines published by societies and associations seem to feel that their money is well spent. Few of them can actually say that people have called them and have given them orders as a result of seeing the ads, but they do claim that when they make sales calls, their prospects frequently remember the ads and are in a positive mode because of the exposure. As an agent explained to me recently, "I always ask prospects I meet for the first time whether or not they have seen my advertisements in the magazines. Some have and some haven't. But in either case it gives me an opportunity to start with a product story. I simply say to them if they haven't seen the ad, 'Let me summarize the points I made in the ad about the product.' And if they do remember seeing the ad, I say, 'Then you remember that the transistor in the ad will deliver 2 watts at 2 gigahertz.' Either way, it's a solid entree to the sales presentation."

How to Get the Right Ad

The biggest problem with agency advertising is seldom in finding the right medium but in getting the right ad to place in the pages of the magazine. It's not exactly inexpensive to have an effective advertisement prepared, and amateur efforts usually do more harm than good. But there is a way out of this seemingly no-win situation.

Most manufacturers who advertise in national publications to generate leads for their sales agencies usually will make the ads available to their agency for local use. With very little work, the ad can often be modified to include the name and address of your agency. A manufacturer's sales manager explained to me that his company will bend over backwards to see that its agencies get the ads that identify them as the local contact. He said: "Our advertising agency has standing orders to create our ads so that with very little effort our name can be made smaller and the agency's name added in bold type. We will send the local magazine the materials they need and in whatever form is required. We send negatives ready for use and/or repro copy, layouts, and illustrations to the magazines that will assemble the ads for the agents. We feel that it's just as important to support our agents on the local front as it is to support them nationally with our own advertising program."

This sales manager further explained that these efforts have given his agencies a national identity that has been hard for his competitors to beat. As he said: "We advertise heavily nationally, and when you include all the local and regional exposure we get by supporting our agencies, we are just about everywhere you look."

What About Cost?

The cost to advertise locally, while it may be small compared with the cost to advertise nationally, is not an insignificant figure for even some of the larger agencies. Consider that the average agency has between eight and ten principals, and each would like them to advertise. Add this to the need to build some continuity in the magazines and you have some pretty heavy expenses. But more than a few of the manufacturers who can be considered progressive in this country share the advertising cost with their agencies as well as supply them with the ads.

"We have a separate appropriation for agency advertising," another manufacturer explained to me at one of the MANA seminars. "We make the same amount of money available to every agency and encourage them to spend it. We run the program pretty much like a coop program in that we pay half the ad space cost up to a certain figure when they send us a copy of the magazine in which the ad runs. When we first instituted this program about ten years ago, we only had eight takers from our team of twenty-two agencies. Within two years, all of the agencies got on the bandwagon. It works! We can point to sales that were the result of contacts made through these ads.''

Where Not to Advertise

It's probably just as important to know where *not* to advertise as it is to know where to advertise. As a general rule, you should select publications that directly cover your market. If you're selling process instruments, for example, the best place to spend your advertising dollars would probably be in the local editions of the Instrument Society's magazines.

The test should be that the publication covers your market directly. You will probably find more than a few magazines badgering you for advertising that cover some rather broad territory. In general, these magazines won't do much more than deplete your advertising budget. The local industry-type publication that is sent to every businessperson in your area won't do very much for you. These publications are usually controlled circulation, which means that the publisher has decided who they are going to be sent to. And, more often than not, the readers included on the publisher's mailing list are operating officers and seldom include the people who will actually specify and buy your products. They'll give you the pitch that they reach the top people, but how often do you sell directly to these people? You want to reach those who buy and use your products.

If the local magazine is sponsored by the local Chamber of Commerce and you're a member, you'll probably have to advertise. But the chances are that it will do little more than reach a general audience. Think of it as your contribution, but don't think of it as a practical way to reach those who you want to influence.

There is one type of publication you want to watch out for. It seems that more than a few hustlers have latched on to a racket that is making them rich, but provides nothing to those who are making them rich. These are local publications that are produced under the name of an organization that is hard to deny, e.g., ''The Voice of Police'' or ''Magazine of Industry.'' The titles sound important. Some even hide behind civil organizations; others seem as though they represent some aspect of the business community. But their only real goal is to get your ad dollars. Sure, they do publish, but their magazines are nothing more than page after page of advertisements that their commission phone salespeople have gathered. Incidentally, the space is sold in these magazines by high-pressure telephone salespeople who usually make a high-gear pitch for the ad early on.

To get off the hook or at least identify the baloney artists, ask them to send you some additional information and a copy of their most recent issue. And, if you really want to see how quickly they hang up, ask one of them to stop by your office to discuss the program.

One way to make sure if you are uncertain about a publication is to ask your principal to have its advertising agency review the publication and give you a report. Ad agencies not only have access to the directories of all the business magazines in the country but most of them also keep records of the frauds that you should watch out for.

HOW TO PROMOTE YOUR AGENCY AND THE PRODUCTS YOU SELL BY DIRECT MAIL

When the cost of a sales call topped $100, more than a few agencies thought they could do the job cheaper by direct mail. Well, if agents could sell products through the mail, their principals would have cancelled their contracts years ago and enlisted the aid of the post office. All the post office asks for is the price of a stamp. But, unfortunately, it just isn't that easy.

However, direct mail can be a powerful tool for the manufacturers' agent. Here's what many savvy agencies have done with the help of direct mail:

1. Motivated their salespeople.
2. Opened the door for those more expensive personal sales calls.
3. Trained salespeople in product knowledge as well as in selling skills.
4. Kept in contact with customers between sales calls.
5. Kept sold customers sold.
6. Prospected for new customers.

7. Reopened inactive accounts.

8. Followed up on screened advertising leads.

9. Brought prospects to trade shows.

10. Built the image of the agency.

11. Broken down resistance that was met during a personal sales call.

12. Distributed samples and product literature.

13. Announced new products and policies.

14. Researched new products and ideas.

As you can see, none of these items actually included the sale of a product, but you can also see that direct mail is a powerful tool to facilitate a face-to-face sale. You should concentrate on direct mail for the following reasons.

Eight Ways Direct Mail Boosts Agency Sales

1. Direct mail can be targeted to individuals you want most to influence.

2. It is a personal medium. Even if you don't use a personally typed letter, your mailing is still keyed to an individual—not a broad audience.

3. It has no competition. When a person reads your direct mail piece, he or she is giving your message full attention. The same person may be tempted to skip your ad in a magazine and read the editorial contents or someone else's ad.

4. It has no size limitations. You can put just about any size piece of paper in the mail. When you advertise in a magazine, you are confined to the sizes and shapes of space offered by the publisher.

5. There are no time constraints on direct mail. If you miss a closing date with a magazine, you're out of luck until the next issue is published. However, the post office picks up the mail every day.

6. You can test your direct mail without blowing your entire ad budget. Mail to a small portion of your list and see if it works. If it doesn't, just do a roll-out with the balance of the list. If

your direct mail piece is a dud, create another and again test a small segment of the list.

7. You can tell a much longer story. If you tell your story well, you can go on for pages in direct mail. It's a proven fact that people will read long copy in direct mail, but the opposite is usually true with magazine advertising.

8. You have a chance to push a reader to take some action. Good direct mail always moves the prospect to the next step in the sales sequence. That may be to send for more literature or to request a demonstration. This is rather difficult to do with magazine advertising.

Four Ways to Use Direct Mail Effectively

Direct mail can be used most effectively in the following ways:

1. To persuade. For example, if you want a specific action, it's a lot easier to motivate a person to send for more information with direct mail than it is in other forms of promotion.

2. To inform. If your goal is to get information into the field, you can usually do it most economically and effectively with direct mail. However, you do have to find out the names of the people who will be your audience.

3. To remind. Agency selling is and always will be a personal type of business. And direct mail, when used to follow up sales calls, can be one of the most effective double-team approaches available to you.

4. To assist people. Too many agencies miss out on a sale simply because they are not at the prospect's office when he or she is ready to place an order. With direct mail, which can be kept for reference, you can lend the hand that gets the sale when other types of promotion might have been ignored or discarded.

Just a simple letter, if well written, can be another very effective form of promotion, along with a piece of product literature, and a reply card for the prospect to return for either additional literature or to set up an appointment.

Direct mail is a very precise science. However, with a little practice, you should be able to do a credible job.

HOW TO PROMOTE SUCCESSFULLY
BY TELEPHONE

More and more agencies are using the telephone as part of their total selling effort. But, as with direct mail, the telephone is a good technique for getting a sale in motion and keeping it on track until the sale is consummated. Many agents do some of their own prospecting by phone or will train inside people to do the job for them. One agent explained how he makes best use of his principals' sales leads: "The leads I get from my principals are all prequalified by the time I get them. The manufacturers either check them out by phone or through a direct mail qualification system. However, since this is no longer a cold-call business, I take the sales front's first step by using the telephone to try to set up appointments or to weed out those who will probably never turn into customers."

This same agent also actively uses the phone after his personal meetings to keep up the momentum. As he explained: "I try to leave the first meeting with a specific task to perform for the prospect. For example, I may promise to get him the answer to some questions he may have or if he doesn't ask for additional information, I always have things to suggest that will be of interest to him. Even if I have the material in my bag, I hold back an order to make the next contact. My products (electronic components) are seldom sold on the first call. It often takes several contacts to do that. The telephone gives me the opportunity to get back either with the information the prospect has requested, or with the information I have more or less lead him to request."

There are companies that you can retain to do telephone selling for you. Some will take on the job of prospecting; others will take on the lead qualification process. These services can be very effective, but be careful who you select. This is a relatively new business, and some of the people are really sharp operators. They may have good records of accomplishment, but you must be certain that they do the job the way *you* want it done. Avoid anyone who is the least bit hard sell. Remember, these people will be representing you on the phone. They must project the right image or else they can do more harm than good.

Eight Tips to Make Your Telemarketing More Effective

1. Identify yourself and your company immediately. There are an awful lot of people—and computers—making sales calls by phone today that your prospect might want to avoid.

2. Identify your prospect's interests quickly. Before you get on the phone, you should have a pretty good idea of his or her interests and how they relate to the product you are selling. If you don't, do your homework first. Make your point right away. Your prospects want to know what's in the call for them. And what you tell them shouldn't only be that you want to sell them your product. You should tell them something that will be of specific benefit to them—and right away if possible. You might even consider just calling to tell the prospect that you are sending a catalog in the mail and wanted to verify the spelling of the person's name. A call such as this establishes contact, gives the prospect something to look for in the mail, and it also gives you an opportunity to call back in a few days to see if the mailing has arrived.

3. Learn how to read voices. As an experienced salesperson, you have already learned how to read the combination of visible body language and voices. But on the telephone, half of the cues will be missing. You have to become especially sensitive to vocal inflections in order to make a go of telemarketing.

4. Go through a dry run. There's nothing like trying out your presentation on someone else to get the bugs out. Also, you might consider taping the practice sessions. It's one thing for a friend to play the part of a prospect on the phone, but the best help will be a combination of your friend's comments and your own observations of the pitch by listening to the tape.

5. Have the answers ready. It's just about impossible to prepare for all the questions you could possibly be asked, but you should know the answers to the most often-asked questions. And you should be able to guide the telemarketing call well enough so that you lead your prospect to ask the questions that you want to answer. This is a technique that most salespeople develop intuitively, but to be effective, it usually depends on careful observation of body language and vocal cues.

6. Establish strong personal contact. You certainly aren't going to ask: "How's the wife and kids?" if this is your first call. However, general conversation usually leads most people to discover a few things they have in common. And these elements are often sufficient to give you an opportunity to establish some form of personal contact.

7. Watch your pace. A telemarketing call should have a specific purpose. You should plan the call so that it doesn't lag and it doesn't overwhelm your prospect.

8. Maintain flexibility. Beginners in telemarketing too often lean on canned presentations. When their prospects take a tack to windward, they can be easily thrown off. You should have a plan to your call, but be able to deviate as the need arises. The trick is to handle the diversion and get the call back on track. All it takes is practice.

Perhaps the best way to get a feel for how you can use the telephone to sell your products is to listen to the pitch that others make. Many of the calls you get won't be for products that relate to ones you sell. But you can benefit from listening to and evaluating the pitches as they come your way. The next time you are ready to hang up on a stock-and-bond sales pitch, hold on and listen. It isn't going to be easy staving off the onslaught, but it will really give you a good idea of how these presentations are made.

One last note on the subject of telemarketing. You have to be persistent without making enemies. It isn't easy. But when you get the knack of reading voices, you'll know when to back off and whether or not to call again soon.

HOW TO USE PUBLICITY TOOLS FOR BEST RESULTS

It's probably easier for a manufacturers' agency to promote by using the techniques of publicity than it is to do the same job with magazine advertising. This requires some explanation before getting into the details of mounting an effective publicity campaign.

Advertising in Magazines

Advertising is the use of paid space. That is, you buy space in a magazine and have the publisher place your ad in this space. If you're very lucky, there may be one or two local or regional magazines that cover your market and territory. And since you will be paying your hard-earned dollars for advertising, you will want to make certain that you get more than a buck back for every advertising buck you spend.

If your goal is to remind people that you are in the territory, your advertising-dollar expectations will not be as high as they would be if you were looking for a proportionate number of new leads. On the other hand, with publicity, you can frequently get more bang for your buck because your goal will be wider exposure, and your only cost will be the preparation and distribution of the press releases. With paid space, you want to make sure that the magazine you choose will hit the right market for your ad before you spend the money. But with publicity, you will probably be sending releases to every publication in your territory that is even remotely related to your field and market. Mass-distributed press releases are best used to make general announcements about such things as new lines, new principals, and new products that you'd like your prospects to see. It's the rifle or the shotgun approach.

Placing a Feature Story in a Magazine

You can target a publicity program to a specific magazine by placing a feature story with the editor. This will take some planning, though. Before you do anything, look at at least a half dozen back issues of the magazine in which you'd like to place your feature story. Check to see what kind of material they prefer. For example, is it how-to? State-of-the-art articles?, etc.

When you know what material the publisher favors, read at least six or more articles in some recent issues to find out the style of writing that is preferred. Many a valuable article never gets into print because the editor sees that it would be too much trouble shaping the material to suit the house style.

If you don't feel comfortable writing a feature article, especially if the target magazine's style is demanding, you might consider hiring a public relations agency to do the job. Many P.R. agencies prefer to work with their clients on a long-term contractual basis, but you should be able to find either a small agency or freelance editor who would be willing to write the article for you. This is called a ghostwriter, and his or her name should not appear in the credits.

How much does a ghost get for this backstage work? Depending on the person and the complexity of the material, the fee for an average 4,000-word article will probably run between $2,000 and $4,000, plus expenses. Expenses include travel and telephone costs as well as out-of-pocket research costs. This may seem like a high figure. But when you consider that a 4,000-word article, with illustrations, will probably occupy 4 to 6 pages in a magazine, you're getting a much better buy than you would if you bought the same space and had ads prepared to fill the space. And, remember, a by-line on an article makes you an authority. While a properly designed ad may bring you more direct inquiries, the ad does little to build your image or the image of your agency.

It's been said that the real benefit of placing an article in a trade magazine is the use of the reprints for years after the article runs. More than a few agents I know who have had articles published in trade magazines send a reprint with every pack of product literature they mail.

If you feel uncomfortable writing a full-length article or are unable to locate a writer for the job, you might consider creating a panel piece. The panel piece is an article based on the input from several people whose opinions are respected. You, of course, are the moderator who puts the piece together, and you share the glory with the people on the panel. However, if you play your cards right you can usually get some of the panel people from among the ranks of your customers and your prospects. Everyone recognizes the benefit of having a name in print, and by putting these people in the limelight, you give them a little ego massage at the same time that you establish your own credentials.

If this approach isn't feasible, you might consider doing a survey piece. For this, pick a topic that is of immediate interest to the people to whom you sell and do a survey on one aspect of the topic. The results in the magazine read by your prospects will add nicely to your stature in the field.

HOW TO MAKE MANUFACTURERS' SALES LITERATURE WORK FOR YOU

Even the biggest manufacturers' agencies seldom create the kind of sales literature produced by their principals. It just doesn't pay. But it does pay to do everything you can to make the most of the efforts of your principals. Here are twenty ways you can work with manufacturers' sales literature.

Twenty Ways to Make Manufacturers' Literature Pay Off

1. *Direct mail.* Don't make the mistake of just mailing out the sales literature your principals give you. The literature should be tailored to

your agency, which includes an imprint of your agency name plus agency addresses and phone numbers. In addition, include a short letter that does some selling. Tell the reader why you are sending the literature and how he or she will benefit from using the products. And you should also include a postpaid reply card, even if all you're offering is just more literature. Make sure that your prospect can get in touch with you easily.

2. *Sales presentations*. Manufacturers' literature can be used as is in a sales presentation, or you might consider having slides made of key pages to punctuate the points you make in your presentation.

3. *Trade shows*. Blowups of key parts of a piece of sales literature can make a big impression at a trade show. Some sales promotion people feel that it's better not to hand out the literature at a trade show. They claim that the literature should be available in the booth only as a sales aid. If prospects want copies, it's best that you take their names and addresses and mail the literature or deliver it in person after the show. The obvious benefit of this is a strong post-show follow-up.

4. *House organs and newsletters*. If any of your principals create case histories as part of their sales literature program, you can make use of this material in your own house organs and newsletters. Prospects like to know about the successes of others before they commit to a purchase.

5. *Inquiry follow-up*. If you do your own advertising and publicity, the manufacturers' literature can be used to handle the follow-up. If your principals do the advertising, they are the ones who should be sending the follow-up literature to the prospects—with the name of the local agency attached. However, sales literature can be used very effectively in personal follow-up calls. Don't use the piece as the focus of the call; simply use it to reinforce the points you would make in your regular presentation.

6. *Sales meetings*. Good manufacturers' sales literature can be the core of a good agency sales meeting. Sales literature is especially helpful when it's necessary to train new agency salespeople, or when product and application refreshers are needed by agency salespeople.

7. *Publicity*. It's unlikely that your principals will include all of the smaller local and regional magazines that exist in your field. This presents a good opportunity for you to make an editorial contact to get the literature reviewed. And the review, if it's done by a local publication, should carry your name and address as the local source.

8. *Displays*. Manufacturers' literature can be the basis for some very interesting office waiting-room displays. If any of your principals allow permanent displays of vendors' products, you can make excellent use of manufacturers' sales literature. If you stock such a customer's display, you will have to check it regularly to make sure that there is literature available at all times. Sometimes it's possible to make arrangements with someone at the plant to store a supply of the literature and to replenish the display whenever needed.

9. *Training courses*. When your principals don't provide formal training, you can often do quite well by using their product literature as the base of a course. It's not enough just to have your salespeople read the literature; a program must be developed from the literature that includes not only training but testing material. If you base your training on applications as well as product features, you will be presenting material to your sales in a way that will be most easily used in the field.

10. *Publication advertising*. The art and copy used to create your manufacturers' sales literature can frequently be used to make space advertising for use in the journals that serve your market and territory. Most progressive manufacturers will be glad to send you duplicates of their literatures' art and copy negatives for you, a local ad agency, or even the publication's art department to use to create an effective space ad.

It's usually a good idea to check first with the publication in which you are going to advertise for its halftone screen specifications. The halftone process creates the little dots you see in printed pictures. Depending on the paper and the press used, the size and spacing of these dots can vary considerably. There is hardly a manufacturer that won't spend a few bucks to give you the right halftone screen if you're going to spend your money to advertise its products.

11. *Sampling*. Many products sold by agencies can be demonstrated or at least shown in a customer's office. If you're lucky enough to have a few of these products in your line and to have manufacturers that produce good sales literature, you have a winning combination. Here's how to do it: As you give your demonstration, use a marker to emphasize the points you make on the sales literature. Then leave both the sample and literature for the prospect to evaluate. Even if you have to collect the sample later, you can leave the marked-up literature as a powerful reminder.

12. *Contests*. Contests are probably best associated with consumer product selling. However, with a little imagination, you can turn a manufacturer's catalog into an application contest, for example. Mail out the catalog, include an entry blank and you're in business. The prizes should be awarded for ideas and interesting applications—not for the largest sales.

13. *Film and slide presentation*. Having sales literature in the hands of a prospect during your presentation can slow things down a lot. Rather, make slides of the important topics you'll cover from the literature and use them during the presentation. The slide or filmstrip material should only be used for support. Your personal presentation has to be strong to make this work.

14. *Feature articles*. There's usually more than enough good information in manufacturers' sales literature to create feature stories. More often than not, the application stories in the literature will be of biggest interest to magazine editors.

15. *Mailing inserts*. If you make regular mailings of a newsletter, you can make the package more effective by inserting some product literature. If possible, try to tie in the feature of the newsletter with the product literature you are sending. I've heard of some agencies that make inserts for each other. These agencies sell noncompetitive products to the same markets, and include the mailings of their fellow agencies. If you go this route, make certain that the material you include in another agency's mailing is clearly identified as being sold by you—not by the agency making the mailing.

16. *In-plant shows*. This is a little different from the in-plant displays, mentioned earlier. The in-plant displays usually last for quite a while. However, in-plant shows are usually scheduled for a week or two at most. When you do an in-plant show, you're going to be there talking with prospects. The material you use should be developed to support your personal presentation.

Most in-plant shows concentrate on products, and use sales literature in a minor role. Therefore, you must pick and choose carefully. Select only the material that will reinforce the points you make during the presentation.

17. *Recruiting personnel*. The sales literature you get from your principals may be the best tool you have to tell the product story to

prospective employees. The use of the literature, along with a practiced eye, will give you a feel for a prospective employee's reactions. If, after reading the literature, the candidate seems interested and asks intelligent questions, you might be on the right track.

18. *Teaching*. More than a few agents teach courses at local schools. What better way to make a point than to use the sales literature of one of your principals?

19. *Sales call follow-up*. Successful consultants know the value of sending a detailed conference report to a client within a few days of the meeting. In a sense, agents are consultants selling the products of their principals, but very few take the time to acknowledge a call or meeting. A short note summarizing the main points of the call, plus some appropriate sales literature, and you have a very effective sales call follow-up program.

20. *Microfilm library*. Today, many large and small companies store suppliers' product literature on microfilm. If you have customers and prospects with microfilm systems, make sure that your principals' literature is in the file.

All of these tips are tried and true, but you have to make sure that the techniques you choose will be appropriate for your operation. It is often possible to combine two or more of these approaches into a unique use of a principal's sales literature.

PROMOTE REGULARLY

So far, techniques and approaches that can be used by just about any agency have been highlighted. However, you should keep in mind that continuity, more than just about anything else in a promotional campaign, makes it work. A first-rate ad only run once will not get you your money's worth. But an ordinary ad run regularly will. You, of course, must make sure that you know the difference between creative sales promotion and gimmickery. A bad ad run in every issue of a magazine is going to do more harm than good.

Advertising is important for the sales agency, but you won't be able to sell products directly from your advertising. You will, however, be able to build demand for the product and an image for your agency. Do it regularly, and you'll wonder why you never advertised before.

CHAPTER **8**

How to Build and Manage a Sales Force

What is it about salespeople that makes some more successful than others? I'm sure you've seen two salespeople who are seemingly equal in all respects: Both have good territories, excellent experience, and similar personal and professional backgrounds. However, one will shine and the other will limp along.

The question you really want answered is this: "How do you get the average salesperson to perform like your superstar?"

HOW TO MOTIVATE YOUR SALES FORCE

Assuming that you have salespeople who meet the basic requirements, who know the line, and who have some experience, the difference between a mediocre performance and success can usually be traced to motivation. However, it's important to recognize that there is no secret motivational technique that once mastered will make every salesperson a superstar.

Unfortunately, the word motivation has been used in connection with many techniques that are, at best, short-term fixes. At worst, many so-called motivational systems are completely impractical attempts to solve complex problems with everything ranging from management Muzak to arcane fads such as hypnotism.

In a practical sense, motivation is really the application of all of the elements that contribute to success. Put very simply, motivation and good management are really the same thing. To be successful managing a sales force, you must take into account all of the factors that have been identified as positive motivators, and they must be used regularly as part of your total sales management program. In other words, success depends on a systematic approach. The following factors have been identified as critical to selling success:

1. Proper salesperson selection.
2. Effective communication and feedback.
3. Fair compensation and rewards.
4. A high-quality and style of management.
5. Effective training.

Let's look at each in some detail.

Proper Salesperson Selection

Good selection techniques are the foundation of a strong sales force. But it's obvious that selection itself isn't a motivational tool. However, when the characteristics of a successful salesperson are spelled out, the people you select will be more responsible to both the economic and noneconomic factors of motivation.

Communications and Feedback

Unfortunately, most discussions of feedback are limited to the procedural aspects and are seldom related to the motivational aspects of working with agency salespeople. To be effective, you should broaden the concept of feedback to include all methods and procedures that let salespeople know reliably, clearly, and accurately exactly how they are doing. This should include reports, meetings, coaching sessions, newsletters, telephone sessions, and buddy-calls in the field.

Fair Compensation and Rewards

Make no mistake about it: Money is a motivator—and a very powerful motivator. But when money is used in a simple carrot-and-stick approach, such as in a sales contest, you will probably be wasting your time. Agency salespeople want to make a lot of money, but they want to do it in a progressive way. That is, they want to build a career that is defined in terms of regular and steady income growth. Spurts represented by occasional sales contests don't build for the long pull.

Money means different things for different people. For some, it means security; for others, it means status; and for still others, it means independence. It will be difficult to motivate all of your salespeople using the same approach. You will have to get to know each, and decide just what is going to work with each individual. When you can relate your compensation program to any of these elements, you will be in a position to exert considerable motivational force.

Remember, even though you can motivate with money, it should still be part of an overall motivation program that includes other elements.

A High Quality and Style of Management

Sound, fair, and intelligent management is as much a motivator as a good compensation program. People are motivated by people who impress them, who show strong leadership skills, and who have a humane outlook on the practical aspects of business management. In fact, considerable research has shown that an informed manager can have a much longer lasting effect on motivation than any hotshot compensation program. Don't read this as: Pay pennies and smile. I'm talking about an integrated approach to motivation that considers all the needs of the individual.

Effective Training

It's safe to say that without effective training, your sales team will never reach peak performance. However, with the wrong training, you can actually have a negative effect.

The chances are that the people you hire will already be effective salespeople. This means that you shouldn't waste their time and your money on any of the typical selling–training programs. However, you should invest in training that will help them understand the products they sell, the markets they serve, and the needs of their customers. More and more manufacturers have recognized this need and are developing programs for their agencies that give them this backup.

In this case, knowledge is the motivator. A salesperson who is secure in his or her knowledge of the product and its use is a lot more assertive when he or she sells. In fact, considerable research has shown that those who don't do well selling usually fail because of lack of knowledge, not because they lack the selling skills.

HOW TO WORK PRODUCTIVELY WITH THE PEOPLE YOUR PRINCIPALS SEND INTO THE FIELD

In a sense, the people your principals put in the field represent sales force potential for you. Far too often, manufacturers' agents view factory people as either a necessary evil or unwelcomed intruders. But talk with the agents who look on factory people as extra help and you'll see an effective team.

Many larger manufacturers that sell through sales agencies have a network that is supervised by regional sales managers. The smaller companies or those with limited territories seldom go this route, but will frequently put people into the field on an as-needed basis to work with the agencies. In either case, both the agents and the manufacturers have to recognize early on that the relationship is one of two businesses working together, not one of sales manager and employee.

Plan for Your "Joint" Calls

Calls made by agents with people from the factory should be planned very carefully in advance. Some agencies refuse to make calls with a "wandering" salesperson from the factory who just drops in unannounced.

Planning for these joint or "buddy" calls should be based on the needs of the customers in the territory—not just to satisfy the feeling that some factory people have about checking out customers once in a while. It's best to be ahead of the manufacturer by planning these visits rather than responding to a manufacturer's request for a few days in the field.

The most productive joint calls are those that are geared directly to a specific customer's needs. They may be to solve an immediate problem, or they may revolve around planning for new products or new product applications. Whatever the case, careful planning before the actual meeting is important. There's nothing worse than a group of people from the factory, from the agency, and from the customer meeting without an agenda and some goals in mind.

Here are a few dos and don'ts to guide you in working with people from the factory:

- Do identify specific problems and deal directly with them. When you, your principal, and your customer take the time to meet, the meeting should be productive and not waste time.

- Don't be defensive about things that may not have been accomplished. Productive meetings solve problems and don't reprimand individuals. If any kind of reprimand is needed, it should be done without the presence of the customer.

- Don't run to the principal every time a problem arises. Try to work it out yourself. But if input is needed, show what progress you have made on your own before bringing in the principal.

- Don't reject ideas and proposals out of hand. Frequently ideas that sound outlandish at first are practical but just different. Be sure you have all the facts before you make any judgments or accept the judgment of the others involved.

- Do recognize that it's human nature for the manufacturer to want its products attended to before you deal with any of your other principals. You can make a big mistake by allowing all of your principals to think that they are number one in your agency. The truth will come out sooner or later. It's best to be straightforward about the relationship, stressing exactly what you are doing for the principal, rather than to create a smoke screen.

In addition to the people your principals will send into the field, you will have to work with a number of individuals at the factory who will only be voices at the other end of the telephone. You may get to meet these people when you visit the plant, but they will probably never be sent into the field to work with you. These people include everyone from shipping clerks and secretaries to engineers, production people, and accountants.

You can do your business a lot of good by cultivating relationships with these people early on. If, for example, the plant production is limited and the production manager has to decide whether your customer or the customer of another agency gets the next available shipment, a solid relationship could make the difference in your favor. Many of the agencies that create newsletters to keep their principals informed of their activities mail to *everyone* at the principal's plant who is involved directly or indirectly with the agency operation.

How to Choose and Use Incentives Effectively

Generally speaking, the type of sales incentive that works well with salaried salespeople is of limited value to those selling for a manufacturers' agency. Salaried salespeople look at incentives, especially cash rewards, as a way of adding to a *fixed* income. They are usually paid a salary no matter how much they sell. However, many people who sell for manufacturers' agencies have their income tied very closely to their productivity. Most are paid a base or draw, but the real opportunity lies in their ability to sell aggressively and to earn a larger income based strictly on their ability to perform.

This difference is significant when it comes to planning an incentive program for agency salespeople. They are usually more interested in increased opportunity to sell than in short-term bonuses. More than a few agency owners have told me that the traditional cash and merchandise incentive programs fall flat when they use them. However, when it's possible to offer an expanded territory to an especially effective salesperson, this act is highly motivating. And more agencies are offering bonuses based on individual production when the agency grows.

On this last approach, some agencies insist that there is a whole-show increase over the previous year before any bonuses are paid. This means that the more productive salespeople are going to make sure that everyone pulls their weight. Of course, each salesperson is rewarded according to his or her individual productivity.

Sales contests are seldom effective unless they are tied in with something that has a long-term benefit. For example, a principal introducing a new product will often include a few extra points of commission or special bonuses for outstanding initial sale of the product. These short-term benefits are valuable, but the entire program becomes even more meaningful when the salespeople realize that their efforts will be rewarded not only for the added early spurt but will continue to pay off once the product takes hold.

More and more, multi-person agencies are offering their prized employees a piece of the action as an incentive. Lawyers have used this technique successfully for years. Hard-working young lawyers are chosen for partnership on their ability to contribute to the growth of the firm. In fact, one of the most important people in a law practice is called the "rainmaker." This is the person who brings in business for the firm. In a sales agency, everyone has to be a rainmaker.

How you choose to make a person part of the firm is best left up to you and your lawyer and accountant. Some ways might be to make stock available at a reduced price, offer stock without cost as a bonus, or establish a stock purchase plan that includes special bonus options. Since the laws governing this activity change so frequently, check with your accountant before you make a decision.

How to Bolster a Sagging Territory

Territories sag for many reasons. You could have an inefficient salesperson covering the area, or the sag could be the result of conditions that are not under the control of the salesperson. Let's look at the first condition.

Assuming that the person covering the territory has been productive in the past, it will be necessary to analyze specific performance. This is best done by making calls with the individual. However, just going into the field isn't enough. You should work closely with the individual in his or her preparations for the calls being made, and also watch the follow-up closely. As you know, everyone has a slump once in a while. They will either come out of it without needing special help or will need a little encouragement to resolve the problems. If, however, your field calls have been unsuccessful and you have identified the problems, you will have to help the individual not only to recognize them but to help him or her to resolve the difficulties.

A sagging territory that is not the result of declining sales efforts is a whole other thing. The important question you have to resolve is whether the drop-off is the result of long- or short-term conditions. Agencies dependent on military contracts, for example, are forever going up and down. But if you've been selling OEM components to a large manufacturer of consumer goods for years and they suddenly slow down noticeably, you'd better find out quickly whether it's a long- or short-term condition.

Competition, of course, is always something which has to be monitored. The sag could be the result of an aggressive sales campaign by one of your competitors. It seldom pays to get into a price war, but it does pay to determine just what the competitor has done to take away the business. This is more than an exercise; it can often point up shortcomings in your products and your way of selling that could, if uncorrected, lead to problems with other customers.

Preventive medicine is usually a lot more effective than bandages. Waiting for a territory to sag means that you and your salespeople are going to have to run twice as hard to correct the problems. However, if you monitor all of the variables regularly, you should be able to detect trends that could lead to the slump. Of course, it's a lot easier to take care of smaller details before they get blown out of proportion and become a definite slump.

How to Back up Your Sales Force With a Computer

Just the in-office benefits of a computer will make it worthwhile for even the smallest agency to have. For example, you can put your customer and prospect list on a computer to make mailings and to help you plan a territory management system. However, most agencies agree —even those whose products include hardware and software—that they are better off buying existing programs rather than writing their own.

Many of the programs on the market today were designed by agents for their own use and were then expanded as commercial products. Even though numerous programs claim to do the same things, it's best to look carefully at all of them before you decide to buy. You want to make sure that the program you select will do everything you want it to do today, and that it has the capacity to expand as your agency grows.

Frequently the programs available include general office packages that provide office management as well as accounting packages and territory management systems. If you are also acting as a distributor— taking title to goods and storing them—you will need a different program than is generally used to handle a strict commission operation. But there are more than a few of these programs available, too. Perhaps the best place to find them is in the advertising pages of *Agency Sales* magazine. You can get a sample copy by writing to MANA, 23016 Mill Creek Road, P.O. Box 3467, Laguna Hills, California 92654.

Many agencies are supplying their field people with lap-top computers to take with them into the field. This equipment, at the very least, lets the field salesperson record his daily activity. At best, they can use the computers with modems to communicate directly with a factory— often from a customer's office—and get immediate information on stock, specifications, and prices. This innovation has been responsible for some excellent service and some distinct competitive advantages for the agencies that invested in the hardware and software.

In addition to computers, many agencies are now using facsimile equipment (FAX) to communicate with customers and principals. This equipment has the distinct advantage of being able to transmit over phone lines relatively faithful images of drawings, tables, and other graphics that cannot be sent by computer. However, facsimile transmission is relatively slow when compared with the transmission of data from one computer to another.

HOW TO PLAN AN EFFICIENT TERRITORY

With sales call costs increasing more and more each year, manufacturers' representatives should study their travel habits regularly and tighten up their plans for covering their territories.

Evaluating accounts and prospects, deciding how much time to spend with them, and analyzing call frequencies and routing patterns can pay big dividends in helping you make the most of the miles you travel, and position you for tougher times to come.

The Territory Plan

Some plans sputter, others hum. Three key facts that make the difference:

- *Realism*. Does the plan provide for in-depth coverage of "A" accounts—without giving some "C" accounts that left-out feeling?
- *Completeness*. Could you justify the plan to every account as well as to your company, or are there "stones left unturned"?

- *Workability*. The comment of one sales representative: "The problem is not planning. It's easy to make a plan. But to carry it out is very hard to do." If this is a problem for you, this special analysis will help you find out why and how to get on track.

Your Hierarchy of Accounts

Regular accounts make up the cornerstone of your business, but not all contribute equally. And while you know which accounts are big and which are small, which are good and which are not so good, differentiations like those don't cut it. A quantitative measure is needed. You get this by establishing a hierarchy of accounts—determining relative importance through an analysis of each account. Here is a five-step way to do that:

1. Estimate the dollar volume you expect from each account over the next twelve months. Do not restrict yourself to last year's figures. Include potential. Identifying your territory's potential and figuring out how to reach it is an invaluable byproduct of your territory plan. Note how specific considerations affect your estimate.

For example, account X is a mushrooming business and you are positive that your sales to them will increase. Account Y has a buyer with whom you have just recently developed a good rapport, and for that reason alone your sales to them are likely to increase. At account Z, you share the business with an entrenched competitor, and your most optimistic estimate is for a marginal increase. When figuring potential, set your sights as high as you dare.

2. Assess the probability of achieving your estimate for each account. Your dollar-volume estimates are something to shoot for, but you want to be as realistic as possible. Go over each estimate and carefully assess your chances of reaching it in this manner:
    - If you feel your chances are very good, assign a rating between 80 and 100 percent.
    - If you feel your chances are good, assign a rating between 60 and 80 percent.
    - If you feel your chances are fair, assign a rating between 40 and 60 percent.

3. Determine the expected value of the account. Multiply the dollar figure by the probability percentage, which gives you the ex-

pected value of the account. It tells you what you are likely to achieve with each account over the next twelve months. It boils down to your best estimate. Here is how it works with account X:

Dollar estimate	$18,000
Probability percentage	90%
Expected value ($18,000 multiplied by .90)	$16,200

As far as account X is concerned, you have established a mathematically reachable goal of $16,200 in business over the next twelve months.

4. Use the expected value figures to set up your hierarchy of accounts. After figuring the expected value of each of your accounts, use the chart of existing accounts and list those in order of importance. Then group the accounts according to volume and assign each an A, B, or C classification.

If you have a great many accounts and prefer a finer separation, add a D and even an E category. Where you draw the line for each category is up to you, but a typical separation runs like this:

A	10% of accounts
B	30% of accounts
C	30% of accounts
D	20% of accounts
E	10% of accounts

5.   Figure the hours per year each account is worth. The expected value figure can tell you how much time per year each account is worth. Here is how to do it:

John Arnold, like many salespeople, works roughly 2,000 hours per year (40 hours a week multiplied by 50 weeks). His sales volume is $300,000 per year. This means Arnold is generating $150 an hour in sales.

Arnold's expected value, for instance, from his Empire account is $7,500. This means that Arnold can profitably spend 50 hours a year at Empire. If an average call, including travel and waiting time, takes up about an hour, then Arnold should be calling on Empire no more than once a week.

Expected value, then, can help you implement your territory plan.

The idea is to go "by the book" rather than by guesses, which can send you where the money isn't. One sales member, in fact, listed his biggest single time-waster as "flying by the seat of my pants."

The Sample Chart of Existing Accounts will help put this discussion into perspective.

Consider establishing a hierarchy of accounts for prospects also, especially for your active list of prospects. This can help you plan callbacks proportionate to the prospect's potential volume and projected classification. An "A" prospect, for example, may be worth seven or eight callbacks; a "B" prospect, six callbacks, and so on. When a prospect is sold, refigure the expected value and transfer the name to the proper place on the existing accounts list.

Call-Frequency Routing Plans

There are a number of factors that will determine how often you call on a given account: territory size, number of prospects and customers, geographical spread, etc. This is where the ABC classifi-

Sample Chart of Existing Accounts

Rank	Account	Expected Value	Classification	Hours per Year
1.	Nomad	$45,000	A	51
2.	Lewis	29,100	A	33
11.	Comco	19,600	B	26
12.	Best	14,700	B	21
13.	Brown	13,500	B	20
19.	Mountain	9,700	C	15
20.	Filler	9,000	C	14
21.	Fry	7,500	C	12
22.	Gordon	7,000	C	12
23.	Ajax	4,900	C	8
Expected value of sample A accounts:				$ 74,100
Expected value of sample B accounts:				47,800
Expected value of sample C accounts:				38,100
Sample accounts TOTAL				$160,000

Average per hour for shown accounts: $80 in sales (dividing $160,000 by 2,000 hours).

cation of accounts proves helpful. It simplifies your call-frequency planning.

A profitable plan takes into consideration

- How often you need to call on each customer to keep and expand the business, as well as
- The most practical routing patterns to accomplish that goal.

It may be useful at this point to take note of a sales truism, so that it doesn't adversely influence your call-frequency planning. The truism is that the more often you call on an account, the more sales you are likely to make. This may be so, but only up to a point. Beyond that point, those extra calls yield no additional business, but do cost time. "A" accounts, in particular, can be overworked. For example, a sales representative averaging six calls a month on an "A" account could conceivably do just as well as the account with one call a week.

Using the ABC classification as a guide, you may decide, for instance, that "A" accounts should be called on three times a month; "B" accounts twice; "C" accounts once. Geography, of course, may dictate adjustments. Cutbacks in the number of calls are best made in reverse order of account importance—C, B, A. In any event, the call frequencies you have decided upon are tentative at this point. How they are firmed up depends on routing patterns that best fit your territory.

Routing patterns depend on territory makeup, location and spread of "A" accounts, presence or absence of large cities within the territory, and even access to superhighways and turnpikes.

Three Basic Routing Patterns

The following routing patterns will help you to cover your territory more efficiently:

1. *Straight line and return.* A New Jersey agent, for example, with a territory that runs from Newark in the northern part of the state to Atlantic City in the southern part uses a straight-line pattern. He travels north–south on one road, and returns south–north on another, with carefully planned crossovers on each leg of the trip. The roads he uses are chosen to allow him to cover "A" accounts on every complete trip.

2. *Circular or roundabout.* Depending on territory size, primary

roads, and location of "A" accounts, this may be more practical than a straight-line approach. The idea is to plot your circle of calls so that you come full circle—all planned calls completed—by the time you return to the starting point.

3. *Area or cluster.* It may be practical to divide the territory into areas. For example, an area might center around a large town or city, or many of your "A" accounts may be clustered in one or two areas. Areas are sometimes mapped as circles and may overlap.

You may want to review your present routing patterns and look for ways to improve them. Of course, a good map of the territory is necessary. Plot your accounts on the map, color-coding the accounts by classification. It is easier to experiment with possible patterns when "A" accounts are in one color; "B" accounts in another; etc.

Establish a Master Schedule

The master schedule provides a long-range view of your territory plan (see Sample Master Schedule below). It is based on the call frequency you have chosen for each account, modified by the routing pattern best suited to accommodate those frequencies. In fairly large territories, the master schedule might take in several months' time. Over that period the master schedule might indicate: Each "A" account

Sample Master Schedule*

Classification Frequency	Account	No. of Calls per Master Schedule	Call
A	Nomad	26	Once a week
A	Lewis	18	Three times a month
B	Comco	12	Every other month
B	Best	8	Every third week
B	Brown	8	Every third week
C	Mountain	6	Once a month
C	Filler	6	Once a month
C	Fry	4	Every 6 weeks
C	Gordon	4	Every 6 weeks
C	Ajax	3	Every other month

* Schedule based on six-month period (July through December).

must be called on five times; "B" account three times; "C" account twice; "D" once; "E" every other master schedule.

Your weekly call schedule is based largely on the master schedule and is best made up on the prior weekend. Leave room on the weekly schedule for unplanned calls (prospecting). The weekly schedule also gives you a record of calls you were unable to make because of a diversion or an emergency. These may have to be fitted into your next week's schedule.

The importance of the master schedule is that it guides you each week. It tells you where you should be going that week and does away with "thinking from scratch" each weekend. It also solidifies your territory plan and sees to it that you spend the optimum amount of time with each customer.

This schedule can, of course, be varied to meet changes in your schedule. And you should arrange to make phone calls to customers and prospects on a planned basis, too. Regular phone calls reinforce your program and give you an opportunity to get immediate feedback.

Now that you've learned some basic guidelines for increasing your own efficiency in covering your territory, here are some further steps you can take to ensure success in meeting this objective. Basically, it involves taking an inventory of your territorial tools.

Territory Tool Inventory

The following checklist is to help you review the condition of some of your territory coverage tools. Place a checkmark in the box that applies:

	Is Missing	Needs Updating	Is in Good Shape
1. My hierarchy of accounts list	☐	☐	☐
2. My expected value list	☐	☐	☐
3. My account classification list	☐	☐	☐
4. My dollar sale per call figure	☐	☐	☐
5. My call-frequency system	☐	☐	☐
6. My set routing pattern(s)	☐	☐	☐
7. My master work schedule	☐	☐	☐

Now, think hard about each tool not checked as "in good shape." The "missing" tools, of course, are those—for whatever reason—you have never seen fit to use. Decide which of these, if not all, could help you cover the territory more efficiently and profitably.

The "needs updating" checks speak for themselves. What better time than now?

The next step is to develop a work sheet and write down each of the tools you plan to work on, including dates, and the specific changes they may bring about in your territory plan. If you have, in fact, been considering an overhaul in your territory plan, take this opportunity to start from scratch, and use every tool that applies to your situation.

When You Make Changes in Territory Coverage

Whenever you decide to make coverage adjustments—not to mention a basic territory reorganization—some customers may be upset. The "C" account, for example, that the new arithmetic now tells you warrants two calls a month rather than three may feel slighted by the schedule change.

Five steps to keep those who must be cut back on personal contacts as good customers are

1. *Advise in advance.* If you tell Smith in June about a change that is to take effect in September, he is likely to be more reasonable about it. In the interim you can "work" on him if you feel it necessary.

2. *Anticipate the major objection to the change.* Jones, who traditionally works with a thin inventory, may feel you are arbitrarily increasing his risk of running out of stock. Brown, a great coffee companion, may feel hurt in a personal way. Be prepared with answers for these people before you talk change.

3. *Be sure to "close."* You need the customer's agreement to the change just as you need it for an order. Half sold is no sale, and you may have an antagonistic customer on your hands. A customer might say, for example, "One of the reasons I like to do business with you is that you show up like clockwork every week. I'm not sure I like the idea of every other week."

This is a customer you value, but also a small order account running below your dollar sale per-call average. This, however, is not what you want to tell him. But you do want verbal agreement to the change, so you might say: "Mr. Barrett, I am determined to make the new schedule work every bit as well for you as the old one. All I ask is that you give it a chance. Fair enough?"

4. *Set up telephone contact.* Even during the transition period, it's a good idea to break the customer in on more frequent telephone communication. That way, when the change takes place and you substitute a phone call for a personal call, the change won't seem abrupt. The customer will have grown accustomed to it.

5. *Check for problems.* Unhappy customers sometimes respond to a change they dislike with silence. Be sure to get feedback for a reasonable period of time following the change. If there is a problem, you may have to make some adjustments. If there is no problem, drop the subject as soon as you are certain all is well.

If you plan to make extensive revision in call patterns and frequencies, try to tamper as little as possible with your "A" accounts. If an "A" needs to be cut back, go over the above steps carefully with the customer. Even if you plan to increase your calls on an "A"—often the case in a territory overhaul—make sure it is all right with those you contact.

Also, we all have favorite people—customers whose companies we enjoy and with whom we like to extend visiting time. Resist the temptation to leave as is your frequency calls on those few favorites with whom you have an especially good relationship. Unless the business yield justifies all the calls you are in the habit of making on these people—cut back. To make "exceptions for friends" won't really help them but can hurt you.

Old habits are comfortable; even the less than good ones are hard to break. And in territory management, that's a difficulty you must fight, because even if salespeople don't change, territories do. New companies come; others go. A small outfit gets going and develops best-customer potential. A big buyer shifts a product line and your product or service loses favor. For reasons like these, you must review territory coverage periodically.

You have a good incentive for doing so. Even a slight improvement in the way you manage and cover your territory can make it possible to practice more of your skills and use more of your knowledge in front of more prospects and customers than any other factor. If anything "goes with the territory" it's the way you choose to run it. And the way you choose has got to show up in your paycheck.

HOW TO EVALUATE
A MANUFACTURER'S PERFORMANCE

As an agency, you will be subject to evaluation of your performance by the manufacturers whose products you sell. Some of them will do this evaluation randomly and without any formal program. Others will have a regular and planned approach to their agency evaluations. The best advice to prepare for these evaluations is to do the best job you can day by day for the principal. After all, it will be the bottom line that weighs most in every evaluation.

But this evaluation should be a two-way street. You, too, should have a systematized approach to performing an evaluation of your principals.

These are the questions that most agents consider to be most important when evaluating the performance of their principals:

1. Has the manufacturer supplied complete, practical, and comprehensive sales literature?

2. Has the manufacturer responded promptly to questions and requests?

3. Does the manufacturer supply case history and application information that helps the agencies sell?

4. Has the manufacturer kept the agencies informed on new product developments and on product modifications?

5. Does the manufacturer keep the agency up to date on competitive activities?

6. Are all of the manufacturers' policies spelled out clearly and enforced equitably?

7. Are the advertising and publicity leads worthwhile, well-screened, and sent on time to be helpful?

8. Are the manufacturers' visits to the territory helpful?

9. Are the people at the factory who are assigned to work with the agency as helpful as they can be?

10. Is the field reporting system practical and helpful?

11. Are the agency comments given a fair hearing by the individuals at the factory to whom they are directed?

12. Is the commission system in keeping with the standards of the industry?

13. Is the agency agreement comparable with the agreements made with other manufacturers?

14. Are the factory's customer service policies effective?

15. Is the credit policy practical?

16. Are the people at the plant up front with the agency people when there are problems?

17. Is there a Rep Council? If so, how effective is it in translating the needs of the agencies and the manufacturers?

Not all of these questions will apply to all situations, of course. However, there are enough to give you a good start in developing your own system of principal evaluation.

One final word: You should let your principal know that you are doing this evaluation, and then make sure that he/she gets the results. These evaluations should not be used as means to wield power. Rather, they should be used by both parties to help build stronger and more productive relationships.

CHAPTER **9**

Practical Financial Management

If there's one aspect of the agency business that makes tough, business-getting salespeople wilt in their tracks, it's the thought of bookkeeping. I wish there were some magic answers to make it easy, but there aren't. In this chapter, however, you'll get some ideas that have worked for a lot of agents on a lot of different aspects of financial management.

This is not a short course on bookkeeping and accounting. The chances are that you will be able to handle your basic bookkeeping yourself or at least with the help of a part-time or freelance person. But when it comes to tax planning and tax filing, you should get professional advice. You may be able to sort through all the government papers and give the fed and the state exactly what they are after, but unless you keep up with the changes in the law, you will probably never know how much money you are entitled to legally.

If you find that a CPA offers more than you need and are willing to pay for, there are a few franchised accounting and bookkeeping services that might fit your needs. These firms work with local franchises who offer direct and personal help, and who process all of your records through a centrally operated and computerized service.

At first, it may be difficult to decide which route to take. However, if you work backwards and are able to determine just what kind of financial assistance you need, you will be in a better position to decide whether a full CPA service, a bookkeeper, or a financial service will be best for you. Bear in mind, though, that if you are called in by the state or the IRS for a tax audit, it's nice to have a licensed and experienced CPA make the trip with you.

HOW TO KEEP RECORDS THE IRS CAN'T FAULT

It's easy to be flip about this and say that as long as you document everything that has tax consequences, you'll be safe. While this is true, it doesn't tell you much more than that if you're not familiar with accounting and taxation. However, since every agency is different and since state laws interact with federal laws, you should get professional advice from someone in your state who has the information on the tip of his or her tongue.

The government most times questions business expenses, looking closely at entertainment, travel expenses, automobile expenses, business gifts, and the like. In most of the cases that have been settled to the agent's satisfaction, the agent had every expense documented in detail.

Under a certain figure, you don't have to get a receipt for a business lunch. But if you keep *all* receipts, even those that are under the minimum required by the IRS, you'll be in much better shape if you are audited. It may seem like a bother, but once you make it a regular habit, you'll feel a lot more comfortable knowing that you have an accurate recordkeeping system.

If you need help keeping track of this information, there are many different systems on the market that can help you organize your business recordkeeping. One of the more practical and complete systems is called Day Log. Not only does it provide all the forms and record sheets you need, it also includes a record retention box to help you stay organized. You can get information on this system by writing to the Bureau of Business Practice, 24 Rope Ferry Road, Waterford, CT 06386.

Depending on the type of operation you run, you will be required to keep different records and for varying lengths of time. For example, if you act as a distributor, you're going to have some rather extensive buy-and-sell records that must be kept. If you're operating strictly as an agency, the chances are that you will only need an accurate record of your commission and other income plus a detailed record of your business expenses.

How Long Should You Keep Records?

If you kept every record relating to taxes, you'd soon be paying more for dead storage than you'd be paying for office space. The answer to this question has to be hedged a bit. Record retention requirements change from time to time, and there are some items you may think should be kept longer than the IRS says you have to. According to Mel Daskal, C.P.A., in a copyrighted report he prepared for MANA, you should consider keeping your records as follows:

Accounting Records

Type	Retention Years
Bank statements	3
Budgets	2
Cancelled checks:	
Dividends paid	4
General	3
Payroll	3
Taxes—payroll	4
Taxes—income	Permanent
Taxes—others	4
Comment: major expenditures of permanent noteworthiness—use your own judgment and keep the checks	Permanent
Cash disbursements journal	Permanent
Cash receipts journal	Permanent
Commission statements to salesmen and representatives	3
Contracts—sales or purchases	3
Credit memos	3
Deposit slips	3

Accounting Records (Continued)

Type	Retention Years
Depreciation records	3
Expense reports—salespeople and others	3
Financial statements—annual	Permanent
General ledger and general journal	Permanent
Inventories	3
Invoices	3
Payroll records, payroll journal, individual earnings records, W-2, W-4, etc.	4
Petty cash vouchers	3
Purchase journal	Permanent
Sales journal	Permanent
Subsidiary ledgers—accounts receivable, accounts payable, etc.	6
Timecards	4
Trial balances—monthly	3

Corporate Records

Type	Retention Years
Article you are now reading	Permanent
Articles of Incorporation	Permanent
Bylaws	Permanent
Charter	Permanent
Contracts and agreements—employment, labor partnership, government, etc.	Permanent
Copyrights and trademarks—all registrations	Permanent
Deeds and easements	Permanent
Leases—expired	3
Legal correspondence of any kind	Permanent
Minutes and minute books	Permanent
Mortgages and notes	6
Patents	Permanent

Corporate Records *(Continued)*

Type	Retention Years
Pension and other retirement plans:	
IRS letter of approval	Permanent
Plan and trust agreement(s)	Permanent
Ledgers, journals and all other accounting records	Permanent
Actuarial reports	Permanent
Financial statements	Permanent
Individual employee account records	Permanent
Anything else related to the plans	Permanent
Personnel records and files	4
Property records	Permanent
Proxies	Permanent
Stock and bond records—certificates, transfer lists, anything relating to stock issued and corporate indebtedness	Permanent
Stockholder lists	6

As you can see from the above listing, almost everything to do with your corporate organization should be saved for eternity!

Correspondence

Type	Retention Years
General	3
Legal	Permanent
Licenses—traffic and purchasing	3
Production	3
Taxes:	
Income	Permanent
Sales and use	Permanent
Payroll	4
Pension and other retirement plans	Permanent

Insurance *(Continued)*

Type	Retention Years
Accident reports	6
Claims—settled	3
Fire inspection reports	6
Group disability reports	6
Insurance policies—all kinds	6
Safety records/reports	6

Tax Returns

Type	Retention Years
Income—federal, state, and local	Permanent
Cancelled checks—in payment	Permanent
Payroll	4
Pension and other retirement plans	Permanent
Sales and use	Permanent

Sales and Purchasing

Type	Retention Years
Acknowledgements	2
Credit memos	3
Credit files	4
Production and sales reports	3
Purchase orders	3
Requisitions	3
Sales contracts	3
Sales invoices and purchase invoices	3

Receiving and Shipping (Traffic)

Type	Retention Years
Bills of lading	3
Delivery receipts	3
Export declarations	3

Receiving and Shipping (Traffic) *(Continued)*

Type	Retention Years
Freight bills	3
Freight claims	3
Manifests	3
Receiving reports	3
Shipping reports	3
Shipping tickets	3
Waybills	3

Personnel

Type	Retention Years
Contracts and agreements	Permanent
Daily time reports	4
Disability or sick benefits records	4
Timecards	4
Withholding statements and all other payroll records	4

ANALYZING AND CONTROLLING SELLING EXPENSES

As important as tax planning is, the ability to analyze and control selling expenses will probably do more to enhance your bottom line than just about any other internal agency activity. This skill, with the help of material supplied by the Research Institute of America and adapted for agency use, is one of the most practical approaches to this problem.

Despite short-term ups and downs, the dynamics of the decade ahead practically guarantee the continued expansion of most markets. But to gain an edge will require unprecedented control of sales efforts and selling costs—at the very time profit margins will be under steadily mounting pressure.

Traditional sales records are often no match for this challenge. Though most of the required data is undoubtedly in a company's possession, it will have to be recomputed, expanded, and analyzed in light of these more demanding needs. Experience shows that relatively little time and money invested in this area will produce results far more spectacular than in any comparable effort.

An agency's sales, of course, are not equally derived from all parts of the operation. A small number of products, a few customers, and limited territories often provide the bulk of the sales volume. And profits probably follow a similar pattern; the major share coming from a fraction of one or more of these categories.

Arbitrarily lopping off unprofitable accounts, services, or territories is not always the answer, because it may leave a company with "unabsorbed" overhead and other costs that are greater than those that can be carried by the profitable part of the business. A realistic solution requires a more detailed knowledge than most agencies have at their disposal—exact figures of where the volume comes from, what it costs to sell, what effect each part has on total earnings.

Selling and sales-related expenses, of course, claim the lion's share of an agency's income. Unfortunately, due to inflation and other factors, that share is growing. Accordingly, the agency should find increasing benefits in knowing which costs are getting out of line and which ones are likely to yield the greatest sales profit. To do this, these questions should be addressed:

Which sales expenses have shown the biggest increase? Are the amounts being spent in proportion to the added volume they bring in? How much does each salesperson cost per $100 of sales he/she produces? Are figures needed on reimbursed expenses, costs per call made or account serviced, or all of these? Let's look at these more closely.

Who Are the Agency's Outstanding Producers?

Orders secured by each salesperson, by month or even more frequently, is the one item that is the most closely watched in all agencies. Yet when a person's performance has become so unsatisfactory as to require drastic action, management can usually see in retrospect that this failure was foreshadowed months earlier by facts which went largely unnoticed. For example, the person's total sales failed to keep pace with the general rate of expansion, or he/she began to neglect some parts of product lines or ignore segments of the market.

The analysis in Figure 9-1 is designed to reveal quickly any lack of balance or other weakness in each employee's sales effort. Note that not all of the four breakdowns suggested will necessarily apply to any

FIGURE 9-1
Form 1

Salesman's Name	Current Year*			Last Year			2 Years Ago		
	Dollars		Percent	Dollars		Percent	Dollars		Percent
Total Company Sales			100.00%			100.00%			100.00%
Man's Total Sales									
by Product									
1									
2									
3									
4									
by Area									
A									
B									
by Type of User (Market Segment)									
a									
b									

one agency. If you can't pick up figures from two years ago, at least post those for last year so that you will have some basis for comparison.

How Much Does Each Salesperson Cost?

Based on each $100 of sales the salesperson produces in reimbursed expenses per call made and account serviced, what is the cost?

Sales produced and basic compensation are obviously only rough measures of each salesperson's performance. To supplement these general indicators, many companies still rely on general impressions and vague judgments. The analysis in Figure 9-2 will help pin down the other measurable elements in sales performance. Once total costs have been related to sales results, management can exercise its judgment meaningfully in the areas where no dollars-and-cents yardsticks are possible, such as personality traits and potential for long-term growth.

FIGURE 9-2
Form 2

Salesman	Jan.			Feb.			Cumu-lative			March			Cumu-lative			April		
Salary or Guarantee																		
Commissions & Bonuses																		
Employee Benefits																		
Total Compensation																		
Transportation Cost																		
Telephone & Wire																		
Other Travel Expense:																		
Lodging																		
Food																		
Entertaining																		
Other Expense																		
Total Expense																		
Days of Travel																		
No. of Accounts																		
No. of Sales Calls																		
Net Sales																		
Travel Exp. per Day																		
Total Exp. per Account																		
per Sales Call																		
per $100 of Sales																		

What Contribution Does Each Salesperson Make?

How does the salesperson contribute to overhead and profit? Which of his/her sales are most profitable? Where does he/she cost the company money?

The profits that each salesperson brings in are one of management's top priority yardsticks. Here are the best opportunities to achieve immediate improvement—by new sales emphasis, different direction of the sales force, closer supervision of territories, and so forth.

Yet it is not advisable to make profitability the starting point for an analysis of sales and selling costs. Reason: Many of the steps recommended in earlier questions are essential for a thorough review of each salesperson's profit performance. Thus, the sample analysis in Figure 9-3 is based on a summary of data previously worked up.

Adapt each form to fit your own operation and need for informa-

FIGURE 9-3
Form 3

Salesman's Name	Sales		Gross Profit		Direct Cost		Contribution		% of Total Contrib.		% of Total Sales	
Man's Total Sales												
Detailed Analyses by Product 1 2												
3 4 by Customer Abbott Alston												
by Area A B C												
by Type of User a b												

tion. If the forms presented here work for you, simply make copies of them and you're ready to get the system under way.

Only a few hours of posting each month is required to keep these records up to date. The payoff will be vital information at a glance that will tell you how productive your agency and agents are, and at what cost.

HOW TO USE A COMPUTER TO YOUR ADVANTAGE

The computer is, perhaps, one of the most practical office machines an agency can own. You can use it to do word processing, create and maintain customer lists, make mailings, prepare graphics and, of course, handle your accounting. A recent survey undertaken by MANA showed how agencies are using their computers:

Customer activity by principal—58%

Customer activity by salesperson—49%

Inventory/accounts receivable—35%

Trends/statistical analysis—22%

Commission summaries by principal—55%

Current/prospective customer file—56%

Total sales summaries—65%

Word processing—72%

Commissions payable—47%

Payroll—16%

Graphics—13%

Mailing list—72%

Engineering design—6%

General ledger—38%

There is another way to harness the power of a computer but with none of the headaches, and that is to have the work done by a service bureau. The same MANA survey revealed the following use patterns for computer service bureaus:

Payroll—27%

Sales analysis—65%

General ledger—39%

Other—12%

Also included in this category are direct mail, lead tracking, and word processing.

Agents who have their own computer systems need software to make it work. The same survey revealed just how agents are using software:

Off-the-shelf software—53%

Custom software—11%

Combination of custom and off-the-shelf software—36%

How to Select a Computer That's Best for You

Unfortunately, most people think about the computer before they think about software. Every consultant I've talked with says that the only way to make an intelligent decision is to decide on your software needs and programs first, then find the computer on which it will run and which will fit your budget and other business needs.

Since it's beyond the scope of this chapter to review *all* of the software programs available for agents, I'll stick to firmer ground and talk about hardware selection. However, if you are confused about software, start by reading some of the ads placed by companies that have created software specifically for agencies.

Here's a ten-point checklist to help you make an intelligent hardware choice:

1.   Make sure that the software you have chosen can be run on the computer you are now considering. We emphasize *now* simply because there have been a lot of features projected in the past that have never materialized. Make it a firm rule: If your software can't be run on the computer you like today, don't buy.

2.   Look at expansion capabilities carefully. This can be an especially difficult job for people with little or no computer experience. It's often hard enough understanding what you are doing with a computer. Projecting your needs and computer capabilities into the future can be even more difficult. If you feel that you need help, get it—but get it from someone without an ax to grind—such as a consultant who isn't selling equipment.

3.   Make certain that the equipment you select is compatible with other equipment you or your principals might own. Many agencies tie in directly to their principals with computers through modems and phone lines. There must be compatibility at both ends to make this work.

4.   Check to see that the computer's random access memory (RAM) has sufficient capacity to handle the software you have chosen, and that it can handle more as the software vendor enhances and modifies the programs. Most experts agree that the minimum for a computer to be used in a sales agency operation should be 256K.

5.   Don't buy before you try. At the very least, you should get a thorough demonstration in the showroom with plenty of time to test the

computer yourself. At best, you should try to make arrangements to use the computer in your office for a few days. You may have to pay the equivalent of a rental fee for this privilege, but it will be worth the expense.

6.   Read every word that reviewers have written about the computer you are considering. There are many computer magazines on the market, and most of them provide well-researched reviews of the equipment. If you are unfamiliar with these magazines, a local library may have some of them. For the names of others that may be more specifically related to your operations, check in the *Readers Guide to Periodical Literature*. This is a tool that the librarian uses. You may not find it displayed in the library, but if you ask the librarian, you should be able to use it.

7.   Check around for a local user's club. Some of the more popular hardware has attracted adherents in the form of user's clubs. These clubs can be large and active depending on the popularity of the equipment you are reviewing. A word of caution: Listen to both sides when you ask for opinions. And ask those who offer their thoughts to give you an idea of exactly how they are using the computer. You can find people knocking a computer for reasons that will be unimportant to you. Ask specific questions, and try to get specific answers.

8.   Get a feel for the vendor and the service you will need. The vendor is going to be your contact when that puff of smoke emerges from the vents in the CRT housing. Probably the best way to get a solid handle on the vendor is to ask others who have bought from him. This shouldn't be too difficult if you first get in touch with a user's club. The club members will have all kinds of tales to tell about the good and bad service they have received.

9.   If you're buying a computer for the first time and will be using it with one of the programs designed specifically for agents, you should acquire some basic familiarity with computers before you venture into the agency program. This can best be done with vendor help and some basic general business programs. If your purchase isn't going to be a big one, you may have to do a little haggling. If it's a larger one, you will probably receive decent support to get you going.

10.   Hardware manufacturers come and go. When they go, you could be in trouble. More often than not, the assets of these companies are picked up by others, which means that you should be able to get

service. This doesn't mean, though, that you should automatically pick the giant that has dominated the market. There are many fine computer manufacturers that have carved a niche in the market that they will continue to hold. But it pays to look.

As you know, or will find out, competition is keen. There are a lot of manufacturers out there who would like your computer dollars. And one of the ways they get your attention is by being first with something . . . regularly. Being first means spending a lot of money on development and rushing a computer to market to counter the latest developments of competitors. This one-upmanship can leave less money for production and testing. When hardware is rushed to market, there can be changes or problems. Even with a solid-gold guarantee and the promise of all kinds of service, you don't want your computer sitting in the repair shop often. It may not cost you anything to have the problems remedied, but it will cost you in the time you have allocated for computer use.

Is there a formula for successful hardware evaluation? Not really, but those who have bought and been bitten urge that you ask hard questions and demand precise, qualified answers. You should test, test, test. If you feel that you don't have the experience to do this, turn to someone to do it for you, even if you have to pay. It will be worth it in the long run.

HOW TO NEGOTIATE A FAVORABLE COMMISSION RATE

Commission rates are negotiable, but only within rather narrow limits and under certain circumstances. If you are taking on a line that has been represented by agencies in other territories for quite a long time, the chances are that you will have to go along with the prevailing rate. However, if you're taking on a line and the company has not worked with agencies in the past and a lot of hard missionary work is going to be needed, there will probably be some room to negotiate.

Negotiation, to be successful, means that both sides get something that they value. If you want a higher rate than the manufacturer might be offering, you will probably either have to justify your requests with some pretty hard figures or you're going to have to put something else on the table. That something else could be the promise to add people, whose expense you will bear, but whose burden can be lightened by a higher preliminary commission. Or you might be willing to do some service work as well as sell the product for an extra point or two. The possibilities are almost endless. But the point is that there can be some flexibility in commission structures.

How do you know when you're even in the ballpark? The answer can be found in the survey of sales commissions that MANA conducts every two years. The surveys aren't done more often simply because the rates don't fluctuate that much. The data include the high and low average figures for the present as well as the period under study. The figures that follow are the most recent available, and since they don't change much from year to year, they are pretty reliable.

FIGURE 9-4

Survey of Sales Commissions

	1985 Survey Results			1987 Survey Results		
		Average of			Average of	
PRODUCT MARKET	Highest %	Average %	Lowest %	Highest %	Average %	Lowest %
Abrasives	11.42	9.04	6.67	9.34	7.34	5.34
Advertising Products & Services	24.23	16.17	8.11	19.07	13.18	7.30
Aerospace & Aviation	9.73	7.44	5.15	11.04	8.63	6.22
Agriculture/Chemicals	13.37	10.24	7.12	7.83	6.12	4.41
Agriculture/Equipment & Machinery	8.68	7.02	5.42	11.31	8.62	5.93
Appliances	6.21	5.21	4.21	6.07	5.10	4.14
Architects & Interior Designers	16.29	11.33	6.37	18.06	12.66	7.26
Arts & Crafts	11.13	8.33	5.54	16.50	11.86	7.22
Automation/Robotics				14.26	11.14	8.02
Automotive/Aftermarket	9.88	7.32	4.77	9.48	7.24	5.00
Automotive/OEM	6.31	5.15	4.00	6.00	4.78	3.56
Beauty Salon & Barber Equipment & Supplies	12.33	9.83	6.33	—	—	—
Building Materials & Supplies	10.68	7.65	4.62	9.90	7.11	4.33
Castings & Forgings	6.05	5.27	4.49	6.16	5.29	4.43

Survey of Sales Commissions *(Continued)*

PRODUCT MARKET	1985 Survey Results			1987 Survey Results		
	Highest %	Average of Average %	Lowest %	Highest %	Average of Average %	Lowest %
Chemicals/Industrial	14.14	11.57	9.00	13.63	10.44	7.25
Chemicals/Maintenance	20.88	15.83	10.79	13.93	10.59	7.26
Coatings	14.02	10.60	7.19	13.98	10.15	6.32
Computer/Hardware, Software & Peripheral Equipment & Supplies	13.13	9.99	6.85	17.12	12.40	7.68
Construction Equipment & Machinery	12.68	9.57	6.47	10.02	8.09	6.17
Controls & Instrumentation	18.14	13.58	9.03	16.83	12.62	8.42
Electrical/Consumer	6.70	5.64	4.58	7.78	6.27	4.77
Electrical/Technical & Industrial	12.60	9.53	6.46	11.54	8.61	5.69
Electronic/ Communications, Audio-Visual & Professional Products	10.38	8.46	6.54	12.14	9.26	6.39
Electronic/Components & Materials	8.40	6.68	4.97	9.56	7.47	5.39
Electronic/Consumer Products	6.53	5.14	3.76	9.41	7.27	5.13
Electronic/Technical Products	12.16	9.61	7.07	14.00	10.57	7.14
Energy	16.14	11.79	7.45	13.50	10.66	7.82
Fasteners	7.46	6.34	5.22	7.68	6.26	4.85
Floor & Wall Coverings				9.14	7.21	5.28
Food/Beverage Chemicals	22.50	15.62	8.75	11.25	8.25	5.25
Food/Beverage Processing	13.47	9.98	6.50	14.57	11.15	7.73
Food/Beverage Products & Services	16.00	15.00	14.00	8.33	6.96	5.60

Survey of Sales Commissions (Continued)

| | 1985 Survey Results | | | 1987 Survey Results | | |
| | Average of | | | Average of | | |
PRODUCT MARKET	Highest %	Average %	Lowest %	Highest %	Average %	Lowest %
Food/Beverage Service Equipment	11.05	8.75	6.45	12.30	9.06	5.88
Furniture & Furnishings	11.86	8.75	5.65	9.71	7.83	5.96
Gas, Oil & Petroleum Products & Services	15.02	10.89	6.77	13.15	9.81	6.47
Glass Industry/Raw Materials & Products	9.33	7.99	6.66	15.25	10.33	5.42
Government	9.79	7.33	4.87	9.43	7.42	5.42
Graphics/Printing	13.97	10.54	7.11	16.24	12.00	7.76
Hardware/Houseware	9.38	7.13	4.89	8.80	6.72	4.63
Health & Beauty Aids				18.25	11.88	5.50
Heating, Ventilation, Air Conditioning	15.56	11.10	6.64	14.88	10.38	5.87
Heavy Duty Truck-Trailer Equipment	8.82	6.99	5.17	7.83	6.31	4.78
Home Improvement	8.10	6.46	4.82	7.86	6.05	4.24
Import-Export	11.82	8.83	5.85	13.07	8.79	4.50
Industrial Equipment & Machinery	16.05	11.53	7.02	15.06	11.04	7.01
Industrial Supplies	13.80	10.29	6.78	12.14	9.08	6.01
Lawn & Garden				8.21	6.42	4.63
Lubricants	13.50	11.25	9.01	13.79	10.28	6.77
Lumber Industry	6.38	5.05	3.73	6.68	4.96	3.23
Machining Equipment & Services	7.57	6.33	5.10	8.36	6.78	5.20
Maintenance Supplies	17.25	13.87	10.50	13.17	10.30	7.43
Marine	12.83	9.81	6.79	10.36	8.11	5.86
Material Handling	13.85	10.34	6.84	13.88	10.07	6.25
Medical Equipment, Supplies & Services	18.18	13.25	8.33	18.90	13.99	9.07
Metals/Processing, Assemblies & Products	7.61	6.22	4.83	7.37	6.15	4.93

Survey of Sales Commissions (Continued)

PRODUCT MARKET	1985 Survey Results			1987 Survey Results		
	Highest %	Average of Average %	Lowest %	Highest %	Average of Average %	Lowest %
Metals/Raw Materials	6.66	5.04	3.42	6.61	5.04	3.46
Mining	12.77	9.41	6.05	10.75	7.00	3.25
Mobile Homes, Accessories & Supplies	7.75	6.35	4.95	9.33	7.25	5.17
Nursery/Florist	10.00	7.45	4.91	—	—	—
Office Supplies & Equipment	13.78	9.89	6.00	16.00	11.16	6.31
Optical Supplies	9.71	8.42	7.14	9.78	7.71	5.63
Packaging & Plastics	8.79	7.26	5.73	10.32	7.93	5.53
Paints & Varnishes	11.08	8.54	6.01	10.64	8.06	5.47
Paper Industry	15.00	11.16	7.32	10.36	7.85	5.33
Photographic Supplies	13.85	10.46	7.07	13.25	10.13	7.00
Plastics	7.51	6.18	4.86	7.79	6.19	4.59
Plumbing	10.54	7.77	5.01	9.83	7.52	5.21
Pollution Products & Services	16.88	12.04	7.21	15.28	10.90	6.51
Powdered Metal/Parts & Components				6.00	5.37	4.74
Power Transmission	10.98	8.12	5.26	10.59	7.97	5.35
Process Equipment	16.67	11.73	6.79	17.12	12.05	6.98
Pumps	17.25	12.96	8.67	14.72	11.03	7.33
Recreational Vehicle/Aftermarket & OEM	8.86	6.98	5.10	8.55	6.43	4.31
Recreational Water Products/Services				8.25	6.45	4.64
Refractories	15.18	11.36	7.54	11.35	9.00	6.65
Refrigeration & Cold Storage				12.00	9.23	6.45
Retail Consumer Products & Services	11.88	8.48	5.08	10.50	7.41	4.31

Survey of Sales Commissions *(Continued)*

	1985 Survey Results			1987 Survey Results		
		Average of			Average of	
PRODUCT MARKET	Highest %	Average %	Lowest %	Highest %	Average %	Lowest %
Robotics	12.39	10.27	8.16	—	—	—
Rubber Products	7.00	5.92	4.84	8.10	6.49	4.88
Safety, Emergency & Security Products	13.39	10.95	8.51	14.06	10.81	7.56
Scientific Research Equipment & Supplies	20.70	14.85	9.00	21.83	15.60	9.36
Screw Machine Products	6.20	5.45	4.70	6.39	5.64	4.89
Sporting Goods Supplies & Accessories	10.97	8.13	5.29	11.32	8.07	4.82
Stampings	5.85	5.20	4.56	5.82	5.09	4.36
Steel Mills & Foundries	8.12	6.52	4.93	7.93	6.79	5.64
Telecommunication Equipment, Services & Supplies				16.50	11.04	5.58
Textile/Apparel Trade	8.37	7.12	5.87	22.50	15.50	8.50
Textile/Carpet, Drapery & Related Materials	6.66	4.33	2.00	—	—	—
Textile/Industrial	6.65	6.01	5.38	8.23	6.57	4.90
Toys, Gifts & Novelties	12.82	9.33	5.85	19.00	13.40	7.80
Transportation	6.33	5.49	4.66	14.50	12.00	10.66
Tubing	6.84	5.64	4.44	6.58	5.25	3.92
Utilities	14.69	10.94	7.19	15.00	11.39	7.78
Veterinary	13.37	8.93	4.50	13.60	10.15	6.70
Water Treatment Equipment & Products	15.30	11.66	8.03	16.53	12.03	7.53
Welding	8.70	7.07	5.45	10.44	8.90	7.36

START WITH GOOD FINANCIAL
MANAGEMENT HABITS

If you wanted to add up columns of numbers, you would have become an accountant. Right? But if you want to be a successful agent, you better learn to handle your financial details on a timely basis. Far too many agencies find themselves in trouble, not because they don't understand the basics of bookkeeping and accounting but because they put off doing the work on time. Even if you have an outside accountant, you are going to have to provide him or her with your records on demand, or you're likely to find yourself in trouble.

It isn't easy to sit down with the checkbook and general ledger when you know that a hot prospect is waiting for you to come over and write up a million-dollar order. But if you want to stay in business, let alone grow, you're going to have to do your financial work accurately and on time.

CHAPTER **10**

How to Get the Most Out of Your Office and Building

Should you have an office at home, or should you run your business from a commercial location? This question is asked so often that I wish there were one answer that would satisfy everyone but, unfortunately, there isn't. However, this chapter will give some agents' experiences to help you decide which way is best for you.

Let's first see how a few agents—some who are relatively new in the agency business and others who have been at it for a long time—run businesses from their homes.

THE BENEFITS OF AN OFFICE AT HOME

"I started my agency seventeen years ago and worked from a converted spare bedroom," one agent told me recently. "My goal at the time was to build the business as fast as I could, and to spend as little

147

money as possible doing it. When you think of saving money, one of the first things that comes to mind is not paying rent. For a one-person agency, renting an office that is seldom used—if you're on the road doing your job—didn't make sense back then.

"After about three years in business, I knew the agency was going to be successful because I had recovered my investment and had another person on the road. I thought I was ready to make the move from my office–bedroom to a small suite of offices in a local building. In fact, I was a few days from signing the lease before things became clear to me. It all looked good on paper, and I could easily afford the rent and extra services. I was even prepared to hire a full-time secretary. However, when I began to look at the goal that I had set for the agency, it became obvious that a separate office just wasn't necessary. My principals weren't concerned with whether or not I worked from my home. Furthermore, none of my customers ever had a need to visit my office. And my part-time typist/bookkeeper worked from her own home and didn't need the space of the office. In other words, the office was really a support system that could be anywhere.

I decided that getting an office wasn't going to do very much for me, so I backed out. Seventeen years later, I still work from my home office. I have three people on the road and two part-time office people who work from their homes. My long-range goal is to phase out, selling the agency to my employees."

For this man, the one-person office works very well. But note that he said that the home office fit well with his agency and business goals. After probing a little, I determined that his goals were not to build a huge agency but only to build an effective agency that he could control without ever having to give up selling to become a full-time manager.

CONSIDERATIONS FOR RUNNING YOUR BUSINESS FROM A COMMERCIAL LOCATION

The next agent you'll hear from had set his sights at a different level. He was just as interested in succeeding as the first agent. However, this man wanted to build a larger business, one that was more than just the sales efforts of a group of individuals. You have to remember that the goals of these individuals reflect their personal lifestyles and their individual ambitions for the business. The first owner planned to phase out of the agency in a few years, gradually relinquishing control and ownership to the individuals who were selling for him. His was a practical plan, under the circumstances he had chosen.

The next individual saw the agency business from an entirely different perspective. He wanted to build an entity. "I started working from my home," he explained. "But I knew right from the start that the home office was only a temporary thing to conserve capital while I was building the agency. Just as soon as I could afford it, which was about two years after I started the agency, I was ready to take space in a local office building."

This man had more in mind than just renting space. He saw the office and the building as part of his total business picture. In fact, he was aware that the building might be up for sale and took the office in order to solidify his position. "It wasn't the kind of an office that I wanted to stay in," he related, "but it was OK and it had other features that I knew could be turned into very productive real estate."

To make a long story short, this agent rented space in the building, bought the building two years later, and moved out almost immediately. He saw the opportunity to break up some of the larger suites into the smaller and more popular office condominiums with central secretarial services. A close financial analysis showed him that he could do better renting space for his agency in another building and renting out the smaller units in the building he owned.

There you have two extremes. Somewhere in between lie 99% of the agents today. To be sure, many agencies are run very successfully from home offices. I've known of agencies that run from home and cover several states with six or more salespeople. On the other hand, it seems that the trend is toward having an office away from home and in a commercial or business location. This doesn't mean that you should automatically set your sights on renting an office somewhere. What it does mean is that you should consider exactly where you want your agency to go and what you are going to need to get there. If you can get there with a home office, that's the way to go. If your plans call for a central location with some permanent office staff and equipment, then you're going to need something more substantial.

Overcoming the Negative Home-Office Image

Some will tell you that a home office is not very professional and that its image is one of a rinky-dink operation. This is not necessarily so. I say not necessarily for one very important reason. The people I know who have home offices and will continue to have them all say that you have to be positive to everyone about your home office—customers and principals alike. The moment you apologize for having a home office, you have automatically diminished your status in the eyes of the person you are talking with.

The truth of the matter is, there is much more of a precedent today for a home office than there ever was before. The growing respectability of entrepreneurs—especially those who come from the professional ranks of business to do their own thing—and the enhanced image of the family as a living and working unit has given the home office the stature it really deserves. Alvin Toffler, the noted futurist, has gone to great lengths to describe the electronic cottages of today. And electronic they are. Some of the home offices resemble some of the NASA control centers. Not only answering machines, but computers, facsimile machines, duplicating equipment, and telex systems make it possible for today's agent to stay in touch with his or her customers and prospects in minutes.

George Toelcke is an agent with a home office in one of the most beautiful parts of the country, Park City, Utah. Apart from being near some of the best hiking, skiing, and fishing in the country, George talked about the advantage of working from his home: "The principal benefit to me is flexibility. I can roll out of bed at seven in the morning and talk to my eastern principals on the phone. I have one product that I sell nationwide. Being in the middle of the country makes it relatively easy for me to do the job for them. And, of course, a major advantage is the fact that I can do all of my paperwork in the evening, at home, without having to get in the car and drive to another office after supper."

On the other side of the coin, agent Dennis Nelson of Marietta, Georgia, had this to say about the value of having an office away from home: "When I started our agency, I chose to begin in an office in the house. An in-home office was convenient and, of course, inexpensive. It didn't take much to convert an extra room into an office using a minimum amount of office furniture and equipment. It also provided the obvious tax advantage.

"I quickly realized, however, that the advantages of having an office in the home were overshadowed by many important factors which pointed me to an outside office. For one thing, future growth was limited. When the time came to hire a secretary and a salesperson, additional space would immediately be needed which was not available in a home-office situation. The need for making a professional presentation to potential customers and principals was also very important."

Dennis did make the move from his home to a very fine office building. He increased his staff and has built a substantial agency. His concluding words on the subject of having an office away from home are these: "Having an office away from my residence helps me work better. It provides me with a stimulus to get up and get out. In my situation, there was a definite need to get out of the house and start a daily business routine. It was important to get dressed up and develop a defined routine of work habits. Because the office is located close to my residence, I still have the privilege of being able to go back to work at night or to go to the office early in the morning, depending on my schedule.

"Another intangible factor of deciding to have an office outside of the home was that it provided me with a personal contact with other peers. It provided a means of professional networking and enabled us to interact with other individuals in the business community."

At Home or Away: Which Is Best for You?

As you can see from the arguments presented by two successful agents, the decision to work at home or not is both intensely personal as well as an important business decision. Since most agencies start out in a home office, the agent at least has an opportunity to see what it's like to work from home before making a decision. Interestingly, many of those who started their agency careers working for another agency that had an out-of-home office claimed that their goal was to have a separate office if they were at first working at home. On the other hand, many former manufacturer sales managers who started agencies and worked from home had no preference one way or the other initially. However, the decision to stay home or to move to an outside office was made mainly on the grounds of what the office could contribute to the growth of the business.

How do you decide which is best for you? This is a decision that must be part of your overall business plan. Here are a few questions you should ask yourself relative to your plans for your agency before you try to make the decision.

1. *Where will the agency be in a year?* In five years? In ten or more years? If your plans include substantial growth that needs a central headquarters for people and office equipment, then you will need to consider moving to an office away from home just as soon as your circumstances and requirements demand it.

2. *Will you have to meet with customers and principals in your office?* No matter how nice your home and your home office is, it is usually a little touchy meeting with important principals and customers

there. The one exception to this is when the home office is truly unique or is located in a very unusual place.

More than a few agencies I've heard of operate out of homes in very desirable vacation areas. A beach home, no matter what size, is quite an attractive place to entertain important visitors. However, it is often difficult to make a good impression even from an impressive tract home in the suburbs. But an agent distributor with a second office on the island of St. Croix never seems to find it difficult to entertain his customers and principals there.

3.   *Will the office interfere with home life or vice versa?* This is a real question from several perspectives. You certainly don't want a barking dog to be heard on your office telephone, and it's not too pleasant to have to leave a family dinner to answer the telephone. Think about this carefully. On the surface it may seem to be a minor problem, but it's one that is easily magnified.

4.   *Are you comfortable working from a home office?* If you feel that you will have to apologize for working at home, you're probably better off getting an outside office. However, if you can speak positively and convincingly of the benefits, the chances are that a home office will work for you. It's a matter of personal style. Know your style before you decide.

5.   *What are the practical considerations?* You may have a small room you can use now, but will it be large enough in a few years? How about taxes and local zoning ordinances? According to local zoning laws, you may not be able to have an office at home. Be sure to check first.

6.   *Is real estate investment an important part of your business plan?* Face it, when you own an agency, you really don't own anything in the sense that your principals own buildings and machinery. You may have a big investment in office machines, but this is an investment that isn't going to make you money unless you use it. However, investing in business real estate is just that—an investment. You do have a shot at building some equity in something tangible. Look at this angle carefully and with some advice from your accountant.

Obviously, there will be other personal questions you must ask before you decide where to have your office. But these six questions seem to be common to all agents, regardless of what they are selling, who they sell for, and where they sell.

To get a handle on the questions that relate to your specific goals and type of business, it's often a good idea to talk with agents who have done what you are planning to do. If there is no one in your territory who has had the same experience you are anticipating, talk with some of the agents who handle the products you sell in other territories.

How to Look at the Home Office From a Tax Advantage

Until about ten years ago, the rules for getting tax deductions for a home office were, to put it mildly, very liberal. Make an occasional phone call from your home office, write a few reports, and you could deduct significant sums. Now, however, the picture has changed dramatically. The change has affected those who took advantage of the law when they really didn't need a home office. But for those who are serious about working out of a home office, the tax breaks are there.

Briefly, you won't be able to take a tax deduction for your home office unless

1. a portion of your residence is used exclusively for the trade or business

2. the home office is used on a regular basis

3. it is your principal place of business or a place of business used by clients or customers for meetings or dealings with you in the normal course of trade or business or . . .

4. it is a separate structure not attached to your home and is used in your trade or business

5. the space is used on a regular basis for storage or inventory and the home office is the only fixed location of the business

6. in the case of an employee, all preceding possible deductions will only apply if additionally: the use is "for the convenience of the employer."

Probably the tightest part of the law is that a specific portion of the home must be used only for the business. You can't use that part of the house for both business and personal use. However, you can dedicate only a portion of a room for business use.

The question of regular use will be easy to demonstrate if you're in the agency business full time and have no place else to hang your hat.

But if you're just starting out and are still working part time for someone else while building your agency, the IRS might get a little suspicious.

Meeting the other criteria will take some serious consideration. Since the IRS has latitude in interpreting the tax laws, you should get the advice of an accountant or an attorney in your area who has had some experience with similar cases.

How to Avoid a Major Home-Office Pitfall

Don't jump at the opportunity to have a home office too quickly; there are some pitfalls you should be aware of. If, for example, you intend to sell your house in a few years, and it has gone up in value rapidly over a relatively short period of time, keep these thoughts in mind. Present laws allow you to defer all gain on the sale of your home if the total sale proceeds are reinvested in another home. In addition, $125,000 of gain is not taxed at all if you're the owner and are over 55 and so elect. However, you could lose both of these benefits if you claim a home-office deduction. You might even lose benefits if you claimed a home-office deduction that is disallowed by the IRS. In other words, if the present value of taxes saved by a home-office deduction is less than the present value of the taxes created at the time you sell the house, you could have problems.

The best advice as of this writing seems to be not to claim the home-office deduction for two years before you intend to sell your house. But, again, get competent advice from a tax professional before you make a move.

WHEN TO BE YOUR OWN LANDLORD

A successful agency can invest only so much in its growth, and the owners can take only so much money from the business before they find that they're really working for the government. One of the best ways to make use of the trajectory of a successful agency is to either buy or construct a building. You should consider one that not only will have rental space, but will have expansion possibilities for your agency. Rarely does it pay to own a building in which you will be the only occupant.

It's impractical to give you the tax implications of property ownership since the laws are constantly changing and vary from state to state. However, let's look at building ownership from the other practical as well as the impractical points of view.

A building gives your agency stature. There's no doubt about it, when a customer or a principal visits the J. J. Smith building—and you are J. J. Smith—you've got stature. And stature does help to stack the negotiating chips on your side of the table. As practical and as efficient as a home office is, a building does make a difference.

Most agents who own their buildings have bought existing buildings. Although there seems to be a recent trend toward agencies building their own buildings. As one agent explained to me, "I looked at a lot of buildings. Some had many of the things I wanted, and others could have been modified for our operation. But when I figured out what it would cost to modify these buildings, it came so close to the cost of building the building myself—the way I wanted it—that I decided not to buy an older building."

This particular agent was also a distributor for several lines of hydraulic components. The building he wanted not only included offices for his agency and offices for rental income, but it also included a large warehouse and shipping area.

Implicit in this approach is a lot of satisfaction. You also have the opportunity to tailor the building to meet your every need. However, suppose that your business turns down and you have to sell the building. If you did too much customization to accommodate your operation, you may be hard pressed to find a buyer whose needs match yours. You certainly don't want a white elephant when what you really need is green cash.

There is a compromise, of course. Architects recommend that you design your building around your basic needs, but include some modifications that suit your special needs. However, they caution builders to consider these modifications in either a limited way or in a way that permits rather easy and inexpensive modification to other use, if other use becomes necessary.

The Practical Benefits of Becoming Your Own Landlord

Real estate, in just about any economy, can be an effective tax shelter. And when you add the advantages to your agency of low rent as well as room for expansion for warehousing, owning a building has some important advantages.

Considering the traditional sale-leaseback deal, buildings are sold to or constructed by a group of investors who are in a position to benefit from the tax advantages. These investors are typically in higher tax brackets, which make it possible for them to take advantage of other tax incentives.

When you look at it from your agency's point of view, it's possible for a lease to improve the balance sheet. If the lease, however, is structured to meet the criteria for operating losses, it doesn't have to appear on the agency's balance sheet at all. Of course, if you obtained a mortgage or issued bonds to build the building, they would show up on your books.

In the kinds of arrangements that make sense for many agencies and agency stockholders, the business conveys the real estate to the buyer at the same time it enters into a lease arrangement with the new owner. It is, of course, possible to make this a three-party arrangement which would include the financial institution that provides the capital.

When this arrangement is made, the benefits often exceed those possible with a typical sale-leaseback. The buyer–leasor gets a tax shelter in the form of depreciation and interest deductions. The seller–lessee can often get 100% financing.

Depending on specific circumstances, it's often possible to get the needed financing from an insurance company, avoiding some of the lending restrictions usually imposed in more conventional real estate loans. However, the ins and outs of these transactions need careful monitoring by your accountant. They are not to be entered into casually, especially considering the fluctuations in interest rates that we have seen over the past ten years.

If, however, you get the go-ahead from your accountant and your lawyer says that your accountant's approach is not going to get you in trouble, the chances are that you will be able to have a building which you could never afford to rent if it belonged to someone else. In general, becoming your own landlord has a lot of very positive advantages. But you should do your homework very carefully before you take the plunge.

Sharing Space With Someone Else

You may not want to work at home but you also may not want to spend a lot of money on rent. This is a dilemma that can often be solved by sharing an office with someone else. A shared office means that all expenses are, of course, shared.

As you might imagine, being a manufacturers' agent offers some distinct advantages to those who consider sharing office space. The major benefit for the other party is that you will probably be out of the office more than you are in it. And when you are in it, you probably won't have many people visiting with you. In other words, your basic needs will most likely be served by sharing an office and secretarial help with someone.

Who are those you can share with best? Sharing with another agency offers a lot of advantages. Consider the possibility of sharing space with an agency that is selling products that don't compete with yours but that might be calling on the same people. You can swap stories and tips and help each other build your agencies. Also, if you share an office with another sales agency, the clerical help that you hire will be working with the same type of business. This can often create certain economies that wouldn't be possible if you were sharing space with, for example, an accountant.

However, I've heard of agents who have shared offices with all kinds of businesses and who have had successful relationships. I would suggest, however, if you decide to share an office, that you do it with some type of business entrepreneur. Even if you are in totally different businesses, both of you will understand the ups and downs and can offer advice or just an occasional friendly ear.

Finding someone to share an office with can be a problem, depending on where you live. If you're in the heart of a big city, there are probably a few newspapers that carry classified real estate ads that specifically list offices to share or that carry ads for those looking for office-mates. In less populated areas, you will probably have to depend on word of mouth and placing some notices on the bulletin boards of the clubs to which you belong.

Should You Locate in the City or in the Country?

This is a question I am frequently asked. Agents often want to know whether a view from the 35th floor is better than a view of a lake. The answer to this question lies in another question: Where do you have to be to best serve your principals and your customers? You may like the idea of looking out your office window and seeing sailboats on a lake, but if you have to drive any great distances to sell, you've asked the wrong question in terms of location.

The real question is one of practical business convenience. Of course, if a metropolitan office and a rural setting have identical advantages, then your problems will be resolved in terms of personal preferences. But if they don't, the answer should lie in the practical considerations.

CO-OPS AND CONDOMINIUMS

The possibility of investing in real estate exists for you even though you might not want or can't afford a building. Buying a co-op or a condominium is a very practical alternative to the purchase of a building.

When you buy into a co-op, you are actually buying a share of the building. Your share entitles you to use the building, but you should make certain that your type of business will be permitted in the building. It's unlikely that you would be excluded from co-op ownership because an agency is essentially a clean and quiet business—the type of a business most co-op owners like to have as neighbors. Your share in a co-op entitles you to vote at the shareholders' meetings. You will also have to pay your share of the monthly building upkeep. However, you don't own your co-op in the usual sense of the word. If you decide to sell it, you must first get approval from the other co-op owners.

A condominium, on the other hand, is similar to a co-op in that members own certain areas and split the cost of maintenance. The difference, however, lies in the fact that you can sell your condominium to whomever you please.

Co-ops and condos represent an excellent opportunity for the agent who doesn't want to buy or build a building to invest in real estate that will—hopefully—appreciate over time. However, when you investigate these properties, check carefully on any loans that may be attached to them since these loans become, in part, your obligation to pay.

RENT VERSUS BUY CHECKLISTS

It's not an easy decision to make, assuming that you have the money or the access to it. But even when money is no object, buying real estate might not be the best move. These points will help you put the decision into perspective.

The Advantages of Renting

- As a renter, the only tie to your space is your commitment to pay rent for the term of your lease.
- You will have a relatively low cash outlay.
- You will have no maintenance costs, except for those of keeping your rental space cleaned.
- You will be responsible for no property or school taxes. However, some rental agreements will include provisions that allow the landlord to raise your rent if their taxes are raised. This is fair, but not pleasant for you, the renter.

The Disadvantages of Renting

- In the long run, it will cost you more to rent because the money you pay to a landlord you will never see again in any form. You are buying nothing but space.
- As a renter, you get none of the tax credits that those who own real estate with mortgages get.

The Advantages of Buying Business Real Estate

- The property you buy brings you important tax advantages. You can write off the interest on your mortgage as well as school and property taxes.
- Buildings and land are usually fairly safe investments, especially during times of inflation.
- Each monthly payment will bring you closer to full ownership.

The Disadvantages of Buying Real Estate

- You will be responsible for property taxes and possibly school and utility taxes.
- Owning and maintaining real estate can tie up a considerable portion of your capital. Even though real estate is generally a safe investment, there is no guarantee that you'll be able to get your money out of it when you need it.

- You may have to spend a lot of your valuable time managing your property.

HOW TO DECIDE BETWEEN ANSWERING MACHINES AND SERVICES

A sales agency must have an address, a phone number, and a place to call, even though it may be the place you call home when you aren't working. Whether you decide to work from home, rent, buy a condo, or build a building, your agency will need a place to call home. The sooner you establish the location, the better off you'll be if you are just starting out. If you are already up and running, you want to make sure that people are able to get hold of you easily.

Getting hold of you easily in the agency business usually means a telephone call. Most customers and principals just don't drop in their agents' offices. If you have someone in your office, wherever it is, during business hours, you should be able to get back to any callers the same day they call. However, if there's no one to watch the store, you will need a surrogate on the phone. This means either an answering service or an answering machine.

Ask ten agents which they prefer and the chances are that you'll get an even split on this subject too. However, the opinions you will get with the answers are usually very strong. Those who favor answering services claim that they like the idea of having a live voice take the call. "I just don't like to talk to answering machines, and I'm sure that others share my feelings," an agent told me recently. He's right, there are many people who are turned off by a machine. However, there are some problems to consider when reviewing an answering service.

The first problem with an answering service is that many of them are obviously answering services. The voice answers your phone and says: "Hello, Jim Smith Agency, please hold." Before you have an opportunity to say anything, you're switched to some insipid music. Then, when the operator does get around to picking up on your call, she is usually pressed for time as other phones ring. And you can hear the other phones and other voices in the background. Obviously, this is not the case with all answering services, but those that are reasonable in cost are also those that can give you the most grief.

There's another problem that some agents cite when it comes to answering services, and that is that the people who take the messages often don't get them right. "It's a person who may make a mistake," is the way an agent who was unhappy with his answering service described the problem.

The answering machine, as I already pointed out, is an impersonal device that some people prefer to hang up on. However, the answering machine doesn't have a problem interpreting what is said. Words spoken are recorded directly on tape, without human intervention. However, machines, like people, are subject to failures. A dirty recording head, a torn tape, the end of a tape, a power failure, you name it and it can cause problems with an answering machine.

In all fairness to answering machines, it seems as though resistance to leaving messages on them has dropped off considerably in the past few years. This is mainly the result of so many people using them at home and at the office. People have simply become more accustomed to using them.

The machines that are available today are considerably more sophisticated than they were even a few years ago. And they are less expensive. Now, for less than $200, you can buy a machine that not only takes messages of any length, but allows you to call it from an outside phone and access the calls by punching a secret code on the touch-tone pad. You don't even have to carry the bulky beeper to get your messages. With some of the machines, it's even possible to sort your messages with fast forward and reverse.

You have to compare the cost of the answering machine with the cost of a tie line to an answering service. And, of course, once you buy an answering machine, your cost is over. With an answering service, you pay for it as long as you use it.

Other Office Machines You Will Need

Whether you have a typist or do your own, you're going to need a typewriter. But before you buy a conventional typewriter, investigate the possibility of buying a small computer with word processing capability. The chances are that you will get more use out of the computer than you will a typewriter. The computer allows you to create paragraphs that you can combine at the touch of a few keys to write a letter. And you can use it to do your direct mail work. Of course, if your customers and principals have computers you can probably hook up with them over the telephone lines with an inexpensive modem. In fact, I hear of more and more agents who have bought little portable computers that they take with them to customers' offices. There, right in front of the customer, they can access a principal's computer with the lap-top computer and get up-to-date stock and price information. This sure makes it easy to clinch a sale when your competitor has to go back to his office to check his stock records.

Facsimile machines can be especially helpful if your factory and customer contacts require the transmission of drawings and forms that can't easily be transmitted from computer to computer.

A copying machine is probably a must for every agency. I don't have to tell you about the mound of paperwork the average agency produces each week, and how much of that needs to be copied for others to use. You may not need a copier with all the bells and whistles offered, but you should consider one that does produce a good image and is dependable. The cost of a copier seems to be directly proportional to the speed with which the machine turns out copies.

If you need lots of paper in a hurry, you pretty much have to reconcile yourself with the fact that an expensive copier will be needed. But if speed isn't a prime concern, look at some of the recent models that have replaceable elements. They give good images, seem to require less service than the more complex machines, and take up relatively little space. You may spend slightly more per copy than you would on some other models, but this is probably a small price to pay.

The last piece of equipment that you may want to consider is the automobile telephone. At the moment, this equipment is rather expensive. But if you spend a lot of time on the road and pulling into a diner to make your calls is a bother, the car phone might be for you.

My guess is that, like all of the other electronic devices that cost so much when they were first introduced, the car phone will become less and less expensive as time goes by. However, the message units charged by the phone company will probably continue to be rather expensive.

PLAN YOUR OFFICE AS AN EXPANDING SYSTEM

Very few agents start out with fully staffed offices in modern buildings. Most start, as indicated, in the home or as shared offices. However, you should consider your purchases in terms of long-range utility. If you can afford it, buy a good word processor, one that will grow with you and be useful once you have a multi-person agency. The same applies to your other office equipment. Of course, if you're working a tight budget, you may not have a choice.

You're going to grow as an agent. Therefore, you should try to plan your office and real estate requirements so that they can grow with you. Buying top-of-the-line equipment means that it will last longer and should be able to do more things for you as you grow. And even if you grow out of the capability of your equipment, if it's top-of-the-line, you should be able to sell it. This is seldom possible with some of the make-do equipment that you can buy for next to nothing.

CHAPTER 11

How to Work Effectively With Subagents

The subagent is, like you the agent, an independent contractor. In general, the benefit to the agent from the use of a subagent is pretty much the same as the benefit to the principal using agents in the first place. But the main benefit to you is that you are able to have coverage where you might not have had it in the past, without spending any money. The subagent, in most cases, is paid when he makes a sale, just as you are.

On the surface it may seem like the only way to go, but there are some pitfalls, which will be covered later. For the moment, though, consider the subagent as a way to solve territorial coverage problems.

WHAT A SUBAGENT CAN DO FOR YOU

The prefix "sub" implies something smaller than what you might think of when you think of a sales agency. However, size bears very little relationship to the subagent. The subagent is defined more accurately by what he or she does, rather than by the size of the agency or the length of time the agency has been in operation. You should note, though, that some large agencies today got their start as subagents, handling lines for other agencies.

The subagent is usually an agency covering a territory or part of a territory that takes on a line for another agency. The subagent provides services or coverage that the agency with the line doesn't want to or can't provide. For example, a principal may want greater coverage of a territory, but the agency with the territory may not see the needed expansion of services as providing a return sufficient to warrant the expansion. In some cases, the subagent provides the answer. In this case, the subagent is already operating in the territory and can provide the needed coverage for the agency with the line. The agent with the line is able to satisfy the principal's request for additional coverage, but he or she isn't faced with the cost of covering what may be an unprofitable section of the territory. The subagent, on the other hand, may be able to do it profitably with his or her organization.

When the relationship works well, it can be one of the most practical ways to build business—yours and your principals'. But it's important that everyone involved go into the arrangement with their eyes open—no secrets from anyone.

Where to Find Subagents

The best subagents are probably the agents in your territory that you already know. Unless you're terribly sure of yourself and your principals, you won't work with subagents who are competing with you in any way. This, as you can imagine, makes it difficult to find an appropriate subagent. Agents, sub and regular, have to call on the same accounts to make the arrangement work. However, the chances are that there are agencies in your territory that call on the same people you call on, but for different products. And the agents with the existing contacts will probably work out best for you as subagents. They won't have to spend a lot of time doing missionary selling. They'll know the buyers and can probably learn quickly about the products they will handle for you as a subagent to be effective almost immediately.

If you are unfamiliar with the agencies that might be appropriate, try asking customers who are in the part of the territory that you are seeking to cover with a subagent. For example, a purchasing agent who can enthusiastically recommend an agent is pretty much a guaranteed winner. And, of course, you can advertise in *Agency Sales* magazine where there is an active trade going on between agents and subagents.

The best subagent is going to be one whom you are comfortable with and who has the business connections in the territory you want covered. The personal equation is going to be important, just as it's important for you to have a good personal relationship with your principals.

How to Manage the Activity of Subagents

If you do it right, you'll have a written agreement with your subagents that describes just how you are to work together. Contractual guidelines will be given later, but for now, let's concentrate on the general working relationship.

Your working relationship will be similar to the relationship you have with your principals. The subagent will probably not want to give you call reports for the same reason you don't give them to your principals. This can be construed as a violation of the independent contractor status and have immeasurable effects on the tax picture of your agency and the subagency. You should expect to get information about specific projects in progress when you want it.

HOW TO CREATE A PRACTICAL WORKING AGREEMENT WITH A SUBAGENT

In the pages that follow, you will find copies of the MANA guidelines for creating a working agreement with a subagent. (See Figures 11-1 and 11-2.) Bear in mind that these are *guidelines* and not legal advice. However, armed with these guidelines, your attorney should be able to create an agreement that will work for everyone involved. At the end of this agreement, comments will be given on some of the major provisions where there are pitfalls and opportunities.

There are two agreements. Figure 11-1 is used when the subagent relationship is one of actual employment. Figure 11-2 is used to establish an independent contractor relationship.

How to Interpret and Use the Sub-agreement Effectively

In the subagent relationship, as in so many other aspects of commercial law, there are contradictions. In general, an agency may not

FIGURE 11-1

Do not use without consulting your attorney regarding state and local laws and conditions.

Note alternative "strike-outs" in paragraphs 4, 6 and 7.

SPECIMEN ONLY

SUB-AGENT (EMPLOYMENT) AGREEMENT

This Contract is made this _____ day of _____, 19____, by and between _____ ("Agent")
and _____ ("Sub-Agent").

1. AGENT'S BUSINESS. Agent conducts a business as an authorized sales agent for Manufacturers ("Principal") in the geographical areas ("Territory") of goods and services ("Product"). and Agent has established a valuable sales solicitation organization. Agent and Sub-Agent recognize and acknowledge that the principal assets of Agent's business include (each of which has been acquired through the outlay of considerable time, effort and expense by Agent). the following: its goodwill: the names, addresses, continued patronage and particular needs and desires of its customers ("Customers") and its Principals; and other private and confidential trade information.

2. SUB-AGENT DUTIES. Agent hereby employs Sub-Agent to render personal services — to act as a sales representative to solicit orders for the Principal's products and to perform such other duties as are directed by the Agent including the timely completion and submission to the Agents of Reports and Call Sheets. Sub-Agent agrees that Sub-Agent will expend Sub-Agent's entire time, attention and energies exclusively for, on behalf of, and at the direction of, the business of the Agent. The parties acknowledge that Sub-Agent holds a position of trust and confidence and has been entrusted by the Agent with confidential knowledge of Agent's methods of doing business including Agent's Territory of operation, routes, Principal and customer names, addresses, particular needs and desires and other private and confidential business information. The purpose of this contract is to promote Principal's products in the Territory below set forth and the long term goodwill of the Agent. The Sub-Agent agrees to diligently and faithfully work the Territory in an endeavor to secure business for the Agent's Principals and use Sub-Agent's best efforts to promote Principal's products.

3. SUB-AGENT TERRITORY, ETC.: Sub-Agent shall solicit orders in the described Territory / for the described products / from the described accounts / for the described Principals, as follows:

      PRINCIPALS: if all of Agent's Principals, check here   ☐
      TERRITORY: if all of Agent's Territory, check here   ☐
      PRODUCTS: if all of Agent's products, check here   ☐
      CUSTOMERS: if all of Agent's customers, check here ☐

4. RELATIONSHIP CREATED. The Sub-Agent is an employee of [the Agent], [the Agent's Principals] **(strike one)** (the "Employer") for the purpose of soliciting sales of Product within the Territory, to the accounts, for Principals as set forth in Paragraph 3 of this contract. The Employer is interested both in the results obtained by the Sub-Agent and means and methods by which the Sub-Agent's services are performed and the Employer has the right to control the manner and means of Sub-Agent's performance under this Contract.

5. SALES POLICIES. The prices, charges and terms of sale of the products ("Sales Policies") shall be established by the Principal. The sales policies shall be those currently in effect and established from time to time by the Principal in its price books, bulletins and other authorized releases.

6. ORDERS AND COLLECTION. Orders for products solicited by the Sub-Agent shall be forwarded to [the Principal], [the Agent] **(strike one)**, and subject to acceptance by the Principal. Sub-Agent understands that all invoices in connection with orders shipped to the Territory shall be rendered by the Principal, direct to the customer, and full responsibility for all collections and bad debts rests with the Principal.

7. SUB-AGENT'S COMPENSATION. Subject to adjustments provided herein, the compensation of Sub-Agent for the term hereof for the services described in this Contract shall be [$_____ per _____, salary, payable in accord with Agent's then current payroll practices with respect to salaries for Sub-Agents.] [commission based on _____% of commissions received by the Agent from the Principal attributable to the Sub-Agent's performance of duties in the Sub-Agent's Territory, etc., as described in Paragraphs 2 and 3, above.] **(strike one)**. Such salary or commission includes compensation for all services performed by Sub-Agent. Sub-Agent acknowledges that Sub-Agent has read and is familiar with the Agent's commission arrangement with the Principal. All commissions earned by the Sub-Agent hereunder are payable only out of commissions paid by the Principal and shall be due and payable to the Sub-Agent on or before the 10th day of the month following receipt by the Agent of payment from the Principal of the sums from which Sub-Agent's commissions are payable. All expenses and disbursements incurred by the Sub-Agent in connection with performance by the Sub-Agent of Sub-Agent's sales activities shall be borne wholly and completely by the Sub-Agent. The Sub-Agent does not have nor shall Sub-Agent hold itself out as having any right, power or authority to create any contract or obligation, express or implied, on behalf of, in the name of, or binding upon the Principal or Agent unless such parties shall consent thereto in writing, except to solicit orders as the same or more particularly defined in this Contract. On termination of either Agent's or the Sub-Agent's right to solicit orders for the Principal, the Sub-Agent shall promptly cease representation of that principal and return to the Agent all promotional material, order forms and supplies provided by either that Principal or the Agent for that Principal.

FIGURE 11-1 *(Continued)*

8. TERM. This Contract shall continue in force and effect for a _____ day probationary period. Thereafter this Contract shall continue in force and effect from year to year (not to exceed 21 years) unless terminated sooner by the first to occur of the following events:

    A. For Cause: (i) The election by one party ("the aggrieved party") to terminate this Contract upon (1) the actual breach or actual default by the other party ("the defaulting party") in the reasonable performance of the defaulting party's obligations and duties under this Contract and (2) the failure of the defaulting party to cure the same within 15 days (the "cure period") after receipt by the defaulting party of a written notice from the aggrieved party specifying such breach or default provided that the defaulting party has not cured the default and the aggrieved party gives written notice to defaulting party of his or its election to terminate within the (10) days after expiration of the cure period; or (ii) Commission of a crime by either party in the course of performance of this Contract shall entitle the other to affect immediate termination upon the giving of written notice; or

    B. Without Cause: (i) On expiration of any one year anniversary date from the date of this Contract, provided written notice of election to terminate is given in writing to the other party thirty (30) days before expiration of the year period; (ii) Either party retains the right to terminate 90 days after notice by giving to the other written notice of such party's election to terminate at least ninety (90) days after the date written notice of such election is given.

    If the Agent terminates Sub-Agent for cause or the Sub-Agent terminates the employment without cause the Sub-Agent's right to solicit business shall terminate on giving notice as provided in Paragraph 12 below and Sub-Agent's right to compensation shall be limited to compensation earned by and payable to Sub-Agent to the date of termination.

    If the Agent terminates Sub-Agent without cause or the Sub-Agent terminates for cause the Sub-Agent's right to solicit new business shall terminate on the date of giving notice per Paragraph 12 below and the Sub-Agent is entitled to (continuing) termination-(residual) compensation equal to the probationary period plus one month for each year of employment completed, in a monthly amount equal to the average compensation earned by the Sub-Agent for the 12 months preceding termination.

9. BUSINESS SECRETS. Sub-Agent specifically agrees not to at any time, whether during or for two years subsequent to the term of acting as a Sub-Agent of Agent, in any fashion, form or manner, either directly or indirectly divulge, disclose or communicate to any person, firm or corporation in any manner whatsoever any information of any kind, nature or description concerning any matters affecting or relating to Agent's Business, including, without limiting the generality of the foregoing, the names, addresses, or particular desires or needs of customers of Agent's Business, the bounds of its routes, the prices charged for products or services with respect to which Agent is authorized to solicit orders for or on behalf of manufacturers or suppliers thereof, the commissions payable to Agent for such solicitations, or any other information of, about or concerning Agent's Business, its manner of operation, its plans, processes or other data of any kind, nature or description, without regard to whether any or all of the foregoing matters would be deemed confidential, material or important, the parties hereto stipulating that as between them, the same are important, material and confidential and gravely affect the effective and successful conduct of Agent's Business and its goodwill, and that any breach of the terms of this paragraph is a material breach hereof. This Agreement shall not be deemed to prevent Sub-Agent from disclosing matters if *all* of the following circumstances exist:

    (1) Such disclosure is necessary to Agent's Business and to the performance of the duties of Sub-Agent;

    (2) Such disclosure does not involve a trade secret or other theretofore undisclosed matters; and

    (3) Sub-Agent makes such disclosure in circumstances and in a manner reasonably calculated to benefit Agent and not Sub-Agent or actual or potential competitors of Agent.

10. NONCOMPETITION. While acting as, and for two (2) years after Sub-Agent's termination, Sub-Agent shall not, directly or indirectly: (1) own an interest in, operate, join, control or participate in or be connected as an officer, employee, agent, independent contractor, partner, shareholder or principal of or in any corporation, partnership, proprietorship, firm association, person or other entity, soliciting orders for, selling, distributing or otherwise marketing products, goods, equipment and/or services which directly or indirectly compete with the Agent's Business or the Products within the boundaries of the Territory; (2) induce or influence (or seek thereto) any person who is engaged (as an employee, agent, independent contractor or otherwise) by Agent or Agent's Principals to terminate their engagement or to engage or otherwise participate in a business or activity directly or indirectly competitive with Agent's Business; (3) either for Sub-Agent or for any other person, firm or corporation, divert or take away or attempt to divert or take away (and during the two years after termination, call upon or solicit or attempt to call upon or solicit) any of the customers or patrons of Agent, including but not limited to those upon whom Sub-Agent called or whom he solicited or to whom he catered or with whom he became acquainted while engaged as a sales representative in Agent's Business; or (4) undertake planning for, or organization of, any business activity competitive with Agent's Business, or combine or conspire with other employees or sales representatives of Agent's Business for the purpose of organizing any such competitive business activity. This covenant not to compete shall be construed as a separate covenant covering competition in each of the separate counties and states in the United States in which Agent transacts its business during the period of Sub-Agent's engagement by Agent as a sales representative; to the extent that any covenant shall be illegal and/or unenforceable in any one or more of said counties or states, said covenant shall not be affected with respect to each other county and state, said covenant with respect to each county and state being construed as severable and independent.

11. GENERAL PROVISIONS. This Contract may be modified or amended in whole or in part from time to time only by the mutual written agreement signed by the parties and delivered by each to the other prior to the effective date of such modification or amendment. Provided Principal has delegated authority to the Agent to include Sub-Agent in any indemnity from Principal to Agent and/or Sub-Agent, to the extent Principal is bound, Principal shall save Sub-Agent harmless from and against and indemnify Sub-Agent for all liability, loss, costs, expense or damages caused by reason of any of Principal's products (whether or not defective or covered by warranty) and any act or omission of Principal or Principal's customers or vendees, including, but not limited to, any injury (whether to body, property or personal or business character or reputation) sustained by any person or organization or to any person or to property whether from breach of warranty, products liability, infringement of any patent rights or other rights of third parties and whether from any violation of municipal, state or federal laws or regulations governing the products or services or their sale which may result from the sale or distribution of the products by the Sub-Agent, and including any act by the Sub-Agent related to the design, alteration, modification or change of the product supplied by the Principal, except as to design alteration, modification or change responsibility of the Sub-Agent expressly assumes responsibility in writing. Agent agrees to include Sub-Agent under all policies of Agent which provide protection or indemnity against liability to customers, consumers or third parties as to any liability or responsibility above referred to on and only to the extent Agent maintains insurance coverage.

    All provisions of this Sub-Agency Contract shall be subject to and shall be enforced and construed pursuant to the laws of the State ("Agent's state") where the Agent's principal office is located, as set forth below. Sub-Agent hereby appoints as its agent for service of process in connection with any action brought by Agent against Sub-Agent hereunder the Secretary of State of Sub-Agent's state of residence at the time such action is brought. In the event of litigation, prevailing party shall be entitled to recover interest as may be provided by law, court costs and reasonable attorney's fees.

    If and in the event any portion of this Contract is void or voidable under any applicable local or state law, such void or voidable provision shall not affect the balance of this Contract which shall remain fully enforceable as if said void or voidable provision had been deleted by mutual consent of the parties.

FIGURE 11-1 *(Continued)*

The parties hereto agree that this Sub-Agency Contract constitutes and expresses the whole Agreement of the parties with reference to the Sub-Agency and compensation for and respect to such Sub-Agency created hereby and all promises, undertakings, representations, agreements and understandings and arrangements with reference to such Sub-Agency representation and compensation are herein merged. No alterations or variations of the terms of this Contract shall be valid unless made in writing and signed by both of the parties hereto.

12. NOTICES. Any notice, demand or request required or permitted to be given hereunder shall be in writing and shall be deemed effective twenty-four (24) hours after having been deposited in the United States mail, postage prepaid, registered or certified and addressed to the addressee at its main office, as set forth below. Any party may change its address for purposes of this Contract by written notice given in accordance herewith.

DATED: _____

Sub-Agent Name _____

Address _____

Signature _____

Agent Name _____

Address _____

Signature _____

FIGURE 11-2

SUB-AGENT (INDEPENDENT CONTRACTOR) AGREEMENT

This Agreement is made on the date shown below, by and between_____
("Agent") and_____ ("Sub-Agent").

1. AGENT'S BUSINESS. Agent conducts a business as an authorized sales representative for Manufacturer ("Principal") in the geographical area ("Territory") of goods and services ("Products"), and Agent has established a valuable sales solicitation organization. Agent and Sub-Agent recognize and acknowledge that the principal assets of Agent's business include the following, each of which has been acquired through the outlay of considerable time, effort and expense by Agent: its goodwill; the names, addresses, continued patronage and particular needs and desires of its customers and its Principals; and other private and confidential trade information.

2. SUB-AGENT DUTIES. Agent hereby appoints Sub-Agent to act as sales representative to solicit orders for the Principal's products. The parties acknowledge that Sub-Agent holds a position of trust and confidence and has been entrusted by the Agent with confidential knowledge of Agent's methods of doing business including Agent's territory of operation, routes, Principal and customer names, addresses, particular needs and desires and other private and confidential business information. The purpose of this Agreement is to promote Principal's products in the territory below set forth and the long term goodwill of the Agent. The Sub-Agent agrees to diligently and faithfully work the territory in an endeavor to secure business for the Principal and use its best efforts to promote Principal's products.

3. SUB-AGENT TERRITORY, ETC. Sub-Agent shall solicit orders in the described territory/for the described products/from the described accounts/for the described Principals, as follows:

TERRITORY: if all of Agent's territory, check here ☐
PRODUCTS: if all of Agent's products, check here ☐
ACCOUNTS: if all of Agent's accounts, check here ☐
PRINCIPALS: if all of Agent's Principals, check here ☐

4. RELATIONSHIP CREATED. The Sub-Agent is not an employee of the Agent or the Agent's Principals for any purpose whatsoever, but is an Independent Contractor. The Agent is interested only in the results obtained by the Sub-Agent who shall have sole control of the manner and means of performing under this Agreement. Neither the Principal nor the Agent shall have the right to require the Sub-Agent to do anything which would jeopardize the relationship of Independent Contractor between the Principal and/or Agent and the Sub-Agent, unless otherwise agreed to in writing. All expenses and disbursements incurred by the Sub-Agent in connection with performance by the Sub-Agent of Sub-Agent's sales activities shall be borne wholly and completely by the Sub-Agent. The Sub-Agent does not have nor shall Sub-Agent hold itself out as having any right, power or authority to create any contract or obligation, express or implied, on behalf of, in the name of, or binding upon the Principal or Agent unless such parties shall consent thereto in writing, except to solicit orders as the same or more particularly defined in this Agreement. On termination of either Agent's or the Sub-Agent's right to solicit orders for the Principal, the Sub-Agent shall promptly return to the Agent all promotional material, order forms and supplies provided by either the Principal or the Agent to the Sub-Agent prior to termination.

5. SALES POLICIES. The prices, charges and terms of sale of the products ("Sales Policies") shall be established by the Principal. The sales policies shall be those currently in effect and established from time to time by the Principal in its price books, bulletins and other authorized releases. Written notice of each sales policy change shall be given by the Agent to the Sub-Agent promptly on receipt of same from the Principal.

6. ORDERS AND COLLECTION. Orders for products solicited by the Sub-Agent shall be forwarded to and subject to acceptance by the Principal. Sub-Agent understands that all invoices in connection with orders shipped to the Territory shall be rendered by the Principal, direct to the customer, and full responsibility for all collections and bad debts rests with the Principal; the Agent shall seek to have Principal refer to the Agent or Sub-Agent, for attention, all inquiries concerning the Principal's products received by the Principal from any source or by any means whatsoever from the Territory or for shipment of product into the Territory. The Agent will promptly furnish the Sub-Agent with copies of all correspondence and documentation between the Company and Customer covering any products ordered from, within or for shipment into the Territory or sold to the Customer within the Territory which Agent considers important to the Sub-Agent's activities, and to furnish the Sub-Agent with a statement on the 20th day of each month covering the amount of commissions due the Sub-Agent.

7. SUB-AGENT'S COMMISSIONS. The Sub-Agent's commission rate is:_____% (if applicable,_____% of the commissions received by the Agent from the Principal attributable to Sub-Agent's performance of duties in the Sub-Agent's territory, etc., as described in Paragraphs 2 and 3 above.) Sub-Agent acknowledges that Sub-Agent has read and is familiar with the Agent's commission arrangement with the Principal. All commissions earned by the Sub-Agent hereunder are payable only out of commissions paid by the Principal and shall be due and payable to the Sub-Agent on or before the 10th day of the month following receipt by the Agent of payment from the Principal of the sums from which Sub-Agent's commissions are payable.

FIGURE 11-2 *(Continued)*

8. TERM. This Agreement shall continue in full force and effect until the first to occur of the following events at which time it shall terminate:

a) the expiration of thirty (30) days after the Sub-Agent gives written notice to the Agent of Sub-Agent's election to terminate this Agreement, which right Sub-Agent is hereby granted and which shall be within Sub-Agent's sole discretion;

b) the expiration of thirty (30) days after the Agent gives written notice to the Sub-Agent of Agent's election to terminate this Agreement which right Agent is hereby granted and which shall be within Agent's sole discretion;

c) the election of one party ("the aggrieved party") to terminate this Agreement upon (1) the breach or default by the other party (the "defaulting party") in the reasonable performance of the defaulting party's obligations and duties hereunder of this Agreement and (2) the failure of the defaulting party to cure the same within fifteen (15) days after receipt of the defaulting party of written notice from the aggrieved party specifying such breach or default providing that the aggrieved party gives written notice of his or its election to terminate within ten (10) days after expiration of the cure;

d) as to any particular Principal where the Principal-Agency relationship is terminated, said termination shall be deemed to effect a termination as to that Principal of the Agent-Sub-Agent relationship, except that the Sub-Agent's right to commissions shall survive such partial termination;

e) by mutual written agreement between both of the parties hereto.

9. BUSINESS SECRETS. Sub-Agent specifically agrees that he will not at any time, whether during or subsequent to the term of his acting as a sales representative of Agent; in any fashion, form or manner, either directly or indirectly, divulge, disclose or communicate to any person, firm or corporation in any manner whatsoever any information of any kind, nature or description concerning any matters affecting or relating to Agent's Business, including, without limiting the generality of the foregoing, the names, addresses, or particular desires or needs of customers of Agent's Business, the bounds of its routes, the prices charged for products or services with respect to which Agent is authorized to solicit orders for or on behalf of manufacturers or suppliers thereof, the commissions payable to Agent for such solicitations, or any other information of, about or concerning Agent's Business, its manner of operation, its plans, processes or other data of any kind, nature or description, without regard to whether any or all of the foregoing matters would be deemed confidential, material or important, the parties hereto stipulating that as between them, the same are important, material and confidential and gravely affect the effective and successful conduct of Agent's Business and its goodwill, and that any breach of the terms of this paragraph is a material breach hereof. This Agreement shall not be deemed to prevent Sub-Agent from disclosing matters if **all** of the following circumstances exist:

(1) Such disclosure is necessary to Agent's Business and to the performance of the duties of Sub-Agent;
(2) Such disclosure does not involve a trade secret or other theretofore undisclosed matters; and
(3) Sub-Agent makes such disclosure in circumstances and in a manner reasonably calculated to benefit Agent and not Sub-Agent or actual or potential competitors of Agent.

10. NONCOMPETITION. While acting as, and for three (3) years after his termination, a sales representative of Agent, Sub-Agent shall not and agrees that he will not, directly or indirectly: (1) own an interest in, operate, join, control or participate in or be connected as an office, employee, agent, independent contractor, partner, shareholder or principal of or in any corporation, partnership, proprietorship, firm association, person or other entity soliciting orders for, selling, distributing or otherwise marketing products, goods, equipment and/or services which directly or indirectly compete with the Agent's Business or the Products within the boundaries of the Territory; (2) induce or influence (or seek thereto) any person who is engaged (as an employee, agent independent contractor or otherwise) by Agent to terminate his or her engagement or to engage or otherwise participate in a business or activity directly or indirectly competitive with Agent's Business; (3) either for himself or for any other person, firm or corporation, divert or take away or attempt to divert or take away (and during the three years after termination, call upon or solicit or attempt to call upon or solicit) any of the customers or patrons of Agent, including but not limited to those upon whom he called or whom he solicited or to whom he catered or with whom he became acquainted while engaged as a sales representative in Agent's Business; or (4) undertake planning for or organization of any business activity competitive with Agent's Business, or combine or conspire with other employees or sales representatives of Agent's Business for the purpose of organizing any such competitive business activity. This covenant not to compete shall be construed as a separate covenant covering competition in each of the separate counties and states in the United States in which Agent transacts its business during the period of Sub-Agent's engagement by Agent as a sales representative; to the extent that any covenant shall be illegal and/or unenforceable in any one or more of said counties or states, said covenant shall not be affected with respect to each other county and state, said covenant with respect to each county and state being construed as severable and independent.

11. GENERAL PROVISIONS. This Agreement may be modified or amended in whole or in part from time to time only by the mutual written agreement signed by all parties and delivered by each to the other prior to the effective date of such modification or amendment. Provided Principal has delegated authority to the Agent to include Sub-Agent in any indemnity provision from Principal to Agent and Sub-Agent, to the extent Principal is bound to Sub-Agent, Principal shall save Sub-Agent harmless from and against and indemnify Sub-Agent for all liability, loss, costs, expense or damages whatsoever caused by reason of any of Principal's products (whether or not defective or covered by warranty) and any act or omission of Principal or Principal's customers or vendees, including but not limited to any injury (whether to body, property or personal or business character or reputation) sustained by any person or organization or to any person or to property whether from breach of warranty, products liability, infringement of any patent rights or other rights of third parties and whether from any violation of municipal, state or federal laws or regulations governing the products or services or their sale which may result from the sale or distribution of the products by the Sub-Agent, and including any act by the Sub-Agent related to the design, alteration, modification or change of the product supplied by the Principal, except as to design alteration, modification or change responsibility if the Sub-Agent expressly assumes responsibility in writing and Principal agrees to include Sub-Agent as an insured in all policies of Principal which provide protection or indemnity against any liability to customers, consumers or third parties as to any liability or responsibility above referred to.

All provisions of this Sub-Agency Agreement shall be subject to and shall be enforced and construed pursuant to the laws of the State ("Agent's state") where the Agent's principal office is located, as set forth below. Sub-Agent hereby appoints as its agent for service of process in connection with any action brought by Agent against Sub-Agent hereunder the Secretary of State of Sub-Agent's state of residence at the time such action is brought. In the event of litigation, prevailing party shall be entitled to recover interest as may be provided by law, court costs and reasonable attorney's fees.

FIGURE 11-2 *(Continued)*

If and in the event any portion of this Agreement is void or voidable under any applicable local or state law. such void or voidable provision shall not affect the balance of this Agreement which shall remain fully enforceable as if said void or voidable provision had been deleted by mutual consent of the parties.

The parties hereto agree that this Sub-Agency Agreement constitutes and expresses the whole Agreement of the parties with reference to the Sub-Agency and compensation for and respect to such Sub-Agency created hereby and all promises. undertakings. representations. agreements and understandings and arrangements with reference to such Sub-Agency representation and compensation are herein merged. No alterations or variations of the terms of this Agreement shall be valid unless made in writing and signed by both of the parties hereto.

12. NOTICES. Any notice. demand or request required or permitted to be given hereunder shall be in writing and shall be deemed effective twenty-four (24) hours after having been deposited in the United States mail. postage prepaid. registered or certified and addressed to the addressee at its main office. as set forth below. Any party may change its address for purposes of this Agreement by written notice given in accordance herewith.

(Agency):_____

By: _____

Title: _____

Address of Agency's Main Office:_____

(Sub-Agent):_____

Address of Sub-Agent's Main Office:_____

DATED:_____

AAG-104-HW

delegate to a subagent the performance of duties which the principal has charged the agency to perform personally. If your contract with your principal states that there are personal services that you must perform, you can't delegate these services to a subagent without the consent of the principal.

Because building sales is the name of the game for agents and their principals, even without specific contractual permission from the principal, you should be able to appoint a subagent to handle a principal's line. Without express instructions to the contrary, the authority to appoint a subagent is usually implied. As a corporation, rather than as a sole proprietor, the right to delegate is usually more obvious. By it's nature, a corporation acts through the use of appointed people.

How to Determine Agency Liability When Using Subagencies

Now that insurance has become a major cost of doing business, it's important to look very carefully at the liability that an agency–subagency relationship creates.

In the absence of a written agreement, liability will be determined by looking at a number of factors. These are the factors that will be taken into account:

- Who appointed the subagent?
- For whose account is the subagent appointed?
- Does the subagent have employee or independent contractor status?
- Does the agency have express or implied authority to delegate powers to a subagent?
- What is the nature and scope of the engagement or employment of the agency and subagent?
- Has there been ratification, consent, or a waiver by the principal or agent?

You should have a written agreement with your subagents, but if you don't, these factors will be taken into consideration when the question of liability is raised.

In most cases, a subagent will have been engaged by the agent in the territory, and the question of liability will be resolved by resorting to this relationship. There are problems, however, when a subagent is engaged by the principal. In this case, the subagent–principal relationship would be used to determine any questions of liability.

There are times when a subagency relationship is stated, but in fact the other agency is working as an employee of the agency. In this case, the liability is one of an employer/employee relationship. However, there are so many possibilities when it comes to liability that you should get competent legal advice when the question of subagent liability comes up. The laws change from time to time and from state to state.

Let's take a look at some of the provisions in the agent's subagent agreement:

Item 1:   The first part of the contract guideline was created to define the agent–subagent relationship. This is pretty straightforward, but don't take it for granted: Read it carefully.

Item 2:   In this section, the guidelines attempt to define just how a subagent is to work in relation to the agent, the agent's principals, and the agent's customers. It's in this section that attorneys will suggest modifications to suit the specific relationship. When these changes are suggested, whether by your attorney or by the attorney representing the subagent, read them very carefully and make sure that you understand not only the obvious points but the implications as they relate to other elements of the guidelines.

Item 3:   Subagent territories are spelled out in this section. Again, there is considerable room for creating an agreement that covers your specific situation. Usually the subagent relationship is created to solve a specific coverage problem for the agent. However, if the relationship prospers, these restrictions may be changed for the benefit of both you and your subagents. If you do change the working relationship, be sure to modify the agreement at the same time. You just might save yourself a lot of headaches if the relationship goes to pot later on.

Item 4:   This is boiler plate, but don't read it lightly. There are some lines that relate to agency termination by a principal that are important for everyone to know and understand.

Item 5:   Under the heading of sales policies, the guidelines outline the relationship that is pretty much standard in the agent–subagent relationship. But you should look at this section at the same time you review the sales policies section of the agreement you have with your principals that the subagent will represent. Make sure they jibe. If there is any conflict, you will find yourself bound by two contracts and unable to perform satisfactorily in some cases. This means trouble—lots of it—unless you are careful right from the beginning.

Item 6:   Orders and collections are pretty much standard and don't require any special remarks other than the general statement. Read it and understand it before you sign anything.

Item 7:   Subagent's commissions are outlined in this section. Again, read and understand this section in terms of the contract you have with the principal that the subagent will represent. There are probably more problems involving commissions than anything else, and most of these problems would never occur if both parties read and thoroughly understood the provisions of this section.

Item 8:   The term of the agreement is pretty much standard for subagent agreements in most fields. All contracts have specified terms, and the agent–subagent's is no exception. Pay particular attention, though, to the references to the agreement you have with the principal.

Item 9:   Business secrets can become a sticky point in some agent–subagent relationships. Since it's usually necessary to expose the subagent to your customer lists and what other information you have generated in order for him or her to be effective, you do want to make sure that the subagent can't walk off with your business. It's very difficult to protect business secrets, but if you remember that any information that you specifically created to make your business success-ful is legally yours, you can keep the picture clear. A prospect list, for example, that is made up by copying names from a published directory won't qualify as a business secret. However, the list of customers that you have built over the years of direct selling would qualify, even though some of the customers might appear on a publicly available list elsewhere. Again, play it safe if you have any questions—get competent legal advice.

Item 10:   In the area of noncompetition, you are really walking in the mist. And you are in an area where more than a few subagent relationships go on the rocks. The MANA guidelines were created to be especially protective in this area simply because it's here that so many legal problems can develop. In general, the courts do like to protect an agent from a predator, but they also find it very difficult to prevent someone from making a living by enforcing some rather strict wording. My advice to you as an agent is to try to see that this provision remains intact, that it isn't changed in any way by the subagent with whom you negotiate.

Item 11: Items 11 and 12 cover all the general elements that weren't covered in the specific headings. Just because these are called general provisions doesn't mean that the points covered are insignificant. For example, this one short line might make the difference between winning a case and losing your shirt: "In the event of litigation, prevailing party shall be entitled to recover interest as may be provided by law, court costs, and reasonable attorney's fees." My advice again is to read every word several times.

Working With Subagents for the Long Term

In general, the subagent relationship is one that is created to solve an immediate problem for the agency or for the principal. Another territory may need to be covered and an existing agent in one territory may be able to take it on with a subagent. Or, an agent may lack the facilities to cover his assigned territory for one or more principals and turn to subagents to take up the slack. In general, these subagent relationships seldom last too long mainly because the agent is often able to set up the facilities needed to cover the territory himself after working with a subagent long enough. However, there are notable exceptions.

Let's face it, when sales are made on a commission, those who make the sales put in effort that they would like to see develop into something more than just commissions. It's not greed, it's just the nature of the entrepreneur to want to share in what he or she helped to create. The subagent, however, is a relationship of convenience. But it has the same psychological elements that can occur in a directly competitive situation.

If both parties enter the subagent relationship with their eyes open, there will be less of a chance for problems to occur. However, it does take a lot of open-mindedness to make the relationship work over the long term.

I've known subagent relationships that have lasted on good terms for years. I've also seen more than a few complaints from agents and subagents after only a few months of working together. When agent and subagent level with each other from the outset and when they put their intentions in writing, they can create working relationships that can be lasting.

CHAPTER **12**

How to Build
A Multi-Person,
Multi-Office Sales
Agency

Some people move from running solo to a multi-person agency as part of their growth plan when they first went into business. Others make the decision later for a number of different reasons. And still others, who like the idea of running alone, never take the step. However, there are more multi-person agencies today than solos. And my guess is that this is a trend that will continue.

MULTI-PERSON OFFICES VERSUS SOLO

Let's look at the business conditions today that favor the multi-person agency.

• More and more larger companies are turning to sales agencies to sell their products. Unlike the smaller companies that were usually dominant on the line cards of agencies twenty or more years ago, these larger companies are often market-driven. That is, although they may make good and innovative products, the force behind the company is usually marketing-oriented. This orientation often sees the success of their marketing plans being in the hands of multi-person rather than solo agencies.

• More and more domestic as well as foreign competition has resulted in stepped-up marketing efforts by the manufacturers who sell through sales agencies. These manufacturers might consider solo agencies, but they recognize that they would need many more of them to cover the territories than they would need if they used larger multi-person agencies. In other words, it becomes less of an administrative job when fewer multi-person agencies are used, rather than more solo agencies. It's a matter of pure convenience, as far as they are concerned.

• Like it or not, manufacturers tend to look at the owner of a multi-person agency as being more adventurous, more of a risk taker than the operator of a solo agency. There may be no basis in fact, but this is often a factor in the decision.

• The larger multi-person, multi-office agencies are frequently able to offer more in terms of backup service than the smaller one-person agency can. When you remember that a lot of B-school types are running the marketing departments of today's manufacturers, you know that they are going to want help in marketing analysis and many other projects that would be difficult for the solo to give them.

Unless you are prepared to fight the battle of one-person versus multi-person as a philosophical effort, plan to be a multi-person agency some day, and if you are one already, think about how you can expand what you have. Unless I miss my guess, the trend to the use and growth of multi-person agencies is going to continue for a long time.

What Is a Multi-person Office?

Before we get into how to build the successful multi-person agency, I think it's important to put the multi-person shop in some perspective. The multi-person agency of today is not necessarily an organization with a large headquarters staff working from it's own building. It's just as likely to be operating from a home office as it is from one of those office condominiums that supply all clerical backup. The point is this: The multi-person agency is really best defined as an agency with more than one person on the road. Whether they own a building or don't is not the question. The factor that's important for the agency as well as for the principals and customers is that the field sales team is made up of several people. Therefore, in the rest of this chapter any references to a multi-person agency will be made in this context. If you are the only person selling on the road but employ a full-time clerical person who doesn't sell, you are not a multi-person agency.

This distinction is important. Too often agents who could and should move up to a multi-person operation fail to do so because they have a mental image of an agency with elaborate and expensive offices to support the multi-person sales force. More than a few multi-person agencies have been profiled in the pages of *Agency Sales* magazine that covered extensive territories with many salespeople that were run either from home offices or from small rented spaces. For the balance of this chapter, think of the multi-person agency not in terms of physical property but in terms of its ability to field a number of salespeople.

The Motivation for Going Multi-person

Generally speaking, the same force that propels an individual to forsake a safe salaried job in order to knock his brains out for a commission is the same motivation that pushes him or her to move from a solo to a multi-person operation. Of course, there are other elements to consider, such as pressure from principals. However, those who start agencies in the first place are generally what used to be called rugged individualists. They want to run their own show. They see lots of good opportunities where lesser motivated people usually see problems, and they have the personal courage to take chances.

In addition to this stylized picture of the agent/entrepreneur, you will also find a practical person who usually knows that it will cost him or her a reduced income for a few years while newly hired salespeople get to the point where they can pay for themselves. And he or she also knows that each and every agency expansion is at once an opportunity as well as a crapshoot.

Most of the agents I know who have built multi-person agencies kept expanding each time they reached breakeven with their previous expansion. That is, they recognized that they had to capitalize on their momentum early on at the expense of short-term gains. In fact, one agent once told me that he was taking home the same money when he hired his third man as he did when he covered the territory by himself. "It is a lot more complicated, and I don't make any more money now than I did when I was alone, but I can't think of a better way to build a business. At least my additions pay for themselves. I don't have to go in the hole to bankroll a lot of machinery as my principals do." This agent was very realistic, and he knew that with the addition of a fourth salesman, which he did shortly after our conversation, he would be bringing in a lot more than he did when he was alone. He was well aware of where the curves crossed.

Running a multi-person agency is not much different from running any other type of business. Early expansion is usually rather expensive, but the growth that follows usually more than makes up for the expense. It's the economic concept or marginal utility working in a positive way for you.

Ten Reasons Why You Should Build a Multi-person Agency

So far the implication has been that the only reason to build a multi-person agency is financial. This is, of course, a very strong motivation, but there are ten other reasons why agents have gone multi-person and why you should at least think about the possibility, as follows:

1. *To maintain steady and predictable service.* Face it, you may be a human dynamo, but you get colds and your car breaks down, and you can only be at one place at a time. As a multi-person agency, you can control these conditions. This factor may be important to you, but it's even more important to your principals, especially when they think that they are sharing your efforts with your other principals.

2. *To get better territory penetration.* One man in a territory often can do little more than get the obvious orders. However, there is usually a lot of business that can go wanting if the coverage is thin. This, incidentally, is one of the reasons manufacturers frequently use when they replace an agency with a factory salesperson. They reason, right or wrong, that there is a lot more business in the territory and that a salaried factory person can go after it full time. They claim that the factory person will go after smaller orders simply because he or she is

on salary and not on a commission. If you want to avoid this problem, the approach is to build safety with a multi-person agency.

3. *To build in continuity.* Because the agency/manufacturer relationship is like a business partnership, both want to see it continue. The one-person agency doesn't offer this continuity. What happens, for example, when you retire? You may sell the agency at the last minute. But suppose that the person to whom you sell the agency doesn't hit it off with your principals? There could be problems all around. However, with a multi-person agency, there is built-in continuity. Your principals and customers will be accustomed to working with the others on your staff. Not only does the multi-person concept make principals feel more comfortable with your operation, it also provides the same sense of strength with your customers.

4. *To build a greater income.* Adding salespeople, all other things being equal, should result in a proportional increase in commissions. However, an increase in commissions doesn't automatically mean an increase in profits. The change in scale usually accounts for at the least the possibility of being more profitable, but it takes good management skills to insure them.

Most agents start out in the business as crack salespeople. They learn how to manage their one-person show in the first few years of operation, and lay the groundwork for being effective managers when they finally have a large organization. Although more of your time will be spent managing your growing multi-person agency than in selling, if you're like others, you'll probably keep a few of your favorite customers to yourself. As one agent who runs a rather large agency said to me: "Servicing a few accounts keeps me humble." What he meant, of course, was that this was his way of staying in touch with what the business really is—a selling machine.

5. *To build a bigger and stronger customer base.* Building a stronger customer base is a decided benefit for your agency and for your principal. The agent who hits the high spots is called a cherrypicker by unhappy principals. And cherrypickers are not among most principals' long-term business partners.

It may not be economical for you, as a solo, to dig in there and get all of the business that's available, but with added staff you can do it. The other benefit to this is that you can head off competition more effectively when you have an in-depth customer base. Anyone trying to nibble away on your business is going to try to get a few satisfied customers in your territory and to build on that. It's a lot easier to knock off a few small customers that you may have ignored in order to get endorsements than it is to take business from one of your big customers. When you have a strong customer base, this is not likely to be a weak spot in your agency.

6. *To expand your roster of principals.* Getting your first principal when you start out is much like getting your first job out of school. You were probably told by that prospective employer to come back when you have some experience. More than a few manufacturers will tell new agents the same thing when you ask for their line. However, once you have a few lines on your card, it becomes a lot easier to pick up more lines. It is, in a sense, a self-perpetuating system, but you do have to work at it.

There's another side to this picture. You may have all the lines you can handle, but there will be those times when you will lose a principal for good or bad reasons. When you have a few good lines, it's a lot easier to sustain the loss until you get the replacement. With only a few lines, each accounting for a large percentage of your income, you are vulnerable. The vulnerability diminishes as your agency grows and as your principal base becomes more diversified.

7. *To expand your customer services.* First and foremost, a sales agency sells. But there are times when additional services are required by principals and customers, and they can become rather important revenue centers themselves. For example, many agencies that sell commercial instrumentation will also offer installation and calibration services. Run right, these peripherals can add an important dimension to your profit picture. Frequently, these added service centers can smooth out the up-and-down sales curves that often make it so difficult to project your case picture in the sales agency field.

8. *To provide input for agency expansion plans.* Having a few salespeople in the field gives you a much broader exposure to what's happening not only in your territory but in the markets in general for the products you sell. This input can be critical when you want to expand, especially when your customer base for the products you already sell is saturated. Many agencies expand horizontally as well as vertically, but it's a lot easier to do it when you have the backup of a multi-person agency.

9. *To provide you with more personal security.* It's already been mentioned that continuity provided by a multi-person agency is impor-

tant from the standpoint of customers as well as principals. However, think about the possibility of selling your agency, over a period of time, to your employees. This kind of continuity not only rewards those who helped you to build the agency, it can also provide a personal cushion in your later years.

I know of quite a few agents who sold their agencies to their employees over a period of years, with the proviso that they be retained to perform certain duties. These duties not only provided additional retirement income, they also made it possible to secure some company benefits that had some rather substantial tax break implications. The tax laws change so often that I prefer not to detail the tax breaks available now. However, you should consider talking with your tax and legal advisor about these benefits if you are planning to sell your agency to employees and want to retain some connection with the business.

10. *To provide you and your principals with ongoing protection.* Building a multi-person agency does more than provide you with the possibility of a sale to fund retirement. It provides you with day-to-day security for as long as you run the agency. The single-person agency puts his or her agency and income in jeopardy in the event of an accident or a serious illness. As compassionate as some principals can be, most simply can't afford to allow a territory to lie fallow for several months while an agent recuperates. The multi-person agency will continue to function with little or no disturbance, which is the reason why most manufacturers prefer to use them.

EVALUATING THE DISADVANTAGES OF RUNNING A MULTI-PERSON AGENCY

As you might have suspected, there are trade-offs involved in growing from a solo to a multi-person agency. But as far as most agents who have made the transition are concerned, the trade-offs are worth it. Let's look at some of the disadvantages.

The first adjustment you're going to have to make is that of adapting to a different lifestyle. You did everything when you ran solo. You knew your customers and principals on a first-name basis. But as your multi-person business grows, you will find that you will have to become more and more isolated from your former contacts and that you will have to become a very productive manager.

The chances are that the first two or three people you add won't affect your lifestyle too much. However, as the team gets bigger, your management responsibilities will definitely make some changes in your lifestyle. As a manager, you will have more people problems to solve and your administrative load will get heavier and heavier. Furthermore, if you build a big enough multi-person agency, you will probably have to give up making sales calls. However, you will probably be able to compensate for this by having more contact with your principals.

I have heard of agency owners who built large and successful multi-person agencies who found that most of the administrative work just wasn't to their liking. Rather than scale back, they hired administrative people to handle the details. You will surely need clerical staff as your agency grows, but you might consider hiring management people to handle the aspects of the work you don't like.

The other major disadvantage of building a multi-person agency is the fact that you may have to do it with borrowed money. This isn't all bad if you have a good source of cash. But if you have to take on investors or partners, you could be in for trouble.

Most agents who have expanded from solo to multi-person claim that you should be able to underwrite the total expenses of a salesperson for at least two years before he or she becomes productive. Adding the first salesperson is often the most difficult financially. However, if you add people in proportion to the growth trends of your agency, the succeeding additions are usually less and less expensive, relatively. As you might imagine, it's a lot easier on the nerves and on the pocketbook to add your tenth salesperson when your agency is earning $5 million than it is to add your first salesperson when your personal income from the agency for the previous year was $70,000.

When you ran your one-person agency, all the commission income was yours. All you had to do was pay your expenses and taxes from this and the rest was yours. As the owner of a multi-person agency, you will have more and different taxes to pay, and you will take only a share of the commission income developed by your salespeople. The amount of the split will vary depending on a number of variables. However, here's a rule of thumb to help you decide when the economic curves cross in your favor. If you retain 40% of the commission income generated by your salespeople, sales must increase by 150% just to provide the same cash flow you enjoyed as a solo agency. Remember, too, that you will have higher service expenses on such items as the telephone.

You should really make some projections for your multi-person agency just as you did when you started your solo business. The number will be more intimidating than those you used for your one-person agency, but they have to be weighed against the increased potential you'll have with the larger operation.

HOW TO GET YOUR MULTI-PERSON
AGENCY STARTED

California agent Gene Fields suggests that you should ask three questions when you plan to expand to a multi-person agency:

1. Do I have the dollar volume or capital to be able to compensate another person adequately?

2. Is the workload sufficient to warrant the addition of another person?

3. Is there a strong enough promise of additional business available for the other person to eventually carry himself or herself?

Gene claims that you have to answer positively yes to these questions before you are ready to take the plunge. I will add another question that requires your serious consideration. Do you have the temperament to manage people and a growing sales agency? You probably do if you worked your way up the sales ranks as an employee and manager for another firm. But it's important to make sure. Talk with the owners of several multi-person agencies before you decide to go ahead. Ask them how being a manager changed their lives. The chances are that you will get positive feedback from all. But be sure to ask all the questions you have that relate to your own personality.

HOW TO FIND THE PEOPLE WHO WILL MAKE
YOUR AGENCY GROW

Many agents have told me that they made the transition simply because they bumped into the right person and wanted to have him or her on board. "I had thought about going multi-person," one agent told me recently. "However, I didn't spend much time making plans until I ran into a man at a local service club who was sales manager for a local firm. He told me that he could go no further in his company and that he was looking for another job. As it turned out, that other job was working for my agency; and that man is no longer just an employee, he's a stockholder and vice president.''

If the truth were known, most agencies think about building a multi-person agency a lot, but they seldom have much time to do anything about it until there is some pressure put on them. Where does that pressure come from? Most often, it comes from the principals who want more of your time and who know that there is more business available in your territory than you are able to dig out with your limited facilities.

"It took some rather direct heat to push me over the top," a midwestern agent related to me. "One of my principals had been making direct and indirect suggestions for quite a while that I do something about covering the large territory I had. I knew that I was stretched thin as one person, and I also knew that I had a large territory for this principal. Finally one day I was told that they were considering taking away a portion of the territory that I wasn't covering too well. I have to admit it, I didn't get into that portion of the territory too often. And I could probably have done without the part of the territory they wanted to take away from me. However, this all seemed like a step backwards. I don't like to give up anything. So I took on another man and assigned him to cover the part of the territory that the principal wanted to split away. This man, of course, also handled the other lines I had. Fortunately, there was enough income from all the lines in that portion of the territory so that the new man was self-sufficient in a little less than a year.''

Finding the right person for a small agency is much more of a problem than adding to an agency that already has a staff of ten. In the first place, the person you select to double your staff of one is going to have to meet all of the goals that you set for yourself. In other words, you're going to be quite critical in your evaluations. And you should be. It's a big step. However, when you add the tenth person to your already successful multi-person agency, you have a lot of history to use to evaluate the candidates.

Where you find the right people can be a problem, but most people solve it by looking first at the salespeople they already know. As I mentioned, many agencies take on that second person mainly because the right person is available, not because the other circumstances are all right.

Talk with purchasing people and your other customers. They may know of a factory person who is interested in moving on. Talk with other agents. They may have some over-the-transom applicants that they liked but were not in a position to hire. Talk to people at the sales clubs in your area, if they exist. In short, spread the word everywhere you can.

If you are planning your expansion properly, you will have your groundwork done long before you start looking for the right person. The right person will have to fit into your scheme of things, so this kind of definition will be important.

Ted Springmeier, president of Wiedemann Associates of Cincinnati, Ohio, a multi-person agency, claims that it's best to find and negotiate with someone who is presently employed, but who has indicated that he or she is thinking of making a career change. This can be a difficult person to find, but when you consider the negative consequences of not looking in the best places, it's worth the effort.

How to Create a Job Description of the Best Candidate

According to human resource experts, you should make up a list of the characteristics you feel are important for the job long before you run ads or talk with people. This list should be used as a checklist. Even though you probably won't find anyone who measures up to all of the criteria you have included in your list, use the list and create a profile of each. When you factor in your personal impressions, the checklist results will give you an anchor in the real and observable world.

More than a few agents try to create their salesperson in their own image. They know that they have been successful, and therefore anyone whose background matches theirs should be right for the job. This is seldom true, and is a very dangerous way to review and select candidates. For example, if you were an engineer early in your career, moved into sales for a manufacturer, and then started your own agency, you probably think that anyone who comes close to this picture has a good chance of success. Don't bank on it.

There are a few characteristics that you can look for that will provide reasonably good predictive indicators. The first you should evaluate is personality. Don't try to be an amateur psychologist at this juncture. However, you should look for the outward characteristics of warmth and a sense of comfort in any type of situation. You should seek a friendly person, but the glad-hander types are seldom the most successful. Look for a person who makes a nice appearance, who speaks without hesitation, and who seems to have the self-confidence needed to dig up sales as well as take them to a successful close.

Self-discipline is critical. Ted Springmeier said: "Of all the desirable qualities that a successful manufacturers' representative possesses, such as ambition, drive, intelligence, honesty, integrity and resourcefulness, the quality I look for and feel is the cornerstone of a successful career as an agent is self-discipline. Why self-discipline? Simply because being an agency salesperson can be very lonely, and self-discipline helps you get through. Also, it takes a lot of discipline to postpone instant gratification for long-range objectives. And the agency business is long range.''

Look for someone who has a realistic sense of his or her own self-worth. There are as many people who think lightly of themselves as those who think that they are the be-all and end-all. However, you know what you would want to be paid if you do the job, and the person you choose should have the same general sense of self worth. It's a mistake to pay too much for someone who is overqualified, and it's just as much a mistake to try to hire cheap. Either way, you could find yourself with the wrong person. When it's just you and another person, and that person turns out not to be the right person, life can be more than miserable.

If you are unfamiliar with the salary and commission range to pay your salesperson, you might be able to get comparative figures from one of the local sales clubs. If you should find yourself talking to a person who seems right in every way but in the salary department, you might be able to sweeten the pot with an added sales incentive. Good salespeople, as you should know, are most productive when their efforts can be translated directly into reward.

Your search will bring you in contact with a lot of people. Many of them will probably impress you as being quite ambitious. Ambition is an important characteristic, but you have to try to see if that ambition translates to a long-term relationship with your agency. Today, people aren't called job hoppers, as they were a few years ago, when they had three jobs in five years. Don't let this deter you if the other characteristics fit in place. Ambition is important, and if you can reward the person adequately, it will be to your advantage as well as to that of your employee.

THE MOST-OFTEN-ASKED QUESTIONS ABOUT THE MULTI-PERSON AGENCY

One of the most popular topics of the MANA seminars on agency management is that of the multi-person agency. One-person agents want to know how to do it, and those who are already running multi-person agencies want to know how to improve their operations. To help those who are unable to attend these informative seminars, MANA capsulized the most-often-asked questions and answers in a special report. Some of them appear below.

Q. When you're a small multi-person agency, what happens when you lose a line?

A. Owners of multi-person agencies appear to be more concerned with this problem than those who run solo operations. This seems to be mainly the result of the personal commitment they have made to the people they either hire or put on as commissioned independent salespeople. The one-person agency may suffer some personal setbacks and have to run harder to replace the line, but he or she knows that no one else is being endangered. However, most multi-person agencies that have faced this situation claim that the adversity often pulled the group together more closely, and that the replacement lines they got were better and more productive than those they lost. However, loss of lines comes with the territory. It's just more of a problem when you're running thin on an expansion program.

Q. How do you get people to join your company when you know that they are capable of starting their own agency?

A. Most people who haven't started their own agency and are thinking about joining an agency really don't have a handle on the problems that are involved, and they don't know the benefits once the problems have been worked out. However, the best way to lock onto these people is to point out that you have a going operation, that you can attract the better lines, and that there will be ownership possibilities when the person proves himself or herself.

Some very capable people are now working for major manufacturers in sales jobs. When the company decides to transfer them and their families for the tenth time, they know it's time to take the plunge. Many of these people are perfectly capable of starting and running a sales agency, but most of them have been locked into the employee role for so long that they prefer to switch to any agency, with the opportunity to own a piece of the show.

Q. Apart from pressure from a principal, is any time better than another to go multi-person?

A. When you know the benefits of a multi-person agency, you have already taken the first step. No one who thinks about retirement or continuity in the event of illness can avoid the consideration of going multi-person. And, assuming that there is no principal pressure on you, perhaps the best time to start making the move is when you're paying more in taxes than you should. Remember, adding people is a business expense. It's better to pay it to someone who is going to make money for you than to the IRS.

Of course, every individual's timetable is going to be different. A person who starts an agency at age 50 and wants out at 65 is going to have to move a lot more quickly than the one who is 35.

Q. When do you know whether your new person is going to work out?

A. Most multi-person agency owners agree that it takes about a year to know whether or not the new person is going to make it. And even this depends on the assignments he or she is given. If your new person is an experienced salesperson, he or she will probably be given strong new business responsibility right away. You should know within a year whether or not this person is going to cut it. On the other hand, if you assign your new people to servicing existing accounts, your only measure will probably be customer satisfaction. This, of course, is important, too. The point is this: Make sure that you define the new person's responsibilities clearly, and that he or she knows them and the goals that are to be accomplished. Only when both of you have a clear picture can you make an effective evaluation.

Q. What about offices? Does adding salespeople automatically mean that you should add offices?

A. There is absolutely no concensus on this point, which means that you can probably do just what you want and it will work. There are some multi-person agencies that flatly refuse to let their salespeople work out of their homes. "We have an image to maintain," one multi-person agency owner explained. He was very concerned with the image of his firm and he maintained regional offices for each of his salespeople. Not all of these offices were in expensive buildings. Many of them were in the new cooperative condo offices that have sprung up all over the country. These offices usually provide phone answering, typing, filing, duplicating, and mailing services. Most agents who have gone this route feel that these offices provide the base they need for regional salespeople.

On the other hand, there are many multi-person agencies whose salespeople work out of their homes, and they do it without making any excuses. Remember that the image of the average manufacturers' agent is still that of an entrepreneur who works from a home office. There is really no stigma attached to it. In fact, there is a growing trend today for many professionals to work where they live. The only point made by multi-person agency owners whose people work from home is this: Don't apologize for it. Treat it as though this is the way everybody does it.

There is one additional point to consider, though. Manufacturers looking for agencies are usually more impressed when sales offices are in commercial buildings. However, it seems that the agency's sales record is the fact that counts most in the final analysis.

Q. How do you divide up the territory when you add people?

A. The answer to this question is tied up in the compensation plan offered. In brief, commission people won't give up territory easily to new people, and this is understandable. It's a lot easier to shift people when they are on straight salary.

Territory division is usually based on the nature of the business. If you're selling biological instruments, for example, you might assign one person to cover hospitals and another to call on the research facilities. There are two different sales involved and the split can make sense.

If, on the other hand, the territory covers five states and you have two people, it doesn't make sense to split this way. It's better to go by geography and have each individual cover both markets.

You really have to review the territory, the market, and

the skills of the people you have, and then make the decision that is best for you and for them.

Q. How do you keep good people happy and from becoming your competitors?

A. There is no simple answer to this complex question. However, you can best protect yourself from a salesperson becoming your competitor by seeing that there is a constantly expanding opportunity for him or her at your agency. For example, you can offer stock in the business for certain performance or based on time with the agency. You can provide additional incentives under certain sales circumstances. And you can include a benefit package that the potential competitor would find difficult to have if he or she were to leave and start an agency competitive with yours. And, probably most important, you can make your agency a place that everyone enjoys working for. You don't have to give away the store. But when people look forward to working for you, you take away one of the most powerful incentives for them to become your competitors.

Q. What about reports and controls?

A. To avoid IRS problems, manufacturers' agencies shouldn't file extensive daily reports with their principals. It's quite possible to jeopardize the independent contractor status. You can have the same problem if you expand your agency with independent contractors. To maintain the distance required for tax purposes, you can't expect daily reports.

However, you do need information to review progress and to plan for the future. You don't want to bog down anyone with paperwork—even a salaried salesperson whom you can legally ask for reports. Most multi-person agency owners I talked with simply either have weekly or monthly reports they ask their people for or they hold regular meetings to go over the status of territories. The weekly reports are not detailed summaries of every minute spent in the field. They are really statements as to the condition of the prospects they are trying to develop and the customers they are serving.

The weekly meeting concept seems to work for agencies with smaller territories. The salespeople can make the meetings without too much trouble. And they are usually held as breakfast or dinner meetings. Some agencies with extended areas have made use of teleconferencing, and this seems to be a growing trend. Other agencies have provided tape recorders and asked their salespeople to make tapes while driving.

GIVE THE MULTI-PERSON AGENCY
SERIOUS CONSIDERATION

For all of the reasons outlined in this chapter, the multi-person agency should be given consideration. It's a concept that serves everyone well—you, your principals, and your customers. It gives you a chance to build something that will be worth money when you are ready to take it easy. It will allow you to attract top principals because they see your commitment and they see that the agency will go on without you someday. And it inspires confidence in customers when they know that there is an organization behind the face they see on personal calls.

CHAPTER 13

How to Build Continuity Into Every Stage of Agency Growth

It's been said by more than a few people that whatever work a person does, he or she must always be a salesperson. As an agent this is obvious. But there is another aspect of sales activity that some people forget or they just plain avoid. That aspect is selling your agency, yourself, and your work constantly to your principals. If you think that it's enough just to sell more than your principals expect each year, you may be in for a rude surprise or two down the line.

An agent I know in the southwest was a star, as far as the numbers were concerned, with all of his principals. Every year, this man exceeded his previous year's sales figures and was responsible for some pretty innovative marketing for his principals. However, about ten years after he started his agency, out of the blue two of his seven principals pulled the plug. "They both had flimsy excuses," the agent said, "but the fact remains that these two principals represented nearly half of my income. Fortunately, I was able to replace the lines quickly. But I wasn't able to recover from the hurt."

The hurt this agent talks of is real. Especially when you consider that the reasons for the termination were trumped up. The real reasons were that this agent did not attend to his principal relationships as carefully as he should have. "I assumed that because I was doing more—much more than they had expected of me—that this was enough. I guess I just didn't do as good a job of holding hands as I should have."

The job of "selling" your principals regularly is as important as the job of selling their products to your customers. Remember, you cannot send your principals regular call reports or you will be in danger of destroying your independent contractor status. And remember also that salaried salespeople are in regular touch with their sales managers. This just isn't the case with the average sales agency. There isn't time, and there is seldom the need for such close personal contact. However, it is important to maintain contact with your principals so that the continuity of the sales situations you are involved in for them, as well as the building of a relationship, continues—*all the time*.

MAKING YOURSELF INDISPENSABLE TO YOUR PRINCIPALS

In truth, no one is ever totally indispensable. However, it is possible—and critical—for an agency to become as close to being indispensable to a principal as possible. As you can see from the example just cited, doing a first-rate sales job is no real guarantee that you will be representing that principal next year. It's the one thing that will lose the line for you faster than anything else if you don't do it right.

I think that the best way to relate the techniques that contribute to being as close to indispensable as possible is to use some case histories.

How to Strengthen the Ties When You're a Brand New Agency

Perhaps the most difficult time in an agency's life to be indispensable is early on. Unless you have started the business with principals who know you and you can hit the ground running, you will have to struggle more than a little to establish the connections that mean longevity in the agency/manufacturer relationship.

Will Travis started his agency after seven years as a salesman and five as a sales manager for a manufacturer. He opened the agency with two principals, neither of which was his former employer. When he got these lines, he was told in no uncertain terms that they liked him, personally, but that they were reluctant to go with a brand new agency. Let's look at the dynamics of this situation for a moment.

The two principals had reservations about going with an untried agency, but they did give Will a personal vote of confidence. At first, Will, who was not accustomed to blowing his own horn, really didn't perceive the situation clearly. And because he was new in the business and had to work as hard at getting new lines as he did at selling the products of his two slightly reluctant principals, he was stretched quite thin.

Will did make a good sales showing, but he soon realized that there was still concern about whether or not he would keep the lines for the long pull. "They were still nervous," Will related. "I was sitting in a prime territory for them and they wanted some assurance that I was going to be around long enough for them to make money on my efforts. Even though my sales were strong for both and they were continuing to improve, they were nervous."

It doesn't take a psychologist to see that the two principals were betting on Will, but that they probably saw the bet as a 50/50 proposition. Even when sales were strong, which they were, the two principals were nervous about whether or not they had done the right thing by appointing a new agency in a prime territory.

After Will became aware of the situation, he took several steps that not only assured his principals that everything was going well, they had laid the groundwork for attracting additional principals. Let's look at each of Will's techniques.

• *Reports.* Regular call reports would put Will in the position of endangering his individual contractor status. However, it's important under any circumstances to let principals know what you are doing for them. In this case, Will made his reports verbally over the phone. "I asked each of the principals for a time that would be good for me to call them. I wrote out my report carefully so that there wasn't any time wasted on either end of the line. Each report contained a status report on projects that were in the works and on new business opportunities that I had turned up."

Will said that this technique was especially effective because it gave his somewhat nervous principals the opportunity to raise questions directly on any aspects of the report. "If there was any question, I could answer it immediately," he said. "If I had sent the reports in writing, there probably wouldn't have been any opportunity for give and take. And the time between reading the report and getting my answers would diminish the value and impact of the material. Also, I'm pretty good at listening between the lines, and I could listen for signs of unsureness and be able to respond to it right away."

Will explained that this reporting process went on for a few months, at which time he suggested that they make the call-in reports monthly rather than every two weeks. Then, after a while, they were made every other month, which is practical for any agency that has proven itself—and Will's agency had by this time proven itself.

• *Field visits.* Early on, Will had discovered that one of his principals' concerns was whether he would be able to make contact at a level high enough within the customers' organizations to be an effective agent. Will scotched this feeling by setting up meetings for his principal with the people within the customer organization who they felt were to be responsible for the sale. It only took two or three of these meetings before Will was able to resolve this uncertainty.

• *Trade shows.* Will explained that his presence at trade shows in his territory was one of the factors that impressed his principals most. "At the shows, everyone from the president to the company sales staff was able to see just what I could do in a sales situation."

Each of these techniques may seem self-evident. But to a new agent faced with the chore of getting new lines and new customers, even the most obvious things may not be seen as being important. Each of these techniques was used to solve a short-term problem for Will Travis, but each was very important in building long-term continuity for Will with his principals.

What Principals Will Look for in an Agency

Let's look at what most principals look for in an agency when they want a long-term relationship.

• *Growth potential.* Most manufacturers want to grow and they feel that growth of their sales agencies should parallel them. Building agency continuity means growing. However, you will often find that your idea of growth and a principal's idea of growth might not be the same.

At it often turns out, your principals will want you to add to your staff at a faster rate than may be practical for your agency. When you encounter this situation, it's best to discuss it out in the open. Explain what your plans are and how they will have an impact on the principal's sales. However, it's best to avoid making a lot of excuses when you don't plan to grow faster than your principal wants you to grow. Stick to what you plan to do, not what you're not going to do.

• *Customer base*. The customer base is an ever-shifting element in the sales situation. Manufacturers want to be able to see continuity in the customer base despite customer personnel shifts. And, of course, they want to see continued growth within the territory. One of the best ways to assure a manufacturer of this kind of continuity is by expanding your customer base.

• *Promotion*. Most progressive manufacturers advertise in the trade press and send the leads that their ads produce to their agencies in the field. These leads should be qualified by the manufacturers before they are sent to the agents, but most manufacturers expect that their agencies will engage in more promotional activity than just following up on the leads.

The continuity-building factor is usually seen in a direct mail program that is sponsored jointly by the manufacturer and the sales agency. Most manufacturers will pick up the postage for the mailing and will also supply sales literature to go with it. The continuity built by direct mail is really of equal benefit to the agency and the manufacturer—if the agency creates its mailing pieces to stress the agency.

Even though your mailings will probably contain product literature on which there is a strong manufacturer identification, the overall effect of the mailing should stress your agency. This is going to build customer continuity for you and at the same time it establishes the kind of contact continuity that manufacturers want to see.

GIVING THE IMPRESSION THAT YOU ARE BIGGER THAN YOU ARE

You may have already decided that you're going to be a one-person agency for as long as you decide to stay in business. Even if this is the case, you still have to look larger than life in order to establish the kind of continuity that makes principals and customers happy. But how do you do this when you're on the road doing what you do best—selling?

There are several ways this can be done, but remember that none of these is a substitute for sales performance. These are the elements of image that principals and customers need to see in order to have confidence in your agency.

• Your stationery should be impressive, but without being gaudy. Even if you're a one-person agency, have a competent artist design your letterhead and have it printed on good paper by a printer who knows what he's doing. And take every opportunity to drop notes to your customers and principals on this letterhead. Many agents claim that it isn't necessary to have every note typed as a formal letter. Just jotting a note on a nicely designed letterhead will do the job. Of course, if the message requires a formal letter, by all means have it typed professionally. By doing this, your principals and customers will see your agency as a little larger than it really might be.

• See that developments in your agency are given publicity in the trade press. *Agency Sales* magazine, published by the Manufacturers' Agents National Association, has a monthly column in which they list agency accomplishments. Getting a press release published, however, isn't enough. Make copies of the published release and send them to your customers and principals with a note that reinforces the idea that you run an agency that is on the move.

• Consider writing an article for a trade magazine in your field on a topic that gives you an opportunity to talk about your agency in growth terms. You might say the same thing to a principal, but it will probably go in one ear and out the other. However, when it's in print, it's cast in stone. In Chapter 7, the public relations techniques you can use to get your agency in print were given. It might be a good idea to review this chapter before you undertake writing an article.

• Call your principals and customers frequently. At first, you may not be able to get through too often. But if you make sure that you have something important or interesting to say to them each time and that you do not bend their ears indefinitely, you will be able to get a regular audience. It's a fact that sales managers think of their agencies as being larger, or at least more active, when they hear from them regularly. But don't make a pest of yourself.

• Take part in a local organization that relates to your business and your principal's business. For example, if there is a local chapter of the Instrument Society of America, and you sell to this market, be more than just a member—run for office or volunteer for projects that will give you high visibility. Yes, this will be time consuming, but there will be other contact benefits that fall out from this activity.

A word of caution: If you work too hard at looking like a big agency when you're not, you just might have the opposite effect. It's one of those situations where you have to watch for reactions carefully, and where you have to make sure that you don't take on so much that it prevents you from running your agency.

How to Maintain Continuity When Your Agency Grows and You No Longer Take to the Road

In a sense, the one-person agency is the ultimate continuity machine. He or she is in touch with customers and principals. But the one-person agency isn't the most efficient sales machine. The most efficient sales machine has enough people covering the territory so that all of the projected volume can be obtained. However, when this takes place, the chances are that you will no longer be in regular contact with the people for whom continuity is an important issue. You will be a manager, an administrator, an owner. In a sense, you just may find yourself back in the same situation you were in when you first started. You may be bringing in the sales your customers want, this time, but they are concerned because they don't see very much of you. This calls for some different continuity strategies. Here are some that have proven effective for many agencies.

• By the time you're the size that you have to be concerned with this set of problems, you will probably have a few people to whom you can assign specific responsibilities for customer and principal continuity. However, no matter how you divide up the responsibility, you should remember that it's important for both customers and principals to have some direct contact with you. If you cut yourself off altogether from both groups, you will probably do irreparable harm to your agency. It may not show up right away, but it will show up sooner or later.

The agency business is a service business, and a service business means that those you serve want to see the top dog once in a while. If you are going to split the responsibilities, always maintain primary contact with your principals. These are the people who are most concerned when they don't see you as often as they did in the past.

• Produce a regular agency newsletter that is sent to both your customers and your principals. The newsletter should be designed to enhance the image of the agency by way of relating agency successes— for agency principals and customers. Application stories about principals' products in customers' installations give you an opportunity to make points on both sides of the street. More than a few agencies have done themselves a lot of good by profiling a specific individual on the customer side and on the principal side in each issue.

Note: You may be tempted to profile someone high up in the organization, but this is not always the best approach. All too often it comes off as a butter-up. You're better off selecting some at mid-management level, and even some of the people at the clerical level, but who bear the brunt of a lot of effort that relates to the sale of your products. Assistants in a purchasing department are overworked and underpaid as a rule. A personality profile in your newsletter not only gives them a boost, it gives your agency a boost when it recognizes the "unsung heroes."

• As the owner of a large agency, you will probably run regular sales meetings for your people. You can combine this needed work with the task of firming up agency continuity by inviting people from both your principals and your customers. You can probably see the wisdom of inviting principals, but why invite the customer whose job is to resist a sales pitch?

The approach here is one that has the customer people tell you just what they need, how they need it, and how you can best serve them. When approached to address an agency sales meeting with this in mind, very few will turn it down. The technique has the double benefit of establishing customer continuity and of getting you some very solid information to use with the customer.

Using Your Salespeople to Build Continuity— As Well As to Sell

It usually doesn't pay to have agency salespeople undertake with customers anything but to sell the products you represent. You can seldom be paid enough to have them conduct market research, for example, for your principals. There are a few things you can train them to do that won't interfere with their selling, but which will add considerably to the establishment of continuity, as follows:

• Encourage your salespeople to talk occasionally with designated people in your principals' offices. You don't want this to turn into a gab fest, but you can use capable salespeople to undertake the chore of talking with customers that you did when you were small and had to do it all yourself. However, monitor these calls at first to make sure that your salespeople know how to handle them. If you can get them to carry on in the tradition you have already established, you will go a long way to binding the ties you have made with your principals.

• If your salespeople have the skills and the interest, you might want to encourage them to take part in business, social, and academic activity that adds stature to your agency. Most colleges and universities offer business courses for adults, either in the evenings or on weekends. Many of these courses are taught by adjunct staff—those who are capable by way of training and practical experience, but who are not full-time faculty. These academic achievements will not only add to the agency credentials, but they will also put your people in contact with individuals in the business community who can lead them to sales contacts.

At the social end of the spectrum, service to a political party or to a charitable organization can result in good exposure as well as contacts. At the business level, membership in a chamber of commerce or in a specialized business group in your area can have a positive effect on agency continuity.

Always Remain Visible, No Matter How Big Your Agency Grows

As your agency grows, you will have to delegate more and more responsibility to others for the day-to-day operations. However, you should always make sure that you remain visible and accessible to customers and to principals. Both want to make sure that their interests are being served. And when they know they can talk with you, they will feel a lot more comfortable. Even though you may be offering only a few reassuring words from time to time, it's important for those on whom you depend—your customers and your principals—to know that they are dealing with an organization *as well as an individual*.

An agent I counselled a few years ago had built a very successful agency. In the fifteenth year he found that his business was coming apart at the seams. He said to me: "In fifteen years, I went from a one-man agency to a seven-person business. We had good lines and the respect of our customers. We had taken pains to make sure that the people we hired were the best. But around the fifteenth year, we began to lose sales to competitors who had been there all along, and who really didn't pose a strong threat in terms of the products they sold and of the aggressiveness of their sales agencies.

"When I began to look beyond the balance sheet, I saw that I had lost much of the personal contact I used to have with principals and customers. And although my salespeople were doing very well in terms of their direct selling efforts, they weren't doing much to promote the image and continuity of the agency.

"I couldn't very well push my people to do these things until I took a few steps myself. The first step was to reestablish direct and personal contact with the key people at all of our principal companies. This was a little tricky because I didn't want to seem as though I was coming on too strong out of the blue. That kind of activity is often sensed as trouble. So I just stepped up the personal contact little by little until it was comfortable for me, and had the effect I wanted with my principals. And I did the same thing with the key buyers in our territory.

"All of this had a price, though. I had become too accustomed to doing a lot of the administrative work in my agency. I was president and I was 'prezzing.' However, this turned out to be a bad use of my time. Even though I still maintain total control over the agency, I have assigned some of my more routine duties to employees we had, and I hired an administrative assistant who was able to take over many of the chores that kept me from being my agency's ambassador."

I think this vignette puts the picture of continuity into clear perspective. This man had gone from a one-man agency where his personal presence had accounted, to a large extent, for his success. But as he grew, he gradually removed himself from the picture and destroyed the continuity that he had built in his early years. Fortunately, he was able to return to the job of providing this continuity before his problems had gotten too far out of hand.

As you can see, continuity is a complex issue involving not only serving your customers and principals' immediate business needs, but serving the emotional needs that are so important in a service business such as a manufacturers' agency.

If all the predictions are correct, the United States is entering the era of a service economy. For many people the transition will not be easy, especially those whose lives have revolved around work that didn't involve much human contact. But for agents, whose work is all human contact, the important fact to remember is that you have to do more than represent good manufacturers, sell well, and deliver on time. You have to establish a system of continuity that makes your agency as important to your customers as the products of your principals that you sell. It isn't easy, but when you can do this, you will not only have a business that will provide you with a better than average income and that will provide you with the psychic rewards that are every bit as important as the financial rewards, but you will be building a business that has value—today, and when you sell it.

14

How to Buy and Merge Agencies, and Take on Partners

Ted Hamilton had run his solo agency for four years, with six top principals, and covered two states. His sales volume had doubled in the first two years, and had increased by close to 70% in the next two years. Was he ready to take on a partner? The answer is no.

Bill Carlin was just finishing his first year as an agent. He covered his expenses, but didn't show a profit for all of his considerable effort. Is he ready to acquire another agency in an adjoining territory? The answer is yes.

If the answers to these questions seem reversed, stay with me for a minute.

From what I have told you about Ted Hamilton, he seems a prime candidate for expansion. But is he a candidate to expand with a partner? To answer this question, you need to know about Ted and his agency. You need to know what kind of an expansion will best benefit his agency, and you need to know whether Ted is suited to having a partner. In Ted's case, he has a very strong personality, and a partnership wouldn't suit him at all. But he has to expand or lose some of his momentum, and possibly some of his principals, when he is unable to satisfy them by working seven days a week.

Bill Carlin, on the other hand, is new in the business, but he had worked for another agency for many years before going out on his own. Although he was in business only a year and hadn't showed a profit, the opportunity to buy another agency was too good to pass up. My advice to him was to finance the purchase and expand immediately.

The point of these two very different cases is that there are no pat answers, that every expansion must be viewed individually with both the people and the business picture being part of the decision matrix. Some agencies aren't ready for an expansion when they are very profitable and in business for a number of years, and others, new to the business, might be ready to take the plunge. To help you get a feel for where your agency is on this question, you might want to use the following checklist.

AGENCY EXPANSION CHECKLIST

• What can be gained by an expansion or an acquisition? There will probably be more than one answer to this question. But the one that should dominate is economics. Will an expansion or an acquisition result in economic gain or a good potential for gain? There's no doubt that there can be considerable personal satisfaction in building a bigger and stronger agency; it's part of any entrepreneur's personal makeup to build. However, these feelings must be tempered with reality.

• What can be lost by an expansion or an acquisition? Of prime importance is that you may make the investment with personal savings or retained corporate money. So, be sure that you can afford it, both in terms of the expense to foster the growth and of the possibility of loss.

• What are the personal factors? Merging and expanding agencies will change your life in many ways. With each step of growth, you will probably find yourself spending less and less time on the road selling. This may be a problem—personally. Most people who become agents do it because they really like the excitement and challenge of making sales. As your agency gets bigger, you will have to spend less time doing this and more time in managing your growing agency. Those who make the change either shift the emphasis in their lives and become full-time managers, or they continue to sell one or two customers just to keep close to their first love.

As one agent explained it to me recently: "When I got to the point where I had to spend all of my time managing and none of it selling, something was missing from my life. I really like to sell. I solved the problem by handling one customer. I didn't pick the cream puff either. I picked the customer we were having the most trouble with. It wasn't that any of my people couldn't have solved the problems, but I needed the intellectual challenge of solving problems on the sales front. And I think that this kind of experience keeps me close to what my business is all about, even though 95% of my time is spent managing and dealing with principals."

• What will the effect be on your principals? Even though most manufacturers are constantly pushing their agencies to expand so they can get more of their time, there are times when an occasional manufacturer will resent an agent's growth. The agent in this unusual position is usually your biggest principal, and the company on whom you spend most of your sales time. This company is likely to perceive your expansion ideas in terms of loss to him. That is, he will probably fear that you may not be able to devote as much time to him with your expanded agency. The smaller principals will like the idea, but you just might find some resistance from your largest principal. You will be wise to explain just how your plans will have a positive impact on *all* your principals when you announce your intentions.

• What will the effect be on your customers? The chances are that most of your customers won't care one way or another, unless you have been giving unusual service in some way to some of them. If you find yourself in this situation, be sure to let these customers know that your plans will in no way diminish the service they have been getting from you.

• What will the effect be on your personal life? Any growth that requires greater participation on your part will have an effect on your personal life. If the expansion will impact dramatically on your life, you should discuss the possibilities with your family and make sure they understand the circumstances. Be sure to make an estimate of when the crunch will be over so that they can plan their lives, too.

HOW TO EXPAND BY OPENING BRANCH OFFICES

Jim Latta opened an agency a few years ago and had a territory for several of his principals that was really more than he could handle.

Fortunately, Jim was able to bring in the business in terms of dollars that his principals felt they should have, but after a few years it became apparent to Jim and his principals that there was considerably more business in the territory than he was able to tap from his one location.

After discussing expansion with these principals, Jim decided that the best approach for him was to open two branch offices. His plan didn't call for opening them both at once, but for opening one as a pilot and then opening the other later.

Jim's plans called for an orderly expansion and the use of people who had experience with his agency to run the branch offices. "I didn't want to open an office three hundred miles from here and staff it with people I didn't know," Jim explained. "My plan was to move one of my top salespeople from the headquarters office to the branch office as manager, and to give him an opportunity to buy some stock in the company. This man had been with me for three years and I knew that he could do the job. I also wanted to make sure that he stuck with us, and the opportunity for him to buy stock was the glue I needed."

Jim discussed his plan with his salesman and got full cooperation, even though the switch required that his branch-office-manager-to-be had to pack up and move his family to another area.

The office that Jim opened was in one of those new office condo complexes. His manager had a good base to work from, but there was no need for support services because they were provided by the backup team at the condo.

After he got the first satellite office under his belt, he had a working plan for the second. However, he didn't have another person at his agency who could move to the territory and take over the office. Jim was able to solve this problem by bringing in a man who had been running a small agency in the area in which the office was needed. This man had acted as a subagent for Jim, so they both knew something about each other before they took the plunge. Jim actually acquired the smaller agency, which gave him a running start.

One thing you should notice from this case history is that Jim Latta didn't make big moves with strangers. As he put it, "Opening a branch office is difficult enough with someone you know. It can be a disaster with strangers." I agree with this notion completely. If you're going to open a branch office, make sure that you have someone run it who knows your agency intimately, or at least knows the agency business well and can adapt to your individual style quickly.

Branch offices don't necessarily have to be full-fledged offices.

More than a few of the larger agency members of MANA maintain branch locations that are based in employees' homes. However, make sure that these "offices" have separate business phone lines that aren't used by the family. An answering service or answering machine is very important in this case. You are probably better off getting one of the machines that allows the user to access calls from any Touch-Tone phone.

SHOULD YOU MERGE FOR GROWTH?

Mergers and acquisitions seem to dominate the business news these days. Large companies are merged or acquired by even larger companies. In fact, mergers seem to be a growth industry apart from the companies themselves that are merged. And the specialists who arrange for these corporate marriages seem to be the heroes of business today.

In most cases, the stockholders of the acquiring companies do well, and in some cases those who own the acquired companies do well. But long term, it seems as though the corporate giants that go around buying up companies are just as active in the sellers' market with their acquired firms only a few years later. In other words, companies, for the acquisition experts, have become the commodities of trade. It's a little like a game of Monopoly™.

Fortunately, mergers and acquisitions in the agency field are undertaken for different reasons. They are done to build bigger businesses for the owners. And they are done to serve customers and principals better. However, like the big corporate mergers, there can be serious problems of compatibility unless everyone knows and understands each other. An agency merger of acquisition is more like a marriage than the joining of corporate giants. The living together of two merged agency owners is a pretty close relationship, and there is seldom any place to hide if disagreements take place.

I believe that agency mergers are a very practical way to build, but only when the parties involved know and respect each other and share common goals. When either party has a hidden agenda in mind, there will be problems.

An east coast agency owner merged with another agency a while back, but didn't tell his new partner that he had planned to retire early. The growth plans of the partner in the dark included some fairly heavy participation on the part of the partner with the hidden agenda. When the acquired agent announced that he was packing it in after a year and a half, the agency nearly fell apart—not because of any weak end position but because of the rancor between the two individuals. The point is this: Put everything on the table. Don't hide anything, and you will have a better chance of making a go of a merger.

HOW TO PUT A VALUE ON AN AGENCY
FOR MERGER OR ACQUISITION PURPOSES

Putting a value on a service business, such as a sales agency, is at best a difficult proposition. Your idea of value and the notion of the owner of the agency you want to acquire will probably be quite far apart. After all, you probably have very little tangible property that can be evaluated. And to put a value on customer goodwill and the continuation of principals is not going to be an easy task.

A valuation by you or your accountant will probably be rejected by the owner of the agency you would like to acquire, and will probably result in more than a little negotiating.

If you and the owner of the agency you would like to acquire can't reach terms that are acceptable to both of you, you should consider using the services of a business broker or an acquisition consultant who makes evaluations.

A valuation serves a major purpose—it predicts what a knowledgeable buyer would be willing to pay and what a knowledgeable seller should be willing to accept. Since there are usually more buyers than sellers, it usually makes sense to approach the valuation from the point of view of the buyer. Many buyers will buy more than one business, but most sellers will sell only once. Because of this consideration, it generally makes sense to consider what the buyer is willing to pay as the value.

In most cases, an acquisitions consultant will provide two prices or values as a result of a complete business evaluation. The first is the liquidation value. This adds the current assets to the auction value of the equipment, real estate, and inventory, and subtracts liabilities. The purpose of this valuation is to project a buyer's financing, which assists in setting the terms of the sale. As you might imagine, this valuation is not especially practical for a sales agency with virtually no assets—even though the agency may be doing millions a year in sales.

The second approach is the fair market value. This is essentially the same as the first, but it presumes a more leisurely and advantageous sale of the assets. And it's a projection of a buyer's downside risk.

The real value for setting the price, however, is found by analyzing the earnings—how much a buyer should be willing to pay for the cash-flow stream over which the owner has control. This has very little to do with the profit which the owner shows the IRS—or even the lack of profit. Rather, the valuator takes that taxable profit and then adds back all the discretionary expenditures such as interest, depreciation, the owner's salary, and fringes, profit-sharing and pension plans, contributions, part of travel and expense, dues and subscriptions, vehicle expenses, and so on. This then produces a number, which is the cash flow, after all absolutely unavoidable expenses. From this, you deduct a reasonable manager's salary and necessary purchases of new equipment.

The result of this activity is the operating earnings, which is defined as the amount of money over which the owner had control, after paying him- or herself a manager's salary.

To this figure, you would apply a multiplier, which depends on the interest rate and performance of alternative investments. Not surprisingly, buyers usually want a much higher return with the risk inherent in any business, plus time and managerial involvement. As of this writing, buyers expect 30% to 35% return, the equivalent of a three-times multiplier. So the average earnings are multiplied by this and the result is the earnings valuation.

Although most agencies lack assets that contribute directly to earnings, there are cases when some assets are involved that will affect the evaluation. There may be real estate; excess cash; inventory, if the agency is also acting as a distributor; and possibly some equipment. These are add-ons to the value. The result is what a buyer should pay for all assets *and* liabilities. That is, part of what he spends goes to creditors and the rest goes to the seller. Subtract the liabilities from the valuation to get the net-to-seller cash value.

Cash sales are the exception, not the rule. The next step, therefore, is a much more involved process. It's based on determining the results or a range of typical deals—very high downpayment, typically 50% to 75%; very low downpayment, possibly 5% although the seller's taxes create a downside floor; and an average of 20% to 40% down. The installment sale value is always higher than the cash value. Played against various interest rates and time periods, the actual value grows out of the various terms, whether or not the seller will stay, and if so, for how long, plus other considerations.

The true market value of a business is at best a nebulous thing. It's far more influenced by the buyer's perceptions of risk and future prospects and the terms of the deal than by the inherent value of the assets involved. And, as you can imagine, the variables in the sales agency business that contribute to this feeling of uncertainty are legion. You have to ask whether the principals will stay with the acquired agency. Will the customers continue to buy from the agency after the merger or acquisition? How about employees? Will they stay? Will any of the top salespeople leave the agency and take business with them? All of these questions are especially important for the acquisition of an agency simply because the assets don't exist in terms of brick and mortar; they exist in terms of satisfied principals and satisfied customers.

If all this sounds disconcerting, take heart. Agencies merge and are acquired every day with little or no trouble. However, when the transactions take place and when they stick, both parties go into the deal with their eyes open.

The typical sales agency acquisition is one in which a larger agency acquires a smaller agency. In this case, there is no doubt who is in control. The smaller agency joins the larger agency with its lines and simply blends into the operation. The terms of mergers such as this usually state that the compensation of the smaller agency will be based on how much business is generated after the merger. When you get right down to it, the smaller agency is operating on a commission basis with the acquiring agency.

HOW TO MERGE YOUR SMALLER AGENCY WITH A LARGER AGENCY SUCCESSFULLY

In Chapter 15, selling an agency as a means of finally getting a lot of money out of your agency will be covered. But for now, I'm going to discuss the best ways to merge your smaller agency with a larger agency, either as a means to personal growth or to divest yourself of a business when you have other interests.

Let's assume that your agency is successful, and that this isn't a fire sale. You've probably had a few offers, but none of them have been especially attractive. You could keep waiting for the right offer—which may never float in over the transom—or you could make use of a variation of the leveraged buy-out technique that is so popular with the big corporate raiders.

In the typical agency sale situation, the buyer has very little money to put into the business. But what he does have is a lot of determination to build a big business. The buyer may come from the outside or might even be made up of a group of individuals. In this case, the seller and the buyer both want to work out a deal in which

- the agency eventually gets transferred to the new manager;

- the former owner is well compensated for the business that he has built, probably with little cash and lots of sweat equity;

- the former owner is able to keep the agency running and the dedicated workers employed because he probably feels an emotional tie to them.

First, get a full set of financials. You should be especially interested in the balance sheet and earnings statement for the last two or three years; projections; and a detailed list of tangible assets that might include inventory, receivables, real estate, automobiles, and other similar bankable items.

Take this material to a banker. Don't go to just any banker, though. Look for one who has shown some creativity and is open to innovative ideas. Remember, most bankers are bottom liners, and the bottom line of even the most successful agency seldom shows much on which a more traditional banker will lend money.

Today, banks are competitive and a lot hungrier than they have been in the past. This, of course, means that you will have a better chance of getting what you want and need than you did only a few short years ago. With the understanding that the future banking business of the ongoing business will go to the bank, you and the buyer seek a loan, using the agency's assets as collateral. This, in effect, can constitute the downpayment for the transaction. And when it's warranted, the bank may even advance operating capital for expansion or modernization.

Be sure to make it completely clear to the bank that you will work out an arrangement, subject to receipt of the financing, in which the new owner will eventually acquire the business, using a portion of the profits of the enterprise to pay the price and the bank loan to make the downpayment. In addition, the current owner, may be the guarantor for all or part of the loan.

Once you have spelled out the deal, imaginative bankers usually see the prudence of such a buy-out loan. The bank will see little or no risk because the loan's collateral is good. And the arrangement is a friendly one. Both sides want it to work. The owner will get more for the business than he would in any other arrangement, and the new owner is able to buy a business which he or she probably couldn't afford otherwise.

To ensure that the agency continues to be successful and that there will be enough profits to pay off both the loan and the selling price, you will have to agree to stay with the agency long enough to train new management fully, and to make sure that your customers and principals stick with the new enterprise. You won't be motivated to cut corners either, because it could hurt the business and the payments might be jeopardized.

This is a fairly simple deal, but it is relatively uncommon mainly because few owners and entrepreneurs are aware of these types of arrangements. Because of this, they rarely, if ever, approach a bank to finance a purchase this way. As a result, many agency owners who lack the alternatives usually sell their business for less or completely finance the purchase out of future profits. This is a much riskier venture mainly because there's no downpayment and the buyer isn't on the hook to the bank. Such a buyer may turn out to be a lot less dedicated to the deal in these circumstances.

The arrangement between you, the seller, and the buyer is quite straightforward. The owner gives his new "partner" a contract that calls for a testing period between them. If the arrangement doesn't work out, the contract would allow for the owner to fire the new manager. If it does work out, the company starts granting him equity participation by way of an option agreement that is exercisable over a period of time. The options are exercised only if the candidate owner remains in the job. If he leaves or if the owner isn't happy with the arrangement, the owner has the right to buy back the options or stock at a prearranged price.

From the owner's point of view, this is a nearly perfect arrangement. He can time his payments to himself to fit his needs in terms of taxes and spending needs. All the payments would be long-term capital gains, so he has the advantage inherent in a conventional installment sale.

Another Way to Slice the Pie

You don't necessarily have to get the initial funds from a bank. The potential owner may be able to raise some or all of the funds from other investors in return for both interest on the loan and an equity position.

In most cases, these deals work quite smoothly. However, there are some problems that can crop up. If the buyer fails to check into the company closely enough, and later discovers liabilities, inadequate capital, or other threats to the business, the whole arrangement could fall apart.

You must also make sure that you draft the employment and stock option contract carefully to catch errors and plug loopholes. Also, if disagreements between partners arise, one could find himself out in the cold. As you might imagine, these arrangements are most effective when both parties want them to work, when neither party has a hidden agenda. And, of course, they should be bound carefully by a written agreement.

If the cash flow forecast is too optimistic and the profits generated by the firm are insufficient to cover the repayment of the loan and the payment of the owner, the deal is going to go sour rather quickly.

Despite these pitfalls, this can be a very effective way to pull two agencies together. Further, you should consider buying key-man insurance to cover the unanticipated problems that could wipe out the best-conceived plan and the most well-intentioned agreement.

HOW TO NEGOTIATE FAVORABLE LOANS TO FINANCE ACQUISITIONS

Let's face it, even the largest manufacturers' agency is not going to be a major account for a bank. However, the smaller the bank and the larger the agency, the closer you come to being able to apply some leverage when you seek expansion capital.

Banks have always had the custom of making loans to favored customers with interest below the price rate. Just because you are not a corporate giant, it doesn't mean that you don't have any bargaining power with a bank. Since banks have become much more competitive and since several lawsuits in 1985 opened the favored customer practices for all to see, you do have some maneuvering room.

Don't be taken in by the new terms that banks use for prime. Your banker may talk of a base rate, an index rate, and even a reference rate. But such a rate by any other name is still the same—the lowest rate charged to commercial customers with the understanding that a few borrowers get even lower rates.

If you want to improve your chances of getting the best rate, you should first determine just how much your account contributes to the bank's profitability, and then you use this information to negotiate a loan. Remember, even though your agency represents a small contribution to the bank's overall profitability, you will still be a valued customer if you have a good history with the bank. And, again, competition has made bankers listen a lot more closely when smaller depositors seek funds.

Many banks have gotten away from the tradition of requesting 10% to 15% of loan value in compensating balances. However, if your agency does maintain large balances or is willing to, you have a powerful negotiating tool for getting a better loan deal. Remember to include the value of the personal accounts you and your company employees have in the bank. These personal accounts can mean a lot to a banker, even though the total deposits are not especially high. The activity of the accounts may be big enough to make the loan attractive at a better rate. If your company uses some banking services, such as payroll and pension plan management, you will have some added leverage in negotiating the loan you are seeking.

When you buy a piece of office equipment, you usually determine the price level at which the seller can make a profit, and then negotiate for a price as close to that figure as possible. You can use the same strategy to negotiate for a loan with a bank. Even though your business may not contribute as much as some of the larger banking customers, you still should have some negotiating room. You may not be able to get the same rate as a major manufacturer who passes millions a year through the bank, but you should be able to shave something from the rate. And in the agency business, shaving even a half a percentage point can be important.

The trick, of course, is to know how the bank earns its profits and then to use that information in your negotiations. The Federal Reserve Bank of New York publishes *Functional Cost Analysis,* annually, that breaks down the average cost of various services for banks throughout the Federal Reserve districts. The report is available at the Federal Reserve Banks in each district.

SHOULD YOU HAVE A PARTNER?

In my estimation, there is a good reason why only 4% of the thousands of MANA members operate as partnerships. That reason is personal conflict. For some reason the same two people can form a corporation, become equal owners, and do well. But as equal partners, most people tend to disagree until their personal differences interfere seriously with the agency.

The corporate form of an agency legally calls for a president, vice presidents, and other corporate officers. The structure, in a sense, tends to force two people to look more closely at their relationship and at their business responsibilities. But in a partnership, there is usually no specified way to resolve disputes. And all too often small disputes turn into bigger problems that can wreck agencies.

CHAPTER **15**

How to Sell Your Agency

For most agents, the sale of their business is the time when they fully realize the effort that went into building the business. You will make a better-than-average salary as an agency owner than will most senior-level sales management people in industry. And you will have the advantage of some pretty impressive perks along the way. But the realization of a large amount of money from the sale of your business is usually the ultimate reward for all the work you have done.

Some agents will have a built-in sale. That is, they may have family members or employees who have been groomed over the years to take over the business. Others may have to resort to an open market sale when they are ready to retire—or to do something else. However, it's a good idea to have someone in the wings to whom you can sell the business. That person should not only be able to carry on the business as you have built it, but should be someone with whom your principals and customers feel comfortable. And that person should understand the terms of the agreement long before it becomes final. In other words, begin grooming the person to whom you will sell your agency long before you sell it. When your principals and customers already know and trust this person or people, if it's a group, it will make things a whole lot easier than introducing them to a stranger.

HOW TO USE THE LEVERAGED BUY-OUT TECHNIQUE SUCCESSFULLY

There is usually one problem that is common to these business sales situations. Although the agency is profitable, it's one of those businesses in which management requires a considerable amount of experience and hands-on attention. Many agency owners have had a number of offers through the years for their business. But most who make these offers either aren't too serious or they really don't understand the agency business. The offers that come out of the woodwork are often fire-sale offers, even when there hasn't been a fire.

What are you to do when you want to sell but don't want to go through the usual process? The answer could be a variation of the leveraged buy-out that is so popular with the businesses on the big board.

In a typical leveraged buy-out situation, the buyer seldom has enough money to complete the sale—assuming that both of you can agree on a value for the business. Usually what the prospective buyer has, though, is the determination to take over the business and to learn what you have already learned as quickly as possible to continue making a profit. When the word buyer is used, it refers to a single individual as well as to a group of individuals, if more than one person is involved. If more than a few are involved, you're usually in better shape than you might ordinarily be with a single individual.

Key Points That Make the Leveraged Buy-out Work

In the discussion that follows, it's important to remember that the buyer and the seller want to work out an arrangement in which the agency will ultimately be transferred to the new owner, and in which the former owner is fairly compensated for the business. In most cases, the original owner will also want to make sure that the agency keeps running pretty much as it has been (assuming that it has been and is still successful) and that dedicated employees are kept on by the new owner.

Here are the steps to take in preparing for a leveraged buy-out deal: First, the seller should prepare a full set of financials. Especially important is the balance sheet, the sales and earning statements for the last two or three years, projections, and a list of the agency's bankable assets. A larger agency will probably have these bankable assets to put on the table: real estate, automobiles, office machinery and equipment, receivables in the form of commissions owed, and inventory if the agency engages in any buy and sell operations.

Then, the buyer takes all this information to a banker—not just any old banker, but a banker with some creativity beyond the bottom-line mentality. It is important to look for a banker who's interested in and open to innovative ideas. Looking for a creative banker doesn't mean that I'm suggesting a shaky procedure. It isn't. It's just that this approach is most often used by larger companies. Smaller companies are usually sold by the traditional guaranteed loan method.

Today, banking conditions are such that it will not be difficult to locate a banker who is open to some interesting business sale possibilities. It may not be enough, however, to find just a creative banker. But when you can promise the banker the agency's banking business, doors generally open up.

With the understanding that the future banking business of the agency will go to the bank, the potential buyer and seller should ask the bank to issue a loan, using the business's assets as collateral. This, in effect, constitutes the downpayment for the transaction. If necessary, the buyer might have to ask the bank to advance operating capital for expansion and modernization. However, this step is usually better left for another time.

At this point, the present owner makes it very clear to the bank that he or she and the buyer will work out an agreement, subject only to the receipt of full financing, in which the new manager will eventually acquire the business by using a portion of the profits of the agent to pay the price and the bank loan used to make the downpayment. In addition, the current owner may be the guarantor for all or part of the loan.

Usually bankers with more than an eye for only the bottom line will see the value of such a buy-out loan. The bank will face little or no risk simply because the loan's collateral is good. And this is a friendly arrangement that both sides want to work. Unlike the leveraged buy-outs of bigger business where takeovers are more often than not hostile, this arrangement is one in which all the parties are working toward success.

In general, the former owner is going to get more for the business than he or she might in most of the other ways a business can be sold.

And the new owner is usually able to buy a business that he or she might not be able to afford under most other circumstances.

To assure that the agency continues to be successful, so that there will be enough profits to pay off both the loan and the selling price, the original owner agrees to stay with the business long enough to train new management. This is seldom a problem with the average agency unless, of course, the owner needs to sell because of health reasons.

You probably aren't thinking about this step now, but from my own experience and from the experience of the hundreds of agents I have counseled over the years, you will want to stay with business for a while—even if the new owner is fully capable of running it right away. From the buyer's and the bank's point of view, your staying with the agency under these terms means that you won't be motivated to cut corners simply because your payments might be jeopardized.

HOW TO AVOID SELLING YOUR AGENCY FOR TOO LITTLE MONEY

These relatively uncomplicated deals are quite uncommon mainly because few owners are aware of the arrangements, and therefore seldom approach a bank with the idea in mind. Because of this, agency owners often sell their agencies for less money than they should. Or, more than a few agency owners will completely finance the purchase out of future profits. This, of course, is a much riskier venture just because there's no downpayment and because the purchaser isn't on the hook to the bank. A buyer, under these circumstances, can often prove to be less dedicated to the deal than he or she should be.

The arrangement described is quite straightforward. The owner of the agency gives his new "partner" a contract that states a testing period between them. If the arrangement isn't successful, the contract should allow for the owner to fire the new manager. On the other hand, if it does work out, the company starts granting him equity participation by way of an option agreement that is exercisable over a stated period of time. It should be noted that the options are exercisable only if the new owner remains on the job. If he leaves or if the former owner doesn't like the way things are going, he has the right to buy back the options or agency stock at a prearranged price.

From the point of view of the owner, this approach is about as close to perfection as you can get. The payments can be timed to fit specific needs, which would include tax considerations as well as spending needs. Also, the payments would be long-term capital gains and would have the tax advantage of a regular installment sale—at least under our present tax law.

Another Way to Get the Money

The system just described is based on getting the money from a bank. However, the potential owner may be able to raise some or all of the money from other investors in return for both interest on the loan and some equity in the agency. In most cases, this arrangement will work smoothly. Nevertheless, there are some factors to look out for:

1. If the buyer fails to do his homework—the financials generally aren't certified because the business is small—he might later discover liabilities, inadequate capital, or other business threats, and the whole deal could fall through. The moral of the story is to put all the cards on the table.

2. If the employment and stock option contract contain any loopholes and if any disagreements occur later on between the new and old owners, there can be problems. This arrangement is most productive when both sides want very much for it to be effective, and when the written agreement protects both sides in the event of a disagreement.

3. If your cash-flow projections are overly optimistic, the profits generated by the agency may not be sufficient to cover the repayment of the loan and the owner payments. As you might imagine, the solution is to make sure at the outset that the projections are conservative rather than overly optimistic.

This is an approach that gives you the opportunity to sell your agency with a considerable amount of safety. And it gives a potential buyer a relatively easy way to acquire the business. But, as just stated, both parties must want to make it work. If either side has a hidden agenda, the deal will probably fall through. In that case, just hope that it falls through earlier rather than later. Better still, hope that the person to whom you sell your agency is as honorable or as motivated as you are.

How to Put a Value on Your Sales Agency

A sales agency is, perhaps, one of the most difficult businesses to appraise. If an appraiser looked only at the physical assets of the average agency, he would see only cars, office furniture, equipment, and little else. If the agency were also operating as a distributor and had inventory or even a building, such assets would be rather easy to evaluate. However, even when an agency owns significant real estate and inventory, the real value of the business is essentially an intangible—the sales history from the point of view of the principals and the good will of the customers. Both of these mean a lot, but are difficult to evaluate.

If you wanted to know the value of a private home, you could go to a real estate broker and get a range of figures that would come pretty close to bracketing the true value of the property. The same would be true if you wanted to buy an automobile. Therefore, it makes sense to talk with a specialist in this field when you are thinking of selling your agency. Such an expert is probably doing business as a business broker or as an acquisitions consultant. Since these people are buying and selling businesses all the time, they are the people who are most likely to be able to help you determine the value of your agency. You could ask your accountant for a figure, but the buyer is most likely to turn it down and start in a series of counteroffer haggles. And, as you might imagine, a homemade evaluation is not likely to pass muster with the Internal Revenue Service.

There is really only one reason for a business evaluation, and that is to predict with a relatively high level of accuracy what a knowledge-able buyer would be willing to pay for your agency and what a knowledgeable seller would be willing to accept. Since many buyers buy more than one business, they're generally more experienced buyers than sellers. This translates to the proposition that it is usually best to approach a valuation of your agency from the point of view of the buyer. In the pragmatic world of commerce, then, what a buyer might be willing to pay is the value of the agency.

In Chapter 14, ways of evaluating an agency in some detail for the purposes of an acquisition were discussed. The same approach is just as practical for you when you want to get a fix on your own agency for the purposes of a sale. Rather than repeat these instructions, please review Chapter 14 for the details.

Apart from the valuation of the physical assets and the difficult-to-measure good-will factors, it's important to consider the value of unearned commissions in computing the worth of a sales agency. These commissions are those which will be payable to the agency when the merchandise they sold is shipped. They are based on firm orders, and they have a significant value that just doesn't appear on an agency's accounting records. The agency has spent time and money to create the orders, but as of an appraisal, their value isn't on the books. However, they must be considered when placing a value on the business.

On the surface, it may seem an easy task to compute the value of these commissions, but consider the possibility that an order may be cancelled after the agency is sold—based partly on the value of the unearned commissions.

Also consider the commissions in terms of a time frame and the future value of money. If the commissions were to be paid today, you can put a firm figure on them. However, assume that you are selling products that will be delivered over a period of several years—and paid for over the same period. The future value of money is something that is rather difficult to anticipate. Just a few years ago when we had double-digit inflation, the situation was a lot different than it is at this time. We are now, in fact, in a period of the lowest inflation in many years.

The actual details of selling your agency are about as varied as there are buyers who are interested in buying your agency. If you doubt this, wait until you have a few offers and see just how different each will be. Not only will the offering prices vary considerably, but the methods of completing the sale will vary considerably, too.

HOW TO FIND A BUYER FOR YOUR AGENCY

The chances are that the person to whom you sell your agency will already be known to you and will, more than likely, be working for you at this moment. According to statistics at MANA, most agencies that are sold are sold to employees of the agency. In some cases, especially with smaller agencies, the buyer will be one person. But when the agency is larger, and therefore more costly to buy, there will be a few buyers involved. In this case, it's usually senior agency management that pools its resources to buy the agency.

But suppose that, for whatever reason, a ready buyer isn't available. What can you do to locate a prospective buyer?

Most of the agents I know who faced this situation claim that they were able to locate buyers within the ranks of the principals that they served. "For years, the sales manager of one of my principals reminded me that he might be interested in buying the agency when I retired," an agent told me recently. About two years before he was ready to retire, this agent had a quiet meeting with the sales manager and began serious talks. When they came to terms that were acceptable to both of them, both met with the owner of the manufacturing firm, not only to tell of their plans, but to ask his blessing. "It went as we both expected and wanted it to go. The president (of the manufacturing firm) was not overjoyed to lose the sales manager, but he did have a number-two man to move up, and the salesman was still in the family, so to speak."

It is occasionally possible to sell your agency to another agency, but this is not one of the most likely prospects. Usually the kind of an agency that would be interested in your agency would be selling similar products to the same market. And the exception that would have to be made in terms of principals, products, and coverage to make it work just might not be worth the effort.

There is a good possibility, though, of selling your agency to another agency—but to an agency that is located outside of your territory that is looking to expand by taking on more geography. Thus, your agency might be welcomed as a branch of a larger agency headquartered outside of your primary territory. The question of conflicting lines is less likely to make the deal unworkable in this case.

Agency Sales magazine, published by MANA, carries a classified section in which agents can advertise the sale of their agencies and others can advertise for agencies that they would like to buy. MANA has also published an extensive guide to the ins and outs of buying and selling an agency, written by accountant Mel Daskal. Write to MANA for the current price of this guide.

You might want to talk with a business broker about selling your agency. These people, though, seldom fully understand the operation of a sales agency. Most are accustomed to dealing with more conventional businesses in which the assets are easily and quickly appraised, and which seldom require more than an average amount of negotiations.

In recent years, accountants have entered the arena by putting business owners and prospective buyers together. Sometimes they will charge for the service. At other times, they are willing to set up the meetings with a promise of the accounting business if the transaction takes place.

THE SECRET OF SUCCESS IN SELLING A SALES AGENCY

Once you run a successful business—and people know it—you will get offers without trying to find a buyer. Today, there is a lot of smart money around, and that smart money is investing in well-managed businesses. An agent I talked with recently told me of how he came to sell his business.

"I really wasn't looking to sell the agency—at the moment, at least. However, my long-range plans did call for a sale in about five years. (The agency had been in business for seventeen years.)

"We have been quite successful, and I did everything I could to create a strong image of the agency on both the customer and principal front. However, I wasn't prepared for the offer when it came. The national sales manager of one of my principals and the regional manager in my territory made an appointment to see me. I assumed that they were on a routine sales call, but when we got behind the doors of my office, they opened up with a pitch to buy the business. Needless to say, I was surprised—also flattered.

"They both had been friends for years and had decided to strike out on their own and wanted to buy an ongoing agency, rather than to start one from scratch. Since they were quite open with me, I was open with them and told them that they were five years too early. As it turned out their plans called for being in business in about two years, and this coincided with the time I had planned to start looking for a buyer in order to make my five-year plan work.

"To make a long story short, we decided to meet seriously about the sale later in the year and decided that if terms could be arranged, they would take over in two years. Everything worked out. The owner of the company that employed them gave them his blessing, and they bought it two years later. There was a three-year pay-out period, during which I remained with the agency to smooth the transition. It all went smoothly, especially considering that I never had to look for a buyer."

Since there are always people on the lookout for successful businesses to buy, you might want to consider using good public relations to get the message out without actually putting the agency up for sale. Making a business attractive, but without letting anyone know it's for sale is a real art. If you're the slightest bit anxious, a smart buyer will smell it. But if you play a cool hand, the chances are that you will have more than a few people making offers just when you want them to.

Hanging in There

As mentioned, selling your agency will be the financial culmination of your agency career. You will have made a lot of money in the meantime, but the final sale will probably set you up for life.

If you think that you can be satisfied playing golf all day long, you'll be mistaken, unless I miss my guess. I have yet to meet an agency owner who was able to sit still after he sold his agency. Many of them told me that they were ready for doing nothing after twenty or so years of running a sales agency. But when the chips were down, they were not more able to handle the usual retirement life than fly. They were still entrepreneurs at heart, and they missed the excitement that goes with building a business.

Many tried to recapture the spirit by working part time for someone else. One agent I know who is more than wealthy by any standards works part time for a small growing agency. As he put it: "This guy needed the kind of help I could provide. He couldn't afford to pay me a consulting fee, so I said, 'Put me on your payroll for a minimum salary and give me some stock options.' It wasn't a crusher for him to do this, and I've been able to do things for him that he couldn't. Sure, he's capable, but he lacks the experience of having done it successfully, and he lacks the time to do it. I am doing the things I like best. I really don't need the money, but I figured that it had to have value to him. What he pays is peanuts to me, but it's a dent in his budget. If I didn't charge him for what I'm doing, it wouldn't seem worth it to him. We both understand this and it's working beautifully. I'm building a new company without killing myself."

I, too, couldn't sit still after I sold my agency. So I have been running the largest professional organization for manufacturers' agents in the country for the past 18 years. When I took it over, there were only 1,700 members. Today we have more than 10,000 members on the books.

I'm sure that someday you will sell a very successful sales agency. And I'm also very sure that when you do, you won't spend much time in the usual retirement pursuits that seem to suit the corporate types.

Good luck—starting your agency—building your agency—selling your agency—and doing the things that really give you pleasure.

Sixty Ideas You Can Use to Make Your Agency Grow

Over the years, MANA has done a lot of research, conducted numerous seminars, and counseled many agencies. Looking over the trends, the problems, and the questions asked, we have developed a list of things that most agents seem to agree on that will help make an agency grow. Some may be old hat to you, and others may seem like a blinding glimpse of the obvious. But if just a few of these ideas solve a problem for you and help your agency grow, we feel that we will have accomplished something.

Each idea is for the agent now in business. There are no ideas to use to get you into business—only tips on how to make your going business go even stronger.

Each point is made only briefly. However, each point is obvious enough so that you should be able to see how it fits in with your present organization.

FINDING THE BEST LINES
AND THE BEST PRINCIPALS

1. Read the business and trade press regularly. Look for start-ups, expansions, and new products your customers need.

2. Stay in active contact with your fellow agents—those in your field and those in related fields. Both are good sources of information.

3. Talk with your present customers—they are often good sources of leads on principals.

4. Contact manufacturers you'd like to represent. Don't knock their present agents, but just let them know you're interested.

5. Don't ask your present principals for names of potential principals—they want more of your time as it is.

6. Be sure your new lines fit in with your existing lines—unless you're planning changes.

7. Don't be afraid to take on a line that a previous agent has had no success with. Decide whether *you* can succeed with it.

8. Make sure that you get all the information you can get on these topics: product specs, pricing, markets, advertising, agency/principal relationships.

9. Be an active MANA member—advertise in *Agency Sales* magazine—and in the MANA directory.

MAKE AN AGREEMENT YOU CAN LIVE WITH

10. Don't go with just a handshake—use the contract guidelines outlined in this book and have your attorney review the contract proposed by the principal.

11. Make sure that the contract states clearly the rights and responsibilities of both parties.

12. Make certain that your rights after termination are clearly stated.

MANAGING YOUR BUSINESS FOR GROWTH

13. Use direct mail, but target your audience. Don't try to make mailings that are all things to all people.

14. Make sure that your mailing has included one of these major goals: inform, persuade, remind, or assist.

15. Be certain that your direct mail talks about benefits, not just features.

16. Get direct mail help from your principals. Most have budgets for this purpose, but they seldom tell anyone about them.

17. Make sure that your principals qualify the advertising sales leads they send you.

18. Develop your own qualifying techniques. The fastest way you can qualify the "qualified" leads sent by your principals is by phone.

19. Take advantage of all the sales literature prepared by your principals. Use it during calls and for direct mail.

20. Get to know the business editors of local newspapers and the editors of local trade and association magazines. They're good sources of leads and will help get your story in print.

21. Sort out your prospects by these categories: deciders, initiators, and permitters. Be sure you know who controls the purse strings.

22. Make active use of samples during sales calls. Research has shown that samples are effective sales aids.

23. Whenever possible, set up in-plant displays, seminars, training sessions, and product demonstrations.

24. Know what your competition is doing, but don't let them force you to respond to their initiative. Be the leader.

25. Sales success is directly proportional to the number of calls you make. If you can comfortably make three a day, be uncomfortable and make four.

26. Every principal wants the lion's share of your time. Make sure that you pick the right lion.

27. Salespeople tend to sell that which sells most easily—that's bread-and-butter. It's the hard-to-sell products that make agents wealthy.

28. Agencies are interested in gross sales; principals are interested in net profits. Learn to be interested in net profits.

29. Work as hard to keep your principals sold on you as you do to keep your customers sold on the product.

30. Make sure that you penetrate your principals' organizations as deeply as you penetrate your customers' organizations.

31. Agents are replaced when they perform poorly and sometimes when they perform too well. There's not much you can do to salvage a poor performance termination. But with a good contract and the proper education of your principals, you can avoid being a victim of success.

32. Don't get caught in the paperwork loop. Extensive reports to your principals can jeopardize your independent status and take up an awful lot of selling time.

33. Stay in regular touch with your customers and your principals. If the time between visits is too long, phone or write a short note.

34. Don't overlook one of the best sources of growth—selling more to those who already buy from you.

35. When you hire new salespeople, don't think of them as expenses, think of them as investments.

36. Subagents are one way to expand. But remember that you, not the subagent, have final responsibility to the principal.

37. Consider going multi-person. It provides continuity, better territory coverage, greater potential for growth, and a stronger professional image.

38. To prevent your salespeople from becoming your competitors, be a good boss, be a good manager, and be a good friend.

39. Know to the penny how much each salesperson costs you and how much each salesperson contributes to profits.

40. Remember that your customers and principals grow and change. Make sure you're in step with them.

41. Position your agency. Make it different from all those with whom you compete, and it will stand out from the crowd.

42. Make only promises that you can keep—and be sure that you always keep them.

43. Emphasize what's important to your customers and principals—not what's obvious.

44. Keep your sales strategy up to date. Make sure that your inside and outside salespeople present this strategy to your customers.

45. Be sure that you profit one way or another from every principal you represent, or at least know when and how you will profit.

46. Make sure that everyone in your agency knows the key people at each principal—personally.

47. Get all the product training you can from your principals, but try to avoid their sales training programs.

48. Make sure that you know exactly what is expected of you by all of your principals. Don't wait for surprises.

49. Find out how other agents representing your principals have succeeded—and failed.

50. Make sure that your principals provide you with competitive information regularly.

51. Get your principals to tell you about their weaknesses as well as their strengths.

52. Do not man a principal's trade show exhibit if it isn't in your territory.

53. Your principals will always be evaluating you. Let them know how they stack up with you.

54. If split commissions are to be paid, be sure that the terms are spelled out before the question arises.

55. If your principals don't have rep councils, urge them to set them up—and participate actively.

HANDLING MISUNDERSTANDINGS

56. When you have a problem with a principal, be frank and open before you take any action.

57. Be sure to live up to the terms of your agreement if you are terminated.

58. If a principal terminates you, insist on a face-to-face meeting, and be sure to get *all* the reasons.

59. If you are terminated, notify all your customers and prospects, but avoid mudslinging.

60. Avoid termination problems by looking for signs of trouble. Don't spend a lot of time looking over your shoulder, but be aware of changes in the way your principals treat you.

APPENDIX

Sources of Additional Information

The Manufacturers' Agents National Association, as part of its on-going research and education program, published a number of bulletins and special reports. The bulletins (listed by number below) are available for sale, but since they are updated regularly, we haven't included prices. If you write to the association, they will send you the prices of the bulletins that interest you, or you can request a price list that will include bulletins produced since the publication of this book. Write to: Manufacturers' Agents National Association, Department HB, 23016 Mill Creek Road, P.O. Box 3467, Laguna Hills, California 92654.

501. Survey of Sales Commissions. Agents report that commissions have stabilized. However, it's important to remember that agencies are being paid for a variety of other services besides selling. Many survey respondents reported that they received additional fees for servicing house accounts, warehousing, aiding in new product development, introducing a new product, and providing design services.

503. When Is a Sale a Sale? Unclear language in the agreement can lead to conflict between representatives and their principals.

504. Product Liability.

505. Exclusive Representation Contracts Are Legal.

507. Company Name—Employee Titles Can Mean Various Liabilities.

510. Class Action Lawsuits.

512. Litigation. Potential litigants need to reevaluate whether easy access to courts and lawyers is a benefit, burden, or disaster.

513. House Accounts: MANA Survey of Agents and Manufacturers. They're a fact of life, but the ways that manufacturers and agents deal with them vary.

514. Sales Meetings: How to Make the Most of Them from Both Sides of the Podium. Who holds them, how often, and how are the expenses handled?

515. Split Commissions: How to Make Them Work for Everyone.

516. Five Fables About Competition.

517. Eight Reasons Why Salespeople Fail.

518. Inside . . . Outside . . . Whose Side? Agents and the manufacturer's production people must work together for smooth, trouble-free service for the customer.

520. How to Create a Marketing Plan. A guiding step-by-step checklist.

521. What Agents and Manufacturers Should Know About Bankruptcy. A summary of the laws and how to decide what help you need in answering questions about financial insolvency.

522. Implied in This Relationship.

523. Inherent in This Relationship. } A three-part series on the principal/agent relationship.

524. It's a Business Venture for Mutual Profit.

525. It's Time to Look at Your Agency/Manufacturer Agreement. The absence of a written agreement, a loose agreement, or even an out-of-date agreement breeds the kind of misunderstanding between a manufacturer and agent that can cause trouble for both parties.

526. Typical Marketing Areas. A map giving suggestions for territorial designations ($8\frac{1}{2} \times 11''$ size).

527. I.U.C.A.B. Roster. A listing of the names and addresses of agents' associations throughout the world. (Member organizations of the International Union of Commercial Agents and Brokers.)

533. Performance Evaluation for Both the Agent and the Manufacturer. An evaluation plan designed to increase productivity on the part of the agent and manufacturer to help them benefit from their relationship.

534. Pre-screening Prospective Principals and Agents: Some Guidelines. Nothing is more fundamental to the agent/manufacturer relationship than choosing the right partner from the start. Effective screening of a prospective partner is essential for both sides.

535. Profile of the Manufacturers' Sales Agency. According to survey results from MANA, the agency of today is more than just an independent sales organization. It's a team of well-educated professional people that is carrying its principals' products to other countries as well as to larger territories. The average agency produces sales for its principals in excess of $4 million annually, covers five states, and fields a team of three highly qualified salespeople.

536. The Two Levels of Sales. Agents and manufacturers alike must remember the need to sell their customers continually—and each other.

538. Manufacturers' Agents Travel Survey. Hotels, motels, automobiles, airplanes: Here's how MANA members cover their territories.

540. Synergy: The Agent's—and Manufacturer's—Ace in the Hole. The crossbreeding involved in selling several compatible items often gives the independent representative an advantage over the direct salesperson.

541. Those Joint Sales Calls: The Agent's and Manufacturer's Guide to Protocol. The "unwritten" rules of procedure for the principal–agent call.

542. The Agent, His Independent Contractor Status and the IRS. An

agent can either be an employee or an independent contractor. If he's an employee, the principal (employer) retains control. If he's an independent contractor, the principal has no right to control the agent's physical actions. This bulletin provides a detailed explanation of the agent and his independent contractor status.

543. Standard Chart of Accounts Designed for Manufacturers' Agents.

544. Record Retention Update. Current recommendations are for shorter periods in many categories. Some suggestions are made for legal reasons, others for practicality.

545. Direct Mail That Works. A short course for the manufacturers' agent.

546. Building the Multi-person Agency. Everyone profits when you practice growthmanship according to plan. Here are some reasons why and pointers on how to go about it.

549. Analyzing and Controlling Selling Expenses.

550. Keeping the Territory Intact. How one manufacturers' agency handles area exceptions, house accounts, and other exclusions.

552. Resolving Commission Misunderstandings. A number of options are available through MANA, lawyer consultation, governmental agencies, arbitration, and litigation. Also included is a list of 25 questions prospective clients might ask the prospective lawyer.

553. A Tighter Territorial Plan Will Increase Your Operating Efficiency. Some plans sputter and some hum. Three factors make the difference: realism, completeness, workability.

554. How to Turn Service Calls into Sales Calls.

558. There Are Added Sales in the Afterglow. Your customer is always a prospect for additional sales. If you aren't thinking about his value to you in terms of future sales, add-ons, and up-grading, you aren't thinking like a professional salesperson.

559. Biggest Potential? It's With Your Established Customer.

563. Good Agency Reporting Techniques Can Furnish Up-to-Date Market Intelligence.

566. Organize Your Office: Guidelines for the Small Agency. Sugges-

tions for organization which will allow you to take on more business and become more productive.

567. Compensation and Incentive Survey. A survey of compensations and fringes paid to the sales force of a multi-person agency.

569. Manufacturers' Agents Product Cash Flow Analysis.

570. Strategies for Agency Growth. The characteristics and skills you need to progress in your business, and a checklist for growth.

572. Warehousing and the Manufacturers' Agent. Stocking agents or agent/distributors: both agree it's profitable. Manufacturers' agents in more and more product specialties are recognizing that a warehousing capability is fast becoming one of their strongest selling points.

573. Selling the Right M*A*N. Unless you're selling to the person who controls the money, has the authority to purchase, and the need for your products and services, you're wasting your best efforts.

579. Becoming Your Own Landlord. There are many benefits to the agency, such as low rent, space for expansion, and warehousing.

581. Average Investment Period: The key to profitable inventory management. An introduction to the procedures that identify the average investment period and the benefits that can come from that inventory management perspective.

582. Maximizing Prospecting Efficiency Through Direct Mail. A properly designed direct mail program can generate more good leads at a lower cost than any other communications medium.

584. When Principals Merge. When two manufacturers who make the same type of product merge their firms, what happens to the two sales agencies which represented them in the same territory? How two affected agencies met the challenge.

586. The Value of Using the Manufacturers' Agent. Selection, expectations of both parties, agreements, and communication training are explored in guideline form.

588. Why Opportunities in Agency Sales Continue to Grow.

606. Planning for Retirement: Some Guidelines for Agents. First step:

providing for the continuity of the agency, a key element in making the best possible sale.

611. How to Keep Your Top Agency Salespeople From Becoming Your Top Competitors. Good interpersonal relationships and opportunities to share in the agency's success usually produce a stable sales staff.

612. How Shaky Is the Handshake Agreement? Plenty—it could be misunderstood, dishonored, or violated. Here's how to handle an oral contract dilemma should one arise.

614. Sales Leads. What do manufacturers want from their agents? What do agents want from their manufacturers?

615. Who Pays? When the visiting sales manager comes to tour the territory, who picks up the check? Here are some current practices.

616. Telemarketing. Practical techniques you can use to make sales calls more effective. Includes a survey of how agents are using the telephone successfully.

618. How Agencies Provide Inside Staff Support. MANA's national survey reveals the staffing activities of members.

619. Compensating Agents for Pioneering New Products. The results of MANA's survey show that agents agree they should be compensated, but there's competition for their pioneering dollar.

620. New Product Research and Market Development. How manufacturers and agencies can work effectively together.

621. Commission Chargebacks on Defective Goods.

622. How to Take Your Case to Small Claims Court. When all else fails, manufacturers and sales agents can use the small claims court to collect outstanding debts. This bulletin instructs how to utilize the legal channels that are available.

624. Sales Costs: Looking at the picture from both sides of the desk.

627. What lies ahead for you, your family . . . Building a successful agency requires careful planning at every step of the way.

628. How Agents Can Communicate Effectively With Customers, Prospects, and Principals. When planning any effective direct mail communication, you have to consider more than just pre-

senting a product or service. Here are several checklists to follow when planning your direct mail campaign.

629. The Most Misunderstood Sales Tool—The Telephone. What are the benefits of prospecting by telephone? Find out how to motivate yourself, "format" your conversation, and learn how to overcome the most common internal roadblocks to telephone selling.

630. How Agencies Are Using the Telephone. More than gadgets and gimmicks, new phone equipment makes it easier and less expensive to do business.

631. Rep Councils: Why They Make It and Why They Don't. Rep councils are one of the most productive ways for agencies and manufacturers to work closely together. To get a better understanding of what makes rep councils succeed, we conducted a series of interviews with agencies and manufacturers for their techniques in developing productive councils.

633. Real Estate: A Major Investment for the Manufacturers' Agency. We conducted a direct mail survey of nearly 2,000 members and interviewed a panel of agents who own their building, who lease the space they use, and who work from their homes. The results are compiled into this bulletin.

634. The Practical and Tax Considerations of Mergers. It is very important for any agency or partnership that merges with another business to be aware of every possible tax complication in such a transition. Some of the types of reorganizations available are examined.

636. A Five-Step Plan to Help an Agency Improve Its Employee Selection. Personality Dynamics, Inc., a professional testing service company whose concepts and research findings have been reported in hundreds of business and professional publications, discusses its techniques that would be most helpful for the owners of manufacturers' agencies to use when selecting employees.

637. Self-Employed Retirement Plans and Individual Retirement Accounts. This bulletin examines three of the most common tax shelter devices—H.R. 10 plans (Keogh), individual retirement accounts (IRAs), and simplified employee pension plans (SEPs).

638. How to Find and Get the Lines That Will Make Your Agency Grow. Techniques for identifying and finding the best lines and best principals, as well as approaching these principals and what you can do to have them seek you out.

639. There's More Than a Contract in a Strong Agency Relationship. A well-written contract is a critical element in building a good agency/manufacturer relationship. But there's more to making a success of this joint sales venture than just a contract. A thorough understanding of the human element and mutual trust are very important too.

640. The Credibility Factor—A key to success for the multi-person agency. How to make the new person in your agency a credible representative as quickly as possible.

641. The Economics of a Sales Agency, or the Trials and Tribulations of Mr. Lance Soopersales. A humorous saga of a sales manager who decides to leave the corporate structure and build his own sales agency. The story takes him through all the paces—both psychological and financial. The article describes in an illustrative way how the NET profits of a sales agency relate to the GROSS commissions paid.

642. Non-Compete Covenants: Holy or Loop-Holey? —It's Up to You . . . The More You Covet, the Less You May Retain. An overview of non-compete covenants and what to look at when considering the use of one. Is it enforceable in your state? Will it be deemed reasonable by the court? How to use a non-compete covenant to get the protection you need by limiting it to the geographical area, time frame, and activities which are clearly necessary to protect your relationships with principals and/or customers.

644. Wrongful Termination: How to Turn a Business Crisis Into a Manageable Risk. Does a principal have the right to terminate an agent, or an employer the right to fire an employee—for good reason, bad reason, or no reason at all—absent a contract or law that restricts it? The law historically says YES! However, current decisions in a growing number of states say NO! Learn what can be done to avoid the problems of wrongful discharge.

647. How to Locate, Screen and Hire the High Performance Employee. Errors made in the hiring and training process, causing

high turnover rates and dissatisfied employers, can cost a firm of upwards of $20,000 per employee.

651. Compensating Agencies for Non-Sales Work. How manufacturers are getting the help they need from their agencies.

659. How Agents And Distributors Work Together.

662. How to Plan and Manage a Gradual Buyout and Phaseout. Plan now, even though the sale may be years away.

666. The Changing Role of the Regional Sales Manager. New responsibilities, new demands, new opportunities for field managers.

667. How to Do Sales Forecasting. Some practical advice for agencies and manufacturers on the art and science of educated guessing.

668. House Accounts. MANA survey turns up strong feelings.

669. How to Prequalify a Principal by Telephone. These techniques give you quick answers in your search for new principals.

672. How To Penetrate New Markets. New markets mean growth for many agencies.

679. How to Calculate the Personal Side of a Buy-Sell Agreement When Partners Decide to Split. In order to make a sound evaluation of an agency and to avoid the problems which can arise from an unplanned split you have to have a lot more at your fingertips than the fair market value of the agency.

SPECIAL REPORTS

I. Rep Councils—How Agents and Manufacturers Can Get the Most From Them.

II. How to Buy or Sell a Manufacturers' Sales Agency

III. Estate Planning and the Manufacturers' Sales Agent. A booklet covering the subject of estate planning.

IV. International Marketing. A portfolio of articles discussing various phases of international marketing.

V. Manufacturers' Agencies and Their Computer Usage. This special report covers numerous areas of agency involvement with computers: surveys, profiles of agencies utilizing various computer facilities, service bureaus, software packages, equipment, suppliers, and so on.

Index